JAY SAMIT

FUTURE PROOFING YOU

TWELVE TRUTHS FOR CREATING OPPORTUNITY, MAXIMIZING WEALTH, AND CONTROLLING YOUR DESTINY IN AN UNCERTAIN WORLD

FOREWORD BY TOM BILYEU

WILEY

Published by John Wiley & Sons, Inc., Hoboken, New Jersey.

Published simultaneously in Canada.

For general information on our other products and services or for technical support, please contact our Customer Care Department within the United States at (800) 762-2974, outside the United States at (317) 572-3993 or fax (317) 572-4002.

Wiley publishes in a variety of print and electronic formats and by print-on-demand. Some material included with standard print versions of this book may not be included in ebooks or in print-on-demand. If this book refers to media such as a CD or DVD that is not included in the version you purchased, you may download this material at http://booksupport.wiley.com. For more information about Wiley products, visit www.wiley.com.

Library of Congress Cataloging-in-Publication Data is Available:

ISBN 9781119772064 (Hardcover)
ISBN 9781119772071 (ePDF)
ISBN 9781119772088 (ePub)

Cover Design: Wiley
Cover Image: © laski/Getty Images

SKY10026384_041921

To that one reader of Disrupt You! who emailed me saying that he didn't believe anyone could become a millionaire. You're wrong.

Contents

Foreword

IF YOU KNOW the premise of this book, then I'll assume that every fiber of your being is vibrating with skepticism. And why wouldn't it be? You're smart. You want to believe, but you know that library shelves are stocked full of books written by charlatans promising things that sound too good to be true, because they are. And don't get me started on the internet. Get-rich-quick gurus are pouring out of every nook and cranny – all too ready to relieve you of a coin or two thousand.

So, what makes this book different with its promise that just about anyone can become a millionaire? If ever there was a claim that's too good to be true, it's that. Right? If that claim was made 1,000,000 times, I wouldn't believe it 999,999 times. I would make just one exception. And that exception is if it's Jay Samit who's making the claim. In that case, I'd believe. Ten minutes with Jay and you just know he knows things – important things. *Useful* things. If you spend an hour with him, you're in awe. If you truly get to know him, you want to sit at his feet and learn. The second I read his previous book *Disrupt You!* I put it on my must-read book list that I keep on my website for people wanting to know who I learn from, because from Jay I've learned a lot.

That's why when Jay came to me a couple years ago and told me that he was going to try an experiment, I was immediately intrigued. When he told me he was going to take an unknown kid raised in poverty, with no money and no connections, and help him generate $1,000,000 in revenue over the next year without giving him money or any intro-ductions, I got the chills. Knowing how powerful Jay's knowledge is, I pitched him on doing a show documenting the journey, but ultimately I got busy with other projects and we only filmed one installment. Now that I've read this book, however, I'm absolutely crestfallen that I didn't see it through. What I would have captured is what follows in these pages – an incredible rags-to-riches story that I wouldn't believe if I didn't know the man behind it.

Make no mistake, what you hold in your hand is an instruction manual. This is as close to one-on-one mentorship with Jay as any of you will get. And what Jay lays out on these pages is nothing less than the elucidation of a formula – a formula for success. A formula for suc-cess that has been tested and shown to work. Now, I know some people will dismiss it out of hand (most without even bothering to read it). Others will say "Sure it worked once, but it would never work for me." I implore you not to be like those people. It's true that no one can guarantee your success. Not myself, not Jay, not anyone. But what will dramatically increase your odds is a blueprint. If you're willing to move forward despite any fears and choose to believe that it's possible, then let me assure you, you're in the right place. You now have the blueprint you've been looking for. Just remember, if you're to build anything of import with it, you're going to be required to pay a heavy price. As they say, if it were easy, everyone would do it.

To all of you willing to put in the work, I will say this: I know many of you are afraid you don't have what it takes. But if my own journey from going from so broke I was scrounging in my couch cushions to find enough change to put gas in my car to building a billion-dollar company shows, it's this: It doesn't matter who you are today. It only matters who you want to become and the price you're willing to pay to get there. Armed with the right information and an unbreakable will, the average human animal is truly capable of the extraordinary.

If you don't believe me, you need only read this book. People often say that success leaves clues, but I'll say it another way – success is a formula. Success has its own laws of physics. Through this book, you're going to see exactly what you need to do if you want to build a thriving business. It's going to be hard as hell (as you'll see through this thrilling

Pygmalion journey), but hot damn, by the end of this you'll know it's possible and you'll know exactly what to do make your own dreams a reality.

One last thing before I hand you over to the game-changing words in this book – I believe in you. If no one has ever believed in you before, let me be the first. I don't need to know you; I just need to know you're a human. Humans are designed to acquire new skills. New skills have utility. If you approach this book sincerely, and put its ideas to use, you will learn. You will grow. You will become capable of the extraordinary. You just have to absolutely, positively refuse to quit.

Go forth and become legendary, my friends.

Tom Bilyeu
CEO of Impact Theory and Co-Founder of Quest Nutrition

PS: I hear people say quite often that the American dream is dead. And maybe it is. But this book will show you that something far better has taken its place. The king is dead. Long live the king.

Introduction

BEING A MILLIONAIRE. We've all had the dream. Picking the winning lottery ticket. Discovering a long-lost Rembrandt painting in the attic. Or perhaps, learning that the Nigerian prince who emailed really is wiring you millions of dollars. No more debt or worries; just Lamborghinis, yachts, and magnums of champagne. But, while most people idly daydream about living the lifestyle of the rich and famous, many people just like you are actually doing it. I have tried to synthesize the most important lessons and knowledge that I have gained over the last three decades into 12 truths that make success possible for anyone. While these truths aren't taught in any business school, they are the foundation for wealth creation in the digital age. This book was written to be your indispensable guide for starting a business, growing a company, or creating a better life for you and your family in this post-pandemic, technologically interconnected, globalized world.

Today, there are a total of 16.5 million millionaires around the world who have amassed an astonishing $63.5 trillion. What is even more amazing is the fact that a new billionaire is created every 48 hours. Think about that for a moment: Every two days a new billionaire is enjoying a life you can only imagine.

Now ask yourself, how did you spend yesterday and today? Are you any closer to your dreams of financial freedom? Or did you trade another

1

precious day of your life for a job that you don't like? A job that will never provide you the lifestyle and independence that you so fervently desire. A job that pays you just enough not to quit, but not enough to live in the style you deserve. Be honest with yourself: Are you truly living life or just paying bills until you die?

How can you break out of this pernicious cycle?

In the history of mankind, it has never been easier than now to become financially independent and spend more time enjoying life with friends and family. The reasons for this massive accumulation of new wealth are simple. With mobile phones and the internet making our world more interconnected, and 7.6 billion potential customers just one click away, you only have to be right for a nanosecond to make millions. The right product or service, at the right time, and you can amass wealth to support your family for generations.

So, the real question is: If all of these millionaires and billionaires have the same 24 hours in a day that you do, what are they doing differently than you? How did they find the opportunities that eluded most people? How can you learn to see the world as they do?

The vast majority of the world's billionaires didn't come from wealthy families or positions of power. Most did not go to top Ivy League universities. And none of them sat at home waiting for the Publisher's Clearing House van to arrive. The honest truth is that most of today's wealthy are no different than you or me. If you would have told me when I was growing up in a row home in Philadelphia that dozens of the people I work with would become billionaires, I would have asked you what you were smoking. Yet, when I first worked with Bill Gates, Jeff Bezos, Paul Allen, Richard Branson, David Geffen, Reid Hoffman, Elon Musk, Brock Pierce, Eric Schmidt, and dozens of others, they hadn't yet attained the wealth that made them internationally famous. But what they had discovered was the secret path to *Future Proofing* their careers and businesses.

The secret is: our world is fundamentally different from the one we were taught about in school. All businesses are tech startups. Sustainability is profitable. The 12 truths in this book will shatter the misconceptions readers have on how to make a career and build a business. Warren Buffett built his wealth by slowly saving and investing over decades (he made 99 percent of his wealth after the age of 50), while social media star Kyle Jenner will be a self-made billionaire by 22. Kyle grew up digital savvy while Buffett still refuses to use a smartphone. Which world do you want to live in?

The 12 truths in *Future Proofing You* are not about luck or astrological signs. They are surely not about grinding it out for 40 years, clipping coupons, and counting your pennies. The truths are all about leveraging a positive attitude in a highly interconnected world. Attitude is something each one of us can learn to enhance and control. You already have within you the power to become a millionaire. You've just never been shown a proven process to follow.

School was designed to get you to fall in line and get a job in someone else's company. Your natural curiosity was shackled into conformity. This book will help you break out of the employee mindset and teach you the 12 truths every twenty-first-century entrepreneur needs to embrace in order to achieve success. Most of your life you have been told to get the safe and steady job by people who had given up on their dreams years before you came along. How is that advice working out for you so far?

There is another way. The simple truth is that self-made men and women just look at the world differently. Where most see problems, Future-Proofers see unmet needs. Where most are afraid of failure, they embrace it and harness it. Those striving to achieve don't worry about what others think. Every billionaire's name that I just dropped was at one point along their journey written off as crazy or foolish. Lastly, where most are afraid to ask for help, a Future-Proofer seeks out mentors to speed them on their journey.

Future Proofing You will walk you step-by-step through the process of attaining wealth and mastering your own life by shattering the misconceptions that hold most people back. This isn't a get-rich-quick scheme, and I am not trying to sell you anything. I want you to succeed for a very selfish reason: Our world needs more entrepreneurs. Entrepreneurs are the backbone of a free and stable society. No democracy can survive without a thriving middle class, and entrepreneurs are our job creators. They solve societal problems and are rewarded for the risks they take. I love living in a world that gets better each year. Each new innovation that creates a Future-Proofer also makes our lives more productive, fun, and rewarding. Airbnb, Waze, and Uber started as half-baked ideas from individuals who believed in themselves. I have had the privilege to work with some of the most successful billionaire innovators on the planet. With this book, I am paying what I learned over the past three decades forward so as to enjoy the astounding innovations that the next generation will create.

How Do You Go about Future Proofing You?

You will only need two things to achieve lasting success and a seven-figure bank account. They are not money or connections. Success doesn't require a college degree nor a high IQ. You don't even have to live in a major city or first-world nation. There are just two things that every self-made woman or man must possess in order to succeed, one of which this book will provide and the other one you must bring with you to the Future-Proofing process.

The only requirements for becoming Future Proof are *insight* and *perseverance* (as you will learn in the following chapters, everything else can be hired). Insight is all about finding opportunities and learning how to quickly capture the value created by changes in our society. We are living in an era of endless innovation where each new app, device, or service creates a new void upon which an insightful entrepreneur can quickly amass wealth. Wealth that can last generations can now be attained in the shortest time ever in history. My friend Brock Pierce, who *Forbes* magazine lists as one of the richest cryptocurrency billionaires, didn't invent Bitcoin. But Brock had the insight to leverage this innovation and make hundreds of millions of dollars in just a couple of years (with no employees, capital, or investors). Social media influencer Tom Bilyeu couldn't find a healthy good-tasting protein bar to help his family lose weight, so he and his friends made one in their kitchen. A couple of years later, Quest Nutrition was a billion-dollar company. Insights are the light that guide you down the path to success. As you will soon discover, the opportunities for success are all around you. You just have to learn what to look for and how to capture the value you create. *Future Proofing You* is the torch to illuminate your path.

While techniques for uncovering insights will be taught in this book, perseverance comes from deep within. You must make a personal commitment to see this journey through to the end. No one is going to hand success over to you. It must be earned. You will also learn how to bolster your perseverance by discovering your purpose. Becoming future proof doesn't happen overnight and it won't be easy. For many, it will take longer than a year, but the moment you commit to *Future Proofing You*, is when the journey begins. As the ancient Chinese philosopher Lao Tzu wrote, "The journey of a thousand miles begins with one step." Only you can take the first step (and since you are reading this book – you are already on your path to prosperity).

But you won't have to walk this road alone. Your perseverance will be aided by the stories and techniques of other millionaires who have made the journey before you. As they share their trials and tribulations, you can acquire tools for coping with setbacks and strategies for conquering obstacles. You will learn to embrace your problems and your failures. You will learn how to prioritize and pivot. You will get an education in converting today's sweat equity into a lifetime of passive income. If you are willing to focus and work one year of your life like most people won't, then you can live the rest of your life in a way most people can't.

To prove that everyone is capable of becoming a *Future Proof* millionaire, I chose to put my knowledge and reputation to the test. While writing this book, I decided to mentor one young man and record his odyssey. This book follows one person's 12-month journey from being a couch-surfing unemployed millennial to a self-made entrepreneur earning his first million dollars. This book documents every step of the way and provides guidance for you to achieve your own results as well as real-world examples from dozens of others who have taken it upon themselves to become Future Proof millionaires. Of the more than 200,000 "success" books currently listed on Amazon that tout ways of how to think and grow rich, **this is the first book ever to prove that its method really works**. *Future Proofing You* will change lives.

PART

I

The Twelve Truths

1

The Growth Mindset

You were not born a winner, and you were not born a loser.
You are what you make yourself to be.

—Lou Holtz

WHILE VISITING A LOGGING CAMP in Myanmar, an American tourist watched how at the end of each day, the loggers secured their elephants with just a small piece of tattered rope tethered to a teak tree. The tourist couldn't understand how such a thin flimsy rope could restrain a powerful 8,000 lb. bull elephant. Having watched the pachyderm haul over a dozen one-ton logs that afternoon, surely, thought the tourist, this massive creature had the brawn to destroy the cord and break free. Quite perplexed, the American asked the trainer, "Why don't the elephants just break free?" The trainer explained that from birth, the elephants are tied up with the same size rope, and since as babies they weren't strong enough to break free, they were conditioned to believe that the rope is inescapable. By the time they are full-grown adults, they stopped trying and accepted their lot in life. What's tying up your future?

Truth #1 – You Must Have a Growth Mindset

If you are reading this book and are broke, here are three comforting facts: you are not alone, it's not your fault, and a year from now you can be a millionaire. While the stock market is at an all-time high, the sad truth is that the vast majority of people are drowning in debt. Americans owe more than $1 trillion in credit card debt and another $1.5 trillion in student loans. According to a recent Bankrate survey, the majority of Americans don't even have the funds to cover an unanticipated $1,000 emergency. As the Covid-19 virus pandemic taught all of us, life can be full of expensive surprises. Your car needs a new transmission, your appendix bursts, or you suddenly lose your job. The smallest financial challenge and you could be just weeks away from being on the street homeless. The income inequality gap in the US has never been wider, with the poorest half of Americans owning just 1 percent of the nation's wealth. According to recent research by the Institute for Policy Studies, 140 million Americans are poor or low-income, living below 200 percent of the Census's supplemental measure of poverty. For almost half the US population, life is a never-ending balancing act of juggling bills and paying off debts.[1]

Before you know it, retirement age creeps up, leaving one third of US households with nothing saved for their old age and the majority (56 percent) having managed to only stash away less than $10,000. Adding to these woes are the facts that younger people will be living longer and the Social Security trust in the US will run out of money by 2034![2] For most people, the golden years aren't so golden, with financial independence and security completely out of their reach.

How Do So Many Fail in a Land So Rich with Opportunity?

There are two reasons most people don't attain wealth: they didn't think they were smart enough to get rich and they were never taught how to create wealth. Let's dispense with the myth about intelligence and money. "There is no relationship between IQ scores and net wealth," according to Ohio State University economist and research scientist Jay Zagorsky. Zagorsky tracked the progress of 10,000 participants from 1979 to the present.[3] While those with higher IQs tended to earn more (each IQ point above average increased earnings from between $202 to $616 per year), smart people weren't any better at holding on to their money and building wealth. Surprisingly, those with higher IQs tended to have more problems. When Zagorsky compared people's IQ scores and their likelihood to have problems such as paying bills, declaring bankruptcy, and defaulting on credit cards, those with the highest IQs were more likely to have financial instability.

What if you didn't get good grades in school? That doesn't matter, either. Standardized tests and rigid curriculums do a poor job of measuring creativity and drive. As we will discuss in later chapters, effort, critical thinking, collaboration, and curiosity are the traits most needed for success. Unfortunately, just like the tethered elephants, too many people internalize failures at school into believing they will fail later in life. Average student Steven Spielberg, the genius director of *Jaws*, *Indiana Jones*, *E.T.*, *Jurassic Park*, and *Saving Private Ryan*, was rejected *twice* by the University of Southern California's film school. (Decades later, multi billionaire Spielberg, whose films have grossed more than $9 billion, showed that there were no hard feelings when he donated $500,000 to USC's School of Cinematic Arts.) Even Nobel Laureate and renowned physicist Albert Einstein failed his entrance exam to the Zurich Polytechnic Institute. A recent study of 700 millionaires found that their average GPA was 2.9 out of 4; C students were the most likely to become millionaires.[4] Forget about how you did in school. You don't become a success by looking in the rearview mirror.

Believing in your ability to succeed is the key to becoming *Future Proof*. Self-perception is more important than any other factor in predicting success. Scientists at Basel University in Switzerland and the University of California analyzed the data of 1,824 people ranging from 16 to 97. "We established that self-esteem is more likely to influence success than vice versa," according to psychology professor Ulrich Orth who led the research.[5] If you think you can or think you can't, you're right. Self-made billionaire Larry Ellison dropped out of two colleges before co-founding Oracle. "I studied everything but never topped," the world's most successful average student Bill Gates once declared, "But today the toppers of the best universities are my employees."

Most parents, having spent their lives struggling to make ends meet, encouraged their children to get good, steady jobs and then retire with a pension. In 1950, the average American family income was $3,300 a year and the median home price was $7,354.[6] In other words, a house cost a little more than two years' wages. The American dream was within reach of most Americans. In postwar America, companies were adding jobs and the average worker stayed at his job for over 14 years. People felt secure in their work, financially secure about their future, and could send their children to college debt-free. The greatest generation lived a Future Proof lifestyle. Such a halcyon world is long gone.

Job Security Is a Myth

Hundred-year-old companies are being displaced by newer, leaner startups. In a booming economy, retailers such as Radio Shack, Payless, Toys-R-Us, Kmart, and Macy's shuttered over 5,000 stores in 2017 displacing tens of thousands of workers. Of the original Fortune 500 companies, only 10.4 percent are still on the list.[7] And when large companies fail, so do their underfunded pension plans. Over 120,000 retired United Airlines workers saw their former employer's pension fund collapse when the company filed for bankruptcy. The same thing happened to the pension funds of the once great industrial giants Delphi and Bethlehem Steel. So where are these so-called secure jobs?

Manufacturing jobs in the United States peaked way back in 1979. Even if factories are coming back to America, they are going to be employing robots, not humans. According to the *Washington Post*, American factories now produce twice as much as they did in 1984, but with one-third fewer workers.[8] Studies show that each factory robot replaces six human jobs. Foxconn, the world's largest manufacture and maker of the iPhone, now has 10 *lights-out* production lines. (The lights are out in the building because no humans work on those production lines.) In 2017, Foxconn announced that their goal was to replace all 1.2 million employees with automation.[9] Our public school system was designed to educate workers with enough reading and math skills to boost factory productivity but not enough skills to venture out on their own. The standardized instruction and conformity we were taught in school leaves most people ill prepared for a postindustrial globalized world dominated by artificial intelligence and robotics.

Only one-third of Americans have a college degree, and yet high school no longer prepares young adults for a trade or even how to find a job. And for those of you who racked up massive college debt, I am sorry to be the one to break the news to you but, research now shows that earning a degree from a major university has no long-term impact on income, job satisfaction, or life satisfaction.

Security doesn't even exist for those working at the most prestigious corporations. Employees at successful tech companies, such as Microsoft, Google, Apple, and Amazon, keep their jobs on average for less than two years.[10] Even for the most educated among us, there is no job security. The adage that security robs ambition needs to be updated: it isn't security that robs ambition, but the illusion of security that robs ambition. The good news is that it isn't too late to change your trajectory and learn how to make money.

Wealth Comes from Creating Money, Not Earning and Saving It

Before diving into the *Future Proofing You* process, it is important to dispel a major misconception about money that hinders most people's ability to create wealth. In the twenty-first century, one doesn't get rich by accumulating and saving money. Slowly reread that sentence again: "One doesn't get rich by accumulating and saving money." One gets rich by *creating* money. Money, and the value it represents, can be created from thin air as if by an alchemist using magic. Wealthy people create money that wouldn't have existed if not for their efforts. To comprehend this fundamental principle, we need to journey back to our formative years and revisit third-grade arithmetic. In elementary school, most math problems went something like this:

If Jeff buys two bananas for one dollar each and sells them to Mark for two dollars each, how much did Jeff make?

In this example, the only way John makes his two-dollar profit is by taking it from Mark's pocket. Jeff wins. Mark loses. While mathematically sound, this equation teaches children that in order to gain money, someone else has to lose money. In game theory, this is known as a zero-sum game. Poker is a zero-sum game. You can't win more money at a poker game than the other players bring to the table. Unfortunately, growing up with a zero-sum perspective is like a horse wearing blinders – it limits the field of view for opportunity. For me to win, you must lose. Taken to the extreme, everyone in the world is your competition. There is only so much money to go around and if you don't take what you can, someone else will get it. As you begin your career, this point of view causes a scarcity mindset. There is never enough money to go around. At work, she got a raise so I can't. Immigrants are taking our jobs. Foreign nations are taking our jobs. Robots are taking our jobs. Technology is evil. Everyone is the enemy. Every day you live with this outlook, your life grows more and more stressful. Your life is reduced to a dog-eat-dog world filled with misery and despair. It is hard to have a positive outlook if this mindset has been drilled into you your whole life (and as you will soon realize, mindset is everything). But there is another perspective that is much more conducive to *Future Proofing You* and living a life of happiness and success.

Compare the zero-sum game problem from your youth with this growth mindset example:

If Jeff starts a company with $1,000 and sells 10 percent of his company to investor Mark for $10,000, how much is Jeff now worth?

The answer: Jeff created a company valued at $100,000 with his $1,000 investment and still retains 90% ownership. So, Jeff is now worth $90,000. Looking at it from another angle, one person with only $1,000 and another person with only $10,000 created $90,000 from thin air. Viola! $90,000 that wasn't printed by the Federal Reserve or borrowed from a bank now exists. Jeff can spend it just as easily as you and I can spend cash. In this example, instead of the transaction being a zero-sum game, by cooperating and working together, both Jeff and Mark made money. Jeff made so much money with this approach that he can stop purchasing bananas a few at a time and buy the whole food market! Now you understand how Amazon, which rarely turned a quarterly profit during its first 20 years in business, made Jeff Bezos the world's richest man with a whopping $188.7 billion. (On January 30, 2020, Bezos made a whopping $13.2 billion in just 15 minutes.)[11] Or how Uber founder Travis Kalanick, who has never made a profit with his company or the other two companies he previously founded, is personally worth $4.8 billion. The proliferation of billionaires today is happening because it has never been easier to create vast sums of money. Startups that are valued by venture capital and investors at more than $1 billion are referred to as unicorns. In 2009 there were just four such rare creatures. As of April 2020, their number multiplied to 465.

Incredibly, each of us has the potential to be a modern-day sorcerer with the Midas touch: we can turn anything we create into gold. What does this have to do with you making a million dollars and *Future Proofing You?* Everything.

The first decision you will have to make in building your fortune is to decide if you want to make money the way John Mackey did with Whole Foods Market – buying items at one price and reselling them at a higher price – or the way Jeff Bezos did with Amazon, by creating a new service with a business model that will be highly valued by investors. Both can earn you money, but only one is likely to make you a millionaire in a year.

Airbnb, Google's search engine, and cryptocurrencies such as Bitcoin are all examples of new business models that created billions of dollars that would not have otherwise existed. Airbnb monetized surplus rooms, thereby unlocking billions of dollars of stored value. Silicon Valley's venture capital firms are all based on this model. VCs look to invest in disruptive ideas that can generate at least a tenfold return on their money. The best of the best, venture capitalists who generate billions of dollars, are tracked on the Midas List. Sequoia Capital's Jim Goetz topped the 2017 Midas List by being the only person to invest in the 55-person mobile app developer WhatsApp, which sold to Facebook for nearly $22 billion after only five years in business. What makes the WhatsApp story even more astounding is that its founder, Jan Koum, just prior to starting WhatsApp, had applied for a job to work at Facebook and was rejected. Without a job, he created his company and became one of the wealthiest billionaires on the planet. Koum, a college dropout and Ukrainian immigrant, made $7.5 billion on an idea he would have gladly given Mark Zuckerberg for free if only Facebook had hired him.[12] Unlike the wealthy industrialists of the twentieth century, today's Future Proofing millionaires and billionaires don't amass wealth, they create it. And, so can you.

To benefit from the opportunities available in the twenty-first century, you must first understand how businesses create value. As I illustrated with the previous arithmetic problems, you need to unlearn how you thought companies made money and look for ways that existing businesses can be disrupted. In my previous book, *Disrupt You!*, I walked readers through all the parts of the modern business value chain from research and development, design and production, through to marketing, sales, and distribution. New technologies such as mobile, social media, and blockchain provide opportunities for small startups to greatly improve upon one part of the chain and dislodge large, less nimble incumbents. Instagram upends Kodak. Netflix destroys Blockbuster and destabilizes Hollywood studios. Airbnb destabilizes the hotel industry. Uber disrupts 17 million taxi drivers. Depending on the industry, businesses can be disrupted at any link upon the chain and thereby release value that can be captured by new startups. (If you haven't read *Disrupt You!*, I highly suggest you do before launching your new business. If this was a college course, *Disrupt You!* would be the prerequisite for enrolling in *Future Proofing You*.) Beating the competition is but one path to financial success.

Fostering a Growth Mindset

Even more than I hate the zero-sum mindset, I hate competition. I am one of the most competitive people you will ever meet and yet, I really hate having to compete. As confident and motivated as I may be on my best day, I am still pretty sure that there is someone out there that is better qualified, better financed, or just plain smarter than me. So, whenever I am starting a new business, I try to avoid competition for as long as possible. You will win every race as long as you are the only runner on the track. To increase my chances of winning, I go where there aren't any competitors. I always focus on the next new thing. I started on the internet in 1978, created software for the first personal computers in the 1980s, pioneered ecommerce in 1996, built a million-member social network in 1998, launched a top 100 mobile app in 2011, and got involved with Bitcoin in 2013. I didn't invent the internet or the smartphone. I didn't create cryptocurrency. I am not even an engineer. I am just an entrepreneur looking for the next opportunity to disrupt the status quo. As the world's greatest hockey player Wayne Gretzky famously said, "I skate to where the puck is going to be, not where it has been."

In my Ted talk *It's Time to Disrupt You!*, I pose this question to the audience, "Ever ask yourself where virtually reality experts or Internet of Things Experts or Bitcoin experts come from?" In reality they are people who started with no more expertise than the rest of us. They are all just self-proclaimed experts who then worked hard to grow and defend the turf they so wisely staked out. They race to where the puck is going to be and then figure out how to skate. I live by the adage, "be the best at what you do or the only one doing it." For if you are the only one doing it, by definition, you are the best. To succeed you need to embrace a growth mindset.

In her 2006 book, *Mindset: The New Psychology of Success*, Stanford Professor Carol Dweck coined the term *growth mindset*. Dweck spent decades researching students' attitudes about success and failure. She wanted to understand why some children could easily bounce back from major failure while others were completely devastated by the most minor of setbacks. The differences among children had less to do with the external circumstances of the specific task at hand and more to do with their preconceived notions of their own abilities. Some students, those with fixed mindsets, believed they were stupid and there was nothing they could do about it. *I'm not bright enough to learn algebra.* For them, intelligence was innate and failure was predestined. Why try when the outcome will always be disappointing? Remember the elephant with the fixed mindset at the beginning of this chapter?

On the other hand, students with a growth mindset saw the world completely differently. These students believe that with work and effort, they can improve and grow smarter. *If I make flashcards, I'll ace the Spanish test.* The more you believe that you can improve, the more effort you will put toward your goals. Over time, students with a growth mindset attain higher achievement and a more positive outlook on life. Positive thinking expands creativity, increases energy, raises intelligence, and even closes more sales. Success doesn't make you happy; being happy creates success. As long as you are in control of your happiness, you are future proof.

Having a growth mindset not only changes how you deal with setbacks; it actually rewires the physiology of your brain. The human brain is not hard-wired from birth. Numerous studies in neuroscience have proven that the connectivity between neurons in the brain's neural networks grow with experience. The brain's plasticity, the degree to which it is malleable, can be improved by basic actions such as asking questions, eating healthy foods, and getting enough sleep. Turns out, science supports everything your mother told you to do as a kid. So how does an adult develop a growth mindset?

The first truth you must accept for *Future Proofing You* is that nothing can be achieved without a growth mindset. Developing and maintaining a growth mindset is the foundation upon which all other great accomplishments can be achieved.

"This growth mindset is based on the belief that your basic qualities are things you can cultivate through your efforts," Carol Dweck writes in her book *Mindset: The New Psychology of Success*. "Although people may differ in every which way in their initial talents and aptitudes, interests, or temperaments, everyone can change and grow through application and experience," Dweck explains.[13]

People with a fixed mindset see having to work hard at something as proof that they are not smart enough or good enough to achieve anything. *I'll never become a real estate agent because I could never pass the exam.* Every aspect of their lives is viewed through a lens of seeing their hard effort as needing to compensate for a lack of talent. A person with a fixed mindset thinks, for example, that they could never play basketball like Michael Jordan because he has *natural* talent. When in fact, a growth mindset is the real reason Michael Jordan became the greatest basketball player of all time.

"I've missed more than 9000 shots in my career. I've lost almost 300 games. 26 times, I've been trusted to take the game winning shot and missed. I've failed over and over and over again in my life," Jordan famously said. "And that is why I succeed."[14]

A fixed mindset not only limits your future, it can prevent you from enjoying every aspect of your life. *Will doing this make me look stupid to co-workers? Will I be rejected?* If every social setting requires you to feel like you have to prove your self-worth, life begins to feel like a never-ending struggle. Quite simply, living with a fixed mindset is exhausting, and that is why too many people give up. Some of the most influential people in your life, parents and teachers, friends and spouses, discourage you from trying because they have given up on their dreams. Parents and spouses don't want to see you hurt as they may have been. If you train your own mind, it will silence all the naysayers in your life.

With a growth mindset, you teach yourself to reframe every fixed negative thought into a potentiality. Instead of thinking, "I tried and I failed," ask yourself, "Are there other strategies I could try?" Start embracing obstacles as opportunities, or as Michael Jordan says, "If you're trying to achieve, there will be roadblocks. I've had them; everybody has had them. But obstacles don't have to stop you. If you run into a wall, don't turn around and give up. Figure out how to climb it, go through it, or work around it."[15]

Remember, your future is mutable. My eldest son wanted to be a Hollywood screenwriter. It is an incredibly difficult industry to break into. Out of the thousands of screenplays written each year, only a couple dozen are produced into movies by the film studios. Many writers give up because, suffering from a fixed mindset and facing constant rejection, they are fearful of people asking the question: Have I seen any of your movies? And having to answer, no. To them, not having sold a script or having a film produced is an acknowledgment of their personal failure. They think of themselves as not good enough because no studio has made their movie. But my son has a growth mindset. For years, when people would ask Benji or his writing partner Dan Hernandez: Have I seen any of your movies? He would always answer, "Not yet." Not yet implies it can and will happen. Today, after a decade of writing, when people ask the question, he can reply, "Did you see *Pokémon Detective Pikachu?* (And his proud father can add, "The second highest grossing film in the world in 2019!")

As with screenwriting or basketball, developing a growth mindset takes practice and effort.

Six Techniques for Developing a Growth Mindset

1. *Stop failing and start learning.* Every time something doesn't work out the way you would have liked, stop thinking of it in terms of winning or losing. You didn't fail, you just figured out a path that

doesn't work. With that one approach out of the way, what is a different technique that might yield a better result? Learn to embrace your imperfections. Imperfections are not career-ending flaws, but rather areas for personal growth and improvement. Once you focus on learning how to overcome obstacles, you will start to enjoy the journey (instead of constantly focusing on the ultimate destination).

2. *You don't need others' approval. You need their criticism.* When you constantly seek validation, you are putting praise ahead of learning. Too many people's careers are ruined by praise instead of propelled by criticism. The only path to success is constant learning and improvement. As an adult, when I was taking painting lessons from a world-famous artist, I didn't want him to tell me how good my watercolor pictures were. I didn't want him to hang it on his refrigerator like a first grader's mother would do. I wanted to know what could be improved. What wasn't working, and why? You should look at every day at work, every interaction with others, as a chance to learn. Your bosses and clients got to where they are by learning things from experiences you may not have had yet. Think of your job, even if it is a job you hate, as you getting paid to learn. You are getting a degree in business without any student debt.

3. *Track your progress with a journal.* Keeping a daily journal is crucial to changing your mindset. It focuses you to take a moment every evening to analyze what worked and didn't work each day. What goal did you set for that day or week? Did you achieve it? If not, what steps could you take to get closer to your goal? People who write down their goals do significantly better in life. According to Mark Murphy, bestselling author of *Hundred Percenters*, "Vividly describing your goals in written form is strongly associated with goal success, and people who very vividly describe or picture their goals are anywhere from 1.2 to 1.4 times more likely to successfully accomplish their goals."[16]

    Pay careful attention to the language you use to describe your goals and your actions. If you are reflecting on the day in dark or negative ways, so shall your actions follow. By focusing on what you learned from disappointing experiences, you are less likely to repeat the same mistakes. The added benefit of carefully choosing the words in your journal entries is that growth mindset censorship will impact how you speak and communicate with others at work and in your social life. Remember, you don't fail, you learn. Replace judging yourself harshly every time you make a mistake or fall short of your goals with self-acceptance.

On those days that really go wrong, we all have a tendency to dwell on our mistakes or misfortunes. Here is a clever trick to free your mind and move forward. Take a blank page in your journal and write down all your negative thoughts about the bad experience. Get it out of your mind and onto the paper. Next, rip out that journal page and throw it away! You are done with those thoughts and are ready to move forward.

Lastly, keeping a journal will give you a sense of purpose. You are on a mission. You are not competing with others as if life is some kind of race. (After all, we all end up buried at the same finish line.) Measure personal growth over speed. That way, any time you are down or hit a roadblock, you can always look through your old journals and congratulate yourself on how far you've come – regardless of how long it took to get there.

4. *Focus inwardly and not on your image.* You don't need others' validation to achieve your goals. Be who you want to be and don't worry about what others think. Take solace in the fact that people who want to bring you down are already below you. The more you build a growth mindset and focus on your internal voice telling you what is possible, the more you will come to realize that haters are speaking their truth, not yours. When anyone tells you *no*, they are not saying you can't do it, they are just informing you that you won't be doing it with them. A growth mindset will have you thinking, "their loss."

Part of growth and acceptance is redefining *genius*. Genius isn't a gift anointed on a select few at birth. "Genius is one percent inspiration and 99 percent perspiration," the inventor Thomas Edison famously proclaimed. Johnny Carson, the *Tonight Show* television host who gave an entire generation of comedians, everyone from Ellen DeGeneres to Jerry Seinfeld, their start by having them appear on his show, said, "Talent alone won't make you a success. Neither will being in the right place at the right time, unless you are ready."[17] The more you keep track of your hard work in your journal the more your will start to internalize the fact that genius is not born, but created.

5. *Learn and grow from the mistakes of others.* Success is not about comparing yourself with others. But we can shorten our road to success by learning from the mistakes of others. Today, we live in a world where the vast majority of all of humanity's knowledge is just a few clicks away. Leverage that tremendous resource. Need help figuring out a new company, client, or industry? Reach out on LinkedIn to people who have been there before. I have yet to meet someone who doesn't want to share their knowledge and feel appreciated for what they have accomplished. And I have yet to meet someone who I can't learn from.

   The more you learn about the mistakes successful people have made along the way, the more willing you will become to take risks and try new ideas. I've run four person startups and managed companies with over 250,000 employees. For decades, I have instructed every person I hire that if they work for me for a year and don't make any mistakes, I will fire them. I do this to free them from being afraid to fail and therefore, afraid to venture outside of their comfort zone. Your business will never grow if your team has fixed mindsets.

6. *Practice gratitude.* Take time every evening when you are journaling and every morning when you first look in the mirror to practice gratitude. Motivational speaker Zig Ziglar aptly noted, "People often say motivation doesn't last. Neither does bathing – that's why we recommend it daily."[18]

   The antidote for self-pity and negative thinking is gratitude. Find something in your life to be grateful for. You may not have a private jet, but be grateful for a roof over your ahead, food in your stomach, and the fortitude to continue executing on your goals. Start with the basic good manners of saying "thank you" when someone helps you, holds the elevator, or just interacts with you in any way. According to a study published in *Emotion* magazine, thanking a new acquaintance makes them more likely to seek an ongoing relationship. (I didn't remember much about the first time that I met the woman who was to become my wife, but when

I received a thank you note from her after our first meeting, my life changed forever.) Gratitude has been proven time and again to improve your physical health.[19] Music industry impresario Ralph Simon, whose label Jive Records signed such acts as the Backstreet Boys, NSYNC, Britney Spears, and Janet Jackson, sends dozens of handwritten notes each week to his friends and colleagues no matter where in the world he is traveling. Even after 25 years of our dear friendship, I still light up when I get a note from Ralph.

Feeling true gratitude silences all the negative emotions floating around in your head. Regret, envy, fear, and resentment lead to anger and depression. Remember the warning Yoda gave to young Luke Skywalker, "Fear is the path to the dark side. Fear leads to anger. Anger leads to hate. Hate leads to suffering." Gratitude enhances your health by reducing aggression. Just spending 15 minutes before you go to bed writing down what you are grateful for, according to a 2011 study published in *Applied Psychology: Health and Well-Being*, will enable you to have a deeper, more restful sleep.

In the morning when you awake, you again have the opportunity to start your day with gratitude. I start each day, as I brush my teeth and shave, saying two affirmations to myself in the mirror, "Today can be better than yesterday, and I have the power to make it so."

A growth mindset is the one trait that separates achievers from failures. It gives you the outlook and perspective to see obstacles for what they really are: short-term events that momentarily get in your way. From positivity and gratitude grow perseverance. Perseverance, by definition, makes you unstoppable.

Notes

1. "Who's Poor in the United States?" Institute for Policy Studies (2019), https://ips-dc.org/supplemental-poverty-measure/.
2. Alexa Lard, "Social Security to Exceed Income by 2020, Run Out by 2034," April 22, 2019, www.usnews.com/news/politics/articles/2019-04-22/report-social-security-costs-to-exceed-income-by-2020-run-out-by-2034.

3. Lee Dye, "You Don't Have to Be Smart to Be Rich," ABCNews, May 16, 2007.

4. Shana Lebowitz, "Why Valedictorians Rarely Become Rich and Famous – and the Average Millionaire's College GPA," *Business Insider* (May 29, 2017), www.businessinsider.com/why-high-school-valedictorians-dont-become-really-successful-2017-5.

5. Etienne Strebel, "Is Self-Esteem the Key to Success?" *Swiss Info* (October 31, 2011), www.swissinfo.ch/eng/sci-tech/is-self-esteem-the-key-to-success-/31463808.

6. Mybudget360, "Comparing the Inflated Cost of Living Today from 1950 to 2014: How Declining Purchasing Power Has Hurt the Middle Class Since 1950," My Budget 360 (February 2014), www.mybudget360.com/cost-of-living-2014-inflation-1950-vs-2014-data-housing-cars-college/.

7. Mark J. Perry, "Only 52 US Companies Have Been on the Fortune 500 Since 1955, Thanks to the Creative Destruction that Fuels Economic Prosperity" AEI (May 22, 2019), www.aei.org/carpe-diem/only-52-us-companies-have-been-on-the-fortune-500-since-1955-thanks-to-the-creative-destruction-that-fuels-economic-prosperity/#:~:text=In%20 other%20words%2C%20only%2010.4,the%20top%20Fortune%20500 %20companies%20(.

8. Ana Swanson, "A Single Chart Everybody Needs to Look at Before Trump's Big Fight over Bringing Back American Jobs," *Washington Post* (November 28, 2016), www.washingtonpost.com/news/wonk/wp/ 2016/11/28/theres-a-big-reason-trump-might-not-be-able-to-keep-his-promise-on-jobs/.

9. Matthew Griffin, "1.2 Million Jobs to Vanish as Foxconn Unveils Plans for Fully Autonomous Factories," *Fanatical Futurist* (January 7, 2017), www.fanaticalfuturist.com/2017/01/1-2-million-jobs-to-vanish-as-foxconn-unveils-plans-for-fully-autonomous-factories/.

10. Becky Peterson, "Travis Kalanick. Lasted in His Role for 6.5 Years – Five Times Longer than the Average Uber employee," *Business Insider* (August 20, 2017), www.businessinsider.com/employee-retention-rate-top-tech-companies-2017-8.

11. Tom Maloney and Tom Metcalf, "Jeff Bezos Adds $13.2 Billion to His Fortune in Just Minutes," *Bloomberg* (January 30, 2020), www.bloomberg .com/news/articles/2020-01-30/bezos-adds-13-2-billion-to-fortune-in-minutes-with-amazon-surge.

12. Avishai Bitton, "7 Entrepreneurs Who Went from Food Stamps to Billionaires," Shockpedia (November 12, 2014), www.shockpedia.com/ 7-entrepreneurs-went-food-stamps-billionaires/.

13. Carol S. Dweck, *Mindset: The New Psychology of Success* (New York: Random House, 2006), 7.
14. Eric Zorn, "Without Failure, Jordan Would Be False Idol," *Chicago Tribune* (May 19, 1997).
15. Ben Frederick, "Michael Jordan: 10 quotes from His Airness, the King," *Christian Science Monitor* (February 19, 201).
16. Mark Murphy, "Neuroscience Explains Why You Need to Write Down Your Goals If You Actually Want to Achieve Them," *Forbes* (April 15, 2018).
17. Judy Wearing, *Edison's Concrete Piano: Flying Tanks, Six-Nippled Sheep* (New York: ECW Press, 2009), 164.
18. Zig Ziglar, *Inspiration 365: Zig Ziglar's Favorite Quotes* (Naperville, IL: Sourcebooks, 2013), 149.
19. "Warm Thanks: Gratitude Can Win You New Friends," *Science News* (August 28, 2014).

1.5

The *Future Proofing You* Experiment

Potential is a priceless treasure, like gold. All of us have gold hidden within, but we have to dig to get it out.

—Joyce Meyer, A Leader in the Making

ONE OF THE GREAT JOYS of writing a book is hearing from you, the readers. I wrote my first book, *Disrupt You!*, as a way of helping others to transform their lives. I wanted to break down the business world in a way that made success accessible to all. *Disrupt You!* flipped the message of most books: in order to change the world, you first must learn to change yourself. The book connected with readers around the globe (and is currently published in 10 languages).

I was humbled and touched by the response. I received emails from thousands of readers. Readers from dozens of countries shared stories with me of how they applied the lessons in *Disrupt You!* to their lives and businesses. I heard from a dentist in Pakistan who went from not being able to support his wife and children to having one of the most successful practices in Islamabad. I heard from intrapreneurs who gained the courage to change old companies from within and from single moms building side hustles that gave them the freedom to quit their day jobs. One young reader, still in his early twenties, even drove

27

hundreds of miles to see me speak and thank me. He wanted to tell me that in just two years of applying what he learned in *Disrupt You!*, he was able to buy his parents and grandparents their own homes. As gratifying as these responses were, the one note that haunted me was from another young man who loved the book, but didn't believe he could make it happen.

At twenty-something years old, he had already given up on his goals. He hated his dead-end job and was drowning in credit card debt. He couldn't envision a future beyond living paycheck to paycheck. He felt trapped and defeated. He didn't think success was possible. I read and reread his email, trying to muster the proper response. By failing to prove to him that success was possible for everyone, I had failed him.

What would it take, I wondered, to convince a millennial – or anyone – that they could achieve financial success? He had written me, I surmised, as a cry for help. His pain gnawed at me and kept me up until dawn. Could I take individuals with very little work experience and no family background in business and mentor them into becoming a self-made millionaire? How long would that take? Could it be achieved in a year? Would they learn the skills to be future proof for life?

This is the story of how I decided to challenge myself and see if I could create a Future Proofing millionaire. For a year, I mentored one individual on how to turn his perseverance into his first million dollars. I took detailed notes of each weekly session and I mapped out the process. My goal wasn't to just mentor one person but to come up with a program by which anyone could Future Proof their life. You now hold in your hand the knowledge and the results of our experiment.

Rules for the *Future Proofing You* Experiment

Before I went searching for a mentee, I needed to set up the guidelines for my *Future Proofing You* experiment. First, I wanted to make sure that the process was repeatable and accessible to all. I was going to mentor someone to do it on their own. I was the coach, but they had to go on the field and run their own plays. To be a fair test, the insights had to be theirs alone. They had to decide what type of business to launch, how to find their niche, and how to acquire customers. The effort too had to be theirs alone. If they didn't internalize the process, they wouldn't be Future Proof.

Since many first-time entrepreneurs blame a lack of money or access to investment capital as the reason for their failure, I needed to find someone who was broke. My mentor would not get a penny from me (though, in full disclosure, I did buy him pizza at our lunch meetings). I also wanted to show would-be entrepreneurs that success could be achieved without raising any capital. He would have to use his skills to create a business that wasn't capital intensive and learn to reinvest his own profits to fuel his first year's growth.

Second, I wanted someone who had no external advantages. I wanted someone with little or no corporate experience. Someone who had only worked entry-level jobs so that every reader could relate. My mentee had to come from working-class roots. No entrepreneurs in the family to use as role models or to lean on for a loan. I also wanted someone with a limited social network. I wanted to find the proverbial fish out of water. Someone new to Los Angeles with no safety net.

Lastly, I was not going to open any doors nor share any of the business connections in my vast global network. I wouldn't ask friends to throw business his way or help him find employees. For this experiment to be truly fair, my mentee would have to build his own universe of contacts and associates. By setting these conditions, I knew that the mentee would feel the sense of pride and accomplishment that comes with achieving something on your own. I needed him to internalize that feeling and use it to catapult him over each new obstacle in his path.

Finding a Mentee

As I noted earlier, the one attribute I was looking for in a subject was perseverance. One cannot teach perseverance. I needed to find someone who was resilient and had overcome many obstacles in their life. Someone who came from a tough background, and though not financially successful yet, worked hard to better their circumstances. I didn't want to invest all of this time (and my reputation) on a quitter. So even if I wasn't sure if the goal of earning a million dollars could be achieved in only a year, I had to find someone who believed it could be accomplished.

Though my methods for quickly generating wealth can be applied by young and old alike, I really wanted to find a millennial. There is a prevailing cultural stereotype that millennials are spoiled and afraid of hard work. Many of my peers have written off millennials as a pampered generation who were given trophies for just showing up and expect accolades for everything they say or do. Having raised two hard-working millennial sons, I didn't believe the entitled narrative. I wanted to find someone who would obliterate those preconceptions. If this book was going to help the largest generation our planet had ever seen succeed, then I wanted one of their own to lead the charge.

In my mind, the rules for engagement were set. I was prepared to bet my entire professional reputation on one person. All that I needed to do now was find my mentee.

> When the student is ready, the teacher will appear.
> When the student is truly ready, the teacher will disappear.
>
> Lao Tsu

One Saturday morning, when I was sitting in the audience at a growth-hacking event in Los Angeles, I watched as the young speaker paced nervously across the stage. Moving like a caged panther that had ingested a case of Red Bull, the nervous young man quickly strode back and forth across the proscenium as he spoke at an ever-dizzying speed. Much like pivoting your head at a Wimbledon tennis match, he was exhausting to watch and difficult to follow. His constant movement distracted the audience from the substantive information in his hundred-plus slide PowerPoint. He had so much he wanted to say and couldn't get all of the thoughts out of his head fast enough. To make concentrating even more challenging, the lanky young man was wearing a gold lamé jumpsuit with matching gold high-top sneakers adorned with the Roman god Mercury's wings. Under the spotlight, his glittery ensemble shimmered like a disco ball bouncing from wall to wall. And yet, underneath his gilded veneer, there was something genuine about him. He was bursting with energy, passion, and ideas. He had taught himself how to do online marketing on the cheap, but didn't know

how to build that into a business. I had found my *Future Proofing You*
millionaire to be.

Vin Clancy grew up in a poor, working-class family in London. He
and his older sister lived in council housing (or as we call it in the
States: government projects) in the gritty Shepherd's Bush neighborhood. A few years before his birth, Shepherd's Bush became internationally infamous when three Metropolitan police officers were gunned
down in a routine traffic stop. Vin's father was a caretaker and his mom
worked when work was available. Throughout his childhood in council housing, Vin was surrounded by poverty, violence, and substance
abuse. At 12 years old, he used to stop by the Blue Hawaii restaurant
on Richmond Road on his way home from school because they gave
out free glasses of pineapple juice. One day, one of the waiters who
was supposed to hand out the juice didn't show up, and young Vin was
offered a job. Earning four pounds for a few hours work, Vin kept the
job all through high school. In his early twenties, Vin worked a series of
odd jobs, including at the popular British grocery chain Tesco. Directionless, Vin even tried a sales job, but soon grew bored and quit. Until
recently, he had been living in the UK on welfare, collecting about
$100 a week. Statistically, a young man with his background was more
likely to end up dead or in prison than a self-made millionaire.

A million dollars isn't cool. You know what's cool? A billion dollars.
> Sean Parker in *The Social Network*

In spite of all these obstacles, or because of them, Vin had
something powerful going for him: perseverance. Unfortunately,
Vin was a go-getter with no idea which direction to go. All that
changed one night in the Odeon Kingston cinema when he became
mesmerized by David Fincher's movie *The Social Network*. Based
on Ben Mezrich's book, *The Accidental Billionaires: The Founding of
Facebook*, the film glorified Mark Zuckerberg's journey from obscure
hacker to the world's youngest self-made billionaire. The Academy
Award–nominated movie was an epiphany for Vin. He saw in Jesse
Eisenberg's performance a character with whom he could relate. He
saw his future and a place to channel his energy. He too was going
to become a rich and famous hacker. But first, he would need to get

a computer and learn how to use it. The local library had computers Vin could use for free, so Vin started there.

Though not a programmer, he taught himself how to use a computer and put all his focus into learning how social media works and, as he would call it, how to "hack the system." Vin networked with others online, learned which tools could help grow a person's social media following and how to interact with followers. Like so many of his generation, Vin's dream was to be famous online and move to Hollywood. He wanted to be a social media influencer, like Kylie Kardashian or British Minecraft reviewer Daniel Middleton, who are paid millions each year just for posting branded social media content. He was determined to become a self-made social media marketing expert and had created a personal following of over 100,000 twenty-somethings without spending a penny. Vin scrimped and saved, sold everything he had in the world, and with stars in his eyes, bought a one-way ticket to Los Angeles. He came to America ready to build his personal Vin Clancy brand. When fame and fortune quickly proved elusive, he tried to pivot his skills to being paid to generate followers for others. Turns out, even in Hollywood, finding paying clients was hard. As a way to find new prospects, Vin started speaking for free at events like the one I was attending.

Flat broke, owning no car or furnishings, he crashed at the ant-infested apartment of two welfare recipients. Still, Vin refused to give up. What sealed the deal for me that Vin was the one was a story he told me of a hack that worked back in England for a new pub.

With over 7,000 pubs in London, generating buzz around a new one opening is quite the task. As the UK's capital, most forms of advertising in the City are prohibitively expensive. With London's rents being notoriously high, a new night spot has to quickly build a clientele or it will go out of business. In my opinion, the solution he came up with was pure genius. He maximized both his profit and the pub's success without spending a cent.

There was no need to buy any social media ads, shoot any glitzy photos, or target Google users. Instead of thinking about the problem from the pub's point of view, he innately focused on the potential customer's journey. How and why do people go to pubs? Who do they go with, and where do they meet those people? From this out-of-the-box thinking, the solution revealed itself. Instead of going on social media sites where people hung out with friends, the campaign created fake profiles on Tinder. Using appropriated photos of hot guys and girls, these "singles" would get a lot of swipes. Once connected, they were let in on the ruse.

"I'm not real, but if you want to find real people like me, check out the action at our new pub." The campaign spoke to the moment and was authentic to how people live their lives. Everyone was in on the joke and shared it with their friends. Soon, the press was writing about the hack and the place was packed. Vin innately understood how to think like a disruptor, or, in his parlance, a hacker.

If I was going to put my entire reputation on the line with the *Future Proofing You* experiment, I needed to make sure that Vin had a growth mindset from day one and believed that he could become a self-made millionaire in a year. So, I used a technique discovered by University of California Riverside professor of psychology Richard Rosenthal. What Rosenthal studied was the effects of self-fulfilling prophecies on student performance. At the beginning of the school year, all the students at an elementary school were given an IQ test, and based on the results, their teachers were told by Rosenthal that certain students were "intellectual bloomers." These students would likely substantially excel in the coming school year. The professor lied. The truth was that the bloomers were chosen completely at random and had no greater intelligence than the rest of their classmates. Rosenthal wanted to see what the effect of teachers believing certain students were special would have on the children's intellectual growth and performance. At the end of the year, first- and second-grade "bloomers" showed a statistically significant mean gain in IQ scores. Just by saying a student was smarter made her smarter. Now known as the *Pygmalion Effect*, this creates a virtuous cycle of change and a self-fulfilling prophecy.

In selecting Vin Clancy for my *Future Proofing You* experiment, I counted on the Pygmalion Effect to improve our odds of achieving success. From the outset, I let Vin know that I had interviewed many candidates and, of all the potential mentees, he had impressed me the most as having the skills, drive, and intellect to be a millionaire. Vin internalized my praise and immediately got excited about how he was going to focus all his energy on making a million dollars. After our initial interview, Vin stayed behind at the restaurant where we met and wrote the following essay to himself (which he only shared with me six months later, when he was achieving inconceivable success):

There's a scene in *Requiem for a Dream* where she goes for a meeting with her psychologist with an extreme power imbalance. She needs money from him, and what he needs from her? Well, you can work it out.

I'm reminded of this scene as right now I'm sitting across the table with a multi-multi-millionaire (may even be a billionaire idk) and I desperately need what he has.

He wants to take someone and make them into a star and a millionaire within one year.

Mentorship, getting them clients, getting thousands of book sales so it's a number one hit when he writes the book, the lot. He is the elixir saving everything that's broken in the crummy business I've slaved over brick by boring brick.

So, we're sitting eating pizza on the beach and I mask my excitement with cynicism like I tend to do (so little is truly exciting, and the thought of being let down and it not happening? Too much.) He was on the founding team of three companies who own the internet to this day. Vice Chairman of a household name which makes a good 10 figures every year. It goes without saying that he knows anyone who's anyone in California, but his involvement in the companies that have changed the world for the last 25 years, and looking for a youngster to mentor before he retires brings a life-changing moment.

He is interviewing people for this role and I am just one of many. He tells me about his experience talking to one of my rivals (fuck that guy, I'm thinking of my head). I have to believe every word he says.

When I was brought home from the hospital to the housing project my parents lived at, a gangster got shot in the kneecaps outside our flat. The turf war had escalated and murders were becoming every week thing. By the grace of god, we moved to a better housing project and we're okay from then on. I had come a long way and MAYBE THIS IS IT WHAT I'VE BEEN WAITING FOR.

I don't really have any control here. I tell my story but am mainly listening as the conversation happens. We're all looking to be led, for a personal savior, because life is hard at whatever stage you have it (even those who have cashed out still go crazy). "We all long to blow up and leave the past behind us" as Eminem once said.

I wanted to say "If you don't mentor me can you find me someone who will?" but I can't accept second place, I have to keep that to myself. Maybe if he says no I can tell him he's making a big mistake (and then say it).

This is only month one in Los Angeles and the number of opportunities should be heartening, but I get so focused that this HAS TO BE THE THING, rather than the abundance of opportunities in this town. I wrote this up and walked out of the restaurant with the only feeling being "fuck that! I'm gonna make it without anyone."

It's the only consolation I can give myself to make myself feel better. My desperation since being on welfare has never left me. Maybe at some point I'll get what I want and it will cease, but for better and worse, remembering the poverty I came from strengthens my resolve that I never wanna go back to where I came from. I came out swinging to a city that was at best indifferent to my existence, and I'll find a way yet to land a knockout blow.

The message that a successful businessman would have only chosen Vin if he knew he could do it gave credence to Vin's self-confidence. Now that Vin believed that he could, he would. Or as Napoleon Hill was fond of saying, "Whatever the mind can conceive and believe, the mind can achieve."

Before turning Vin loose on the world, we discussed the importance of setting daily, weekly, and monthly goals. Setting goals and planning out your day is the easiest way to stay focused. This journaling would have the added benefit of reinforcing his growth mindset. Too many people get trapped in the bottomless pit of answering emails, voicemails, and texts as soon as they come in to work each morning. We agreed that Vin would email me his weekly goals and we would measure the results in our Friday mentoring sessions. To maximize revenue, one needs to also focus on those tasks that can only be performed at specific times of the day. You can't make a sales phone call at 11 p.m. His mantra was going to have to be: daytime is for selling, nights are for writing proposals.

In complete transparency, I must admit something to the readers of this book that I never shared with Vin: he was the only candidate I interviewed. Without a control group to compare results, I thought the more effort I put into cherry-picking the perfect candidate, the less valid and less broadly applicable the results of this *Future Proofing You* experiment would be. Vin was the first person I interviewed, and he ticked all the boxes.

Having selected Vin, the burden was now on me to deliver. My challenge would be to not only mentor Vin in business but to keep him motivated and focused for 365 days. Vin would often tell me that this is the hardest he'd ever worked, and that as a young man it was equally hard to forgo having any semblance of a social life. "I'll go on holiday when this is over," he would frequently lament. Though often exhausted and operating on too little sleep, Vin stayed positive for our entire year working together and persevered.

2

Leveraging Obstacles for Success

It's not that I'm so smart, it's just that I stay with problems longer.
—Albert Einstein

AFTER LOSING HIS ARM in a car crash, a young boy's parents thought it would help their son's self-confidence if he studied judo. The Japanese judo master was impressed with the 10-year-old's attitude and personally trained him week after week. The boy took the lessons seriously, practicing day and night. After three months of vigorous practice, the boy was frustrated that the old master had only taught him one single move. "Sensei, I have worked so hard on this move. I think I am ready to learn another one," the boy implored.

"This move you know," proclaimed the wise master. "This is the only move you will ever need to know." Wanting to be respectful of his old teacher, the boy continued to practice his one move and had the confidence to enter his first tournament. With his sensei looking on, the boy swiftly defeated his first opponent. Then he won his second and third matches, too. As he progressed through each round, the competition he faced grew larger and more experienced. Mustering all his strength, and to the amazement of everyone at the event, the young boy made it into the finals. Now, standing before him, was a teenager nearly twice his size. Seeing the one-armed boy and fearing for his safety, the referee told the sensei that as heroic as the child's accomplishments in

37

the day had been, he was going to call off the match. But the sensei insisted the tournament continue.

The towering teenager was quite skilled and went after the boy again and again. Unable to combat the teenager's size and strength, the boy moved quickly around the mat to avoid getting taken down. Getting tired from chasing the boy, the teenager let his guard down for a second and the boy seized the opportunity to use his one move and win the tournament. As they were leaving the tournament, the boy modestly asked his master, "How did I win against such an experienced opponent with just my one move?"

"Two reasons," responded the sensei with a smile. "First, you truly mastered one of judo's most challenging throws. And second, the only defense for that move is to grab the opponent's left arm."

The boy's problem had become his solution.

Truth #2 – Obstacles Are Opportunities in Disguise

Obstacles, not products, are the source of creating wealth. Solve a problem for your friends, you are popular. Solve for a few million, you become rich. Remove an obstacle for a billion and you change the world. Solving for others is at the heart of every great product, service, or company. Just like the boy's missing arm, the obstacles that have been holding you back all these years can be leveraged to create success.

One of the biggest misconceptions about the business of making money is the belief that wealth is achieved from selling products. Buy low. Sell high. Sure, it may appear that Sam Walton built a multi billion-dollar empire by selling lots of items for a low markup at Wal-Mart, but that's not what made Sam the richest man in America. Before Wal-Mart, there were thousands of retailers selling the very same discounted goods in every major city in America. What catapulted Sam's business to do over $500 billion a year was that he had the insight to see an unmet need. What differentiated Wal-Mart from those that came before is that while all the leading chains built their stores in major cities, Sam focused on the obstacles facing families in smaller towns. He removed the obstacle of having to plan a major shopping trip to the big city to load up on supplies. Walton made buying convenient for the millions of people who lived in rural towns like Rogers, Arkansas; Sikeston, Missouri; and Claremont, Oklahoma. Fifty years later, Jeff Bezos became the richest man in the world by solving the same problem Sam solved. Bezos sold the same products at the same price as his competitors. Amazon didn't focus on having the lowest price. Amazon made it easier for everyone to shop by moving into e-commerce on the internet while the competition was still focused on shopping malls. Bezos saved people time and removed all of the friction from making a purchase. No more loading the family into the car and circling through the parking lot looking for a space to park, only to discover that the items you wanted to purchase were out of stock.

Obstacles are everywhere. Be thankful you have problems, because they are the key to your salvation. The problems you endure everyday are most likely faced by millions of others. Problems don't have to be grandiose things like climate change or harnessing tidal energy – they just have to be inconvenient enough for people to be willing to pay for a solution. Remember, no one ever went into a hardware store wanting to buy a quarter-inch drill bit; what they wanted was a quarter-inch hole.

Like most women, Sandy Stein found herself constantly fumbling around in her purse to find her keys. Tired of this annoying problem, the 52-year-old flight attendant created a key clasp she named Key Finders Purse. It only took Sandy four months to reach $1 million in sales, and within eight months, she had sold more than 1 million units. Stein experienced a problem and recognized that she wasn't alone with wanting a solution to her problem.

So, the first step to solving problems is recognizing them. "It isn't that they cannot find the solution," English writer G.K. Chesterton noted, "It is that they cannot see the problem."[1] As I will repeat again and again in this book, insight and perseverance are the only two things you need to achieve success. This chapter will teach you how to hone your insight skills and identify obstacles that most people overlook.

Finding Problems to Solve

Life is pain ... Anyone who says differently is selling something.
—The Man in Black, *The Princess Bride*

The *3 Problems a Day 30-Day Challenge* is exactly what its name implies. Starting now, put down this book and write down three problems in your life. You must continue to write down three new problems every day for an entire month. Write each problem on a separate 3 × 5 index card and include as much detail as you can (so you don't forget in three weeks why you wrote it down in the first place). *You don't have time to walk the dog. You forgot to order T-shirts for your daughter's soccer team.* It really doesn't matter what the problems are, as long as they are yours personally (for this exercise, avoid the behemoth problems like world peace and curing cancer). In the beginning, the challenge is easy. Problems are all around you. Everyone you talk to has problems. But quickly, within a few days, you'll fail to recognize any major problems. This is where you need to start challenging your assumptions and take your brain off of autopilot.

Most people get stuck after the first few days. They think they have exhausted their list of problems. It is not that their lives are perfect, it is that they aren't paying attention. "Solving problems means listening," says billionaire entrepreneur Sir Richard Branson. To simplify our lives, many of the activities we do on a daily basis, we do on autopilot. We don't need to think about a new route to work, so we follow the same path day after day. We develop a mindset of doing things because that is the way we have always done it.

We accept our circumstances as if we are sleepwalking through life. The *3 Problems a Day 30-Day Challenge* is designed to wake you from your slumber. What isn't working? Where is there friction in your day? Take note of the smallest things and you may find hidden treasure. During the 30 days, concentrate on every moment of your day. Let's take your morning routine, for example. You wake up, grab your medication, and then the telephone rings. You have a nice chat with a friend and then aren't sure if you took your pill already. Most of us on autopilot would just guess and get on with our day. This is exactly what happened to my buddy Larry Twersky. After he finished the call, Larry couldn't remember whether he took his pill. If he did take it before the call and took another one, he could overdose, but if he didn't take his medication, he could get seriously ill. Most people would have just shrugged it off as a senior moment. But Larry recognized it as a problem. How many people forget to take their pills, or take too many, or not enough? How many people take prescription drugs? (Turns out, it's 55 percent of the American population.) In fact, Americans fill 4.3 billion prescriptions annually, according to IMS Institute for Healthcare Informatics.

With the costs of medications and healthcare continually rising, Larry's momentary problem was a multibillion-dollar business opportunity. Larry's solution was insanely simple. He took an inexpensive digital clock, like the kind you would find on a kid's Happy Meal watch, and attached it to a pill bottle lid. Every time you opened the bottle, the clock would reset to zero. So, if his product had existed when he was on that phone call, he could have just looked down at the lid. If it said it's been 12 hours since it was last opened, Larry would have definitively known that he hadn't taken his morning dosage. Thousands of drugstores picked up his TimerCap. From this one simple insight, Larry created a product that can help millions of people stay healthy and prevent accidental drug overdoses. Every moment of every day there is a potential to unmask a major problem and build a billion-dollar solution.

One of the ways to make the most of this exercise is to concentrate on that little voice in your head. You know, the one that is sounding out this sentence as you read it. Every time you hear that voice ask a question, write it down. *Where at the airport did I park my car? Why do hot dogs come in packs of 10 but hot dog rolls come 8 to the package?* Not all questions are problems, but having this heightened awareness will yield better results.

"Problems are nothing but wake-up calls for creativity," writes *Selling Power* author Gerhard Gschwandtner.[2] Get creative with your problems. If you get stuck, just look around at your family, friends, and coworkers. What problems are they complaining about? Or better yet, what problems do they face that you see and they don't?

My friend Dave Carlson was a second-generation roofer. His days consisted of putting on his work boots and climbing up ladders in sweltering heat or freezing cold just to throw a tennis ball tied to a cloth tape measure, so he could accurately measure the size of a roof. The cost of fixing or repairing a roof is a function of calculating the size of the roof. When a tree or hail storm damages your roof, the insurance carrier needs to know how big the roof is in order to estimate the cost of repairing it. As hazardous as Dave's job was, he was amazed how many insurance adjusters in suits and slippery dress shoes unknowingly risked their lives every day climbing up on roofs to survey the situation for themselves. Here was a problem where life and death hung in the balance. One night, while using Google Earth, Dave wondered why aerial photography can't be used to get the roof measurements. Working with a model birdhouse and his engineer brother-in-law, they created EagleView Technologies, which used algorithms to infer the roof's size, shape, pitch, and area. A few years later, the team sold their problem-solving company for $650 million and Dave never had to climb on a roof again. One obstacle, one insight, and Dave – who now has his own island in Central America – is Future Proof for life.

What both TimerCap and EagleView had in common was using existing technologies to solve existing problems. These founders didn't have to invent the digital watch or satellite photography, they just had to apply these tools to solving an unaddressed need. Neither of these founders were engineers, but they knew that an engineer could be hired to build their products. Remember: insight and perseverance are the only two things you need. EVERYTHING else can be hired. (Want proof? Every single person reading this sentence has written at least as much code as Steve Jobs, who co-founded the world's most successful computer company. It was Apple's other co-founder, Steve Wozniak, who wrote code. Steve was just a college-drop-out entrepreneur with perseverance.)

At the end of the month, if you are committed and diligent, you should have a list of 90 problems in need of solutions. Within your list of 90 problems could be the next billion-dollar idea. Now comes the fun part, deciding which opportunity to pursue. Sort your cards along two axes: scale and passion.

Every time I teach my course *How to Build a Hi-Tech Startup* at USC, invariably a student proposes delivering food to the dorms on campus. Yes, students get the munchies at night, but to go through the effort of building a business that doesn't scale when your TAM (total addressable market) is less than 3,000 potential customers is a complete waste of time. Hopefully, your problem's TAM is massive. Down the road, when you are raising money to grow your business, professional investors and venture capitalists will focus on quantifying your TAM. When deciding how big the potential market can be, don't limit yourself to your local city, state, or even country. How many people does the problem affect? Obviously, the more people impacted by a problem, the greater the financial opportunity. In guesstimating the TAM, be realistic in your assumptions. I once read a business proposal that started with the sentence, "If every American ate one rabbit burger per week ... " You may start by testing your idea locally, but concepts such as Uber, Airbnb, Facebook, and Dropbox were able to raise billions of dollars to go international because their TAM was global.

The second axis is even more important to your long-term success. Sort the problems according to your personal passion, as I mentioned previously (Chapter 6 takes an in depth look at perseverance and passion). Tom Bilyeu was part of a successful software startup but felt unfulfilled. He was passionate about nutrition and wanted to help people like his obese mother get healthy. Tom abandoned software and co-founded Quest Nutrition to live a life of purpose. When he started, there were already over 1,600 protein bars on the market, but most were loaded with sugar and other unhealthy ingredients. Quest didn't become the second-fastest growing private company in the US because there was a shortage of energy bars. It grew because its founders were passionately committed to healthy eating. When the company was acquired for $1 billion, Tom was able to devote his energies to his new passion: helping others realize their entrepreneurial potential by starting Impact Theory.

Starting any business is hard. All of the billion-dollar startups I mentioned in this chapter faced constant challenges and unforeseen obstacles, but it was passion that propelled them forward. *Which of your problems is most meaningful to you?*

Having spent the better part of the month identifying problems, the process for finding solutions is fairly straightforward. As the independent vice-chairman of Deloitte, I can tell you that every major consultancy has their unique framework for problem-solving. In fact, entire Harvard Business School courses are dedicated to the subject. I prefer my simple seven-step process that everyone can implement.

Seven Steps for Problem Solving

Step one is identifying the problem. Your 30-day exercise gave you a high-level problem to focus on, but now you need to dig deeper.

The more clearly you establish the goals and performance objectives of solving the problem, the easier it will be to identify the solution. Saying that the floor is dirty is a problem. Saying that brooms just push dirt around a floor better identifies the problem (and can lead to creating an electrostatic solution like Swiffer, which generates $500 million a year in sales for Procter & Gamble).

The second step is to define the goals. What is success? How would you define the problem being solved? Waze didn't magically make millions of cars disappear from the roads, but rather defined success as equally distributing the cars as efficiently as possible. Remember, your business doesn't have to create heaven on Earth, it just has to make people's lives less hellish. Get as much input from as many sources as possible when identifying success. You may find that other people's threshold for dealing with problems is lower or higher than yours. Your goal is to solve for the largest TAM that can be feasibly addressed. When the Swiffer marketing team framed their retailing problem as trying to get a 45-inch broom replacement product into the cleaning supply aisle at the supermarket, their solution became clearer (breakdown the mop handle into pieces so the package could fit neatly on the shelves alongside floor wax and detergents).

My personal favorite step is number three: brainstorming. You'd be amazed how many solutions have been hatched with only a pizza, a whiteboard, and a few erasable markers. Whole books have been written on brainstorming techniques. What all approaches have in common is the need to make everyone participating feel free enough to blurt out any idea. Your team needs to feel that they won't be made fun of or made to feel stupid. Since no one going into a brainstorming session has the complete answer, the trick I use to get people comfortable is to only ask for half of an idea. *I have half of an idea on how to approach this; does anyone have the other half?*

I was chairman of an online crowdfunding commercial real estate company that had a great business concept, but was struggling to get press coverage. Traditional newspaper real estate reporters didn't understand the digital world of crowdfunding, and busy internet writers had no interest in how apartment buildings and shopping centers get financed. By brainstorming, I was able to focus on the real problem. It wasn't about crowdfunding or real estate – the challenge was, where can you find journalists with excess time on their hands? The year was 2014, and the Coachella Valley Music Festival had just gone from being a one-weekend event to a two-weekend massive concert lineup. OutKast, Beck, Queens of the Stone Age, Pharrell, Bryan Ferry, Skrillex, and dozens more top acts were going to draw a massive audience. More importantly, massive press coverage. As I saw it, 600 members of the press were stuck in Palm Springs for the five days between the weekends, with nothing to write about. Now all that we had to do was figure out how to connect crowdfunding of commercial real estate to the world of music. I approached the Hard Rock Hotel in Palm Springs about doing a million-dollar crowdfunding campaign, and the results were massive press coverage, including front-page stories as far away as London. One brainstorming event, and the company was able to attract thousands of investors to our platform.

The more viewpoints you bring to your brainstorming, the more angles with which to look at the problem. This is one of the advantages of having a multicultural team. Different life experiences create different points of view. At this point of the process, you don't have to know if your solution is feasible or even what it would cost – you just need to coalesce around some possible methods. In a world of ever-changing technology, a good technique is to brainstorm solutions to existing problems using the latest buzzwords of the day as possible solutions. Is there a way that blockchain, virtual reality, the cloud, or artificial intelligence could solve the problem? The newer the approach to the solution, the less likely that someone else doesn't beat you to the market. The year that Uber took off, hundreds of startups launched *the Uber of* solutions. VCs funded everything from the Uber of dog walking (Rover.com), the Uber of housecleaning (Handy), the Uber of in-home massages (Soothe), and even the Uber of babysitting (Poppy). As a side note, if you are looking to raise capital for your new business, framing it in terms of another startup with a successful business model is genius. It communicates what you are doing quickly and appeals to all those investors who wish they had a piece of the original company. This approach is so common for fundraising that even bad ideas can get funded quickly.

Step four is to assess your alternative solutions. Some concepts will defy the laws of physics; others may have been tried by others and failed. Whenever and wherever possible, bring data into this stage of the decision-making process. What are consumers willing to pay? How much time or money will your solution save users? Is there a subset of users that would benefit most? Who are they, and why are their needs different? Just as you wouldn't test market a minivan to single guys, make sure you are getting answers from relevant sources. Keep researching and talking with prospective customers until you have just one or two alternative approaches.

Step five is selecting and validating the solution. Most likely, you will not hit it out of the park your first time at bat. Often, the reason something doesn't work is because in the act of testing it, you discover other unmet needs. As unbelievable as this will sound to millennials, when Nokia created the first mobile phone with a camera, it didn't sell because no one understood why they would want a camera on a phone. Nokia made a product that didn't solve a perceived need. To get the devices to catch on, they hired attractive young couples to hang out at busy tourist spots such as Times Square and ask people to take their picture. When the couple handed people a phone, the seed was planted in the future customers' minds that it would be great to always have a camera handy. Within two years of its introduction, people were taking more photos per year on their phones than the total number of photographs shot in the first 150 years of photography!

Step six is all about monitoring the results of your product in the market. Again, the quicker you can analyze your data, the faster you can respond to your market. With over 3 billion people now using social media, you never know where your product will take off. Grey Tech, a small manufacturer of vacuum cleaners and gardening tools in Worchester, England, had one Vlogger in Taipei post about how great the small GTech vacuum cleaned under his bed, and 40,000 units were sold in Taiwan! Thanks to the reach of Facebook, Instagram, TikTok, Snap, and LinkedIn, for the first time in history, every startup has global reach.

Step seven isn't the final step, because step seven never ends. Step seven is about evaluating your solution, the ever-changing dynamic marketplace, and your new copycat competitors. The first person you will educate in business is not your customer, it's your competition. You saw an opportunity that the existing players missed. Don't expect them to stay on the sidelines for long. When Google experimented with the first self-driving cars a few years ago, all of its potential competitors in Detroit, Japan, and Europe laughed it off because the cost of the LIDAR sensors was around $75,000 per vehicle. Today, InGaAs-based sensors from companies such as Luminar are just $3 per unit, and now everyone is jumping into the market.

What Problem Was Vin Clancy Going to Solve?

Before meeting me, Vin Clancy fancied himself a hacker. While by no means an engineer, Vin is a self-taught software enthusiast whose intellectual curiosity made him obsessed with testing out the latest and greatest shortcuts, hacks, and techniques for online marketing. When he started out, he couldn't even afford his own computer and used one at a public community center. To him, figuring out how things worked online wasn't a job, but a fun, engrossing, and free hobby. With no spare change to invest in proper online tools, Vin would spend hours scrounging around the dark corners of the internet for open-source utilities and shareware programs to get what he wanted done for free. In just a few years, Vin had spent enough time in chat groups searching for the latest and greatest that he was able to make a name for himself as a growth hacker, and he developed a small but loyal social media following.

Growth hacking is the art of competing with the big marketers for online attention without spending vast sums of advertising dollars on Google or Facebook. Where other "social media experts" required substantial budgets to reach a target audience, Vin drew satisfaction from achieving the same results without spending a penny. Vin's biggest challenge, however, was trying to figure out how to make a living off of being an expert in free software.

Coming from a blue-collar background, Vin had virtually no exposure to the corporate world of chief marketing officers (CMOs), advertising agencies, and brand managers. He was energetic, brash, and confident. He kept lists of online shortcuts and tricks for getting stuff done on the cheap. He defined his skillset as being a low-cost digital marketer. Unfortunately, this superpower tended to only appeal to those without the funds to pay for proper marketing and so Vin couldn't figure out how to make a living from growth hacking.

In our very first mentoring session, fame was the first roadblock I ran into with Vin. He craved validation. He wanted his mates and family back in England to know that he had made it in America. Before we started discussing what business he would bring to market, Vin made it very clear that Vin Clancy had to be the brand. He was adamant. Sears, Heinz, Ford, Disney, and countless others have named their companies after themselves for the very same reason as Vin. Turning one's name into a well-respected brand shows everyone what a success you are. And a century ago, when companies took decades to build and often stayed in families for generations (the fourth generation of the Ford family still controls Ford Motor Company), tying your name to a business made sense. But in the twenty-first century, when companies such as Katerra, Instacart, and Opendoor can go from concept to over a billion-dollar market cap in two years, founders should maintain a separate entity from their creations.

An independently branded company is easier to sell and leave than one that is intrinsically tied to the founder's name. Sharing a company name with a living founder can also prove a challenge for investors if the founder gets into trouble (as in the case of Martha Stewart's $2 billion home furnishings empire when she went to prison). In 2018, Papa John's namesake John Schnatter had to resign from the company he founded after the pizza chain came under fire for him making a racist comment, which caused their stock to crash 33 percent. In our very first mentoring session, I needed to convince Vin to adopt a brand name without turning him off to our entire mentoring experience. Mentoring is not forcing someone to change direction, but rather, giving them the knowledge from the mentor's experience to make a better-informed decision.

Luckily, I knew the perfect role model for Vin to emulate. Sir Richard Branson is perhaps the world's most famous entrepreneur, and yet he created a completely autonomous brand with Virgin. Sir Richard has launched over 300 companies with the name Virgin. He's had Virgin Music and Virgin Rail, Virgin Active and Virgin Brides, Virgin Comics and Virgin Cruises, Virgin Mobile and Virgin Money. His most recent venture, Virgin Galactic, is even eyeing space tourism. In my opinion, Virgin is the most brilliant brand name of all time. By definition, a virgin is young, innocent, and inexperienced. As a brand that means even when one of Sir Richard's companies fails (remember Virgin Cola?) the core brand grows even stronger because it shows the spirit of trying something new. I shared stories of Branson with Vin and shared how Branson had wanted me to come work for him. The more I talked about Branson's success, the more comfortable Vin was with creating a brand name for his new venture. Richard Branson was beyond famous. As the richest man in England, he was an icon. As he smiled and leaned in, I could see in his eyes that Vin wanted to be the next Branson. (Six months later, Vin would tell me it was the single best piece of advice he received all year and allowed him to create a successful company that was not dependent on him or his name.) Monetizing his personal brand would be put on the back burner for now.

Our process of brainstorming ideas for Vin resulted in two different potential businesses that he was equally passionate about pursuing: an online marketing agency and creating a digital product that he could sell to teach people how to do their own marketing. Having always done his growth hacking on the cheap, Vin was envious of the huge fees traditional agencies charged their corporate clients for the very same work Vin was doing for $100. What scared him about the agency business was he didn't have a clue as to the process of how to get corporate clients with large marketing budgets. The entire agency–client relationship was an opaque mystery to him.

Creating his own product, on the other hand, freed Vin from having to answer to anyone (clients, investors, employees). Vin's concern was that while he understood the ins and outs of online marketing, Vin didn't, in his mind, have a million dollars' worth of something to sell. Given the daunting task of needing to earn $83,333 per month to hit our target of $1 million in a year, we agreed that, at least for now, he had the bandwidth to pursue both ventures.

Vin's Million-Dollar Idea

"You've really had an influence on me," Vin Clancy emailed after reading *Disrupt You!* "After finishing chapter ten I had an idea for a business. It is the first idea I've ever had that isn't 'me' focused! I can't stop thinking about it."

Following what we had discussed, Vin wanted his agency to be the best in the world and to have a generic enough name to accommodate any pivot or client need. After researching available URLs, Vin anointed his aptly new company the World's Best Agency (worldsbestagency.com).

The business model for his new agency was our next discussion. Choosing the right business model is key to creating wealth quickly. For now, we agreed that Vin's agency would focus on the service business model and later Vin could test selling a product under his personal brand. His goal would be to focus on clients that would commit to a multi-month campaign as opposed to a one-time product launch. Building recurring revenue stream clients would mean that he wouldn't have to start each month prospecting from dollar one. By layering in new clients on top of prior ones, his revenues would multiply with the same amount of sales effort.

With Vin's agency model, I knew that sales would be lumpy. One month he could sign on three new clients and another month he could lose clients. But agencies build momentum. As clients' employees move on to to new jobs at other brands, they too will hire the agency that served them well at their last company. While the agency business takes time to grow, a tangible product's sales growth is based on one's marketing spend and sales funnel conversion. My hope was that if Vin reinvested the profits he made with the agency into marketing his product, a million dollars in revenue could be achieved. But how would he get his agency clients quickly?

As with many of you reading this book, your initial business idea or product may be too generic or undifferentiated. It is a lot harder to market an all-purpose home video camera than a helmet-mounted GoPro for outdoor sports enthusiasts. With the GoPro, marketers knew exactly who their customers would be and how to find them. Instead of competing with all the other video cameras on the cluttered shelves of

Best Buy, GoPro could sell their product at sporting goods stores, surf shops, and ski resorts. Launching a social media marketing agency in 2017 was hardly a novel business idea. Facebook had been around for over a dozen years and on any given day, LinkedIn listed over 130,000 social media job listings. Vin needed to find a niche to differentiate his agency.

In the prior chapter's brainstorming discussion, I suggested pairing your problem with the trending buzzwords of the day. Thousands of professional photographers and videographers were in business before drones flew into being. The first people to brand themselves as drone photographers quickly grew a new category of clients ranging from realtors to resort owners. If we had done this experiment back in 2000, we would have focused on the dot com boom. In the first decade of the twenty-first century, when I saw an explosion of companies around the concept of digital music, I was able to IPO a company of mine with just $30,000 in lifetime sales for $600 million. In the fall of 2017, it didn't take long for Vin and me to recognize that the global zeitgeist was coalescing around a brand-new $270 billion untapped market segment: cryptocurrency.

In 2017, everyone from personal trainers to Wall Street tycoons were caught up in the Bitcoin frenzy. Everyone's Facebook feed was filled with stories of how much money could be made. The year began with Bitcoin worth less than $1,000 a unit and ended 2017 with a price just shy of $20,000. The FOMO (fear of missing out) was further being stoked by industry "experts" like Octagon Strategy's Managing Director Dave Chapman predicting Bitcoin to top $100,000 in 2018. With millions of people flocking to invest, Bitcoin and Bitcoin exchanges didn't need any marketing help. But in its massive shadow, Bitcoin planted the seed for an entirely new crop to come to market: the alternative coins.

Alt coins, such as EOS, Ethereum, or Aspire, are cryptocurrencies that are designed to improve upon some of the systemic limitations of the original Bitcoin blockchain. Like miners racing to California in the gold rush of 1848, the stampede to launch initial coin offerings (ICOs) of new and improved cryptocurrencies had begun. By the time Vin and I sat down for our first meeting, over 1,000 altcoins were in the works, all racing to come to market before the quick and easy money vanished as quickly as it had appeared. How would all these new coins find a market and get discovered? If only there was a digital marketing agency that specialized in ICOs.

With that one session completed, Vin now had his plan for Future Proofing in place. He was going to focus on altcoins and launch the world's best agency for cryptocurrency.

As the only social media agency targeting this new sector of cryptocurrency (and therefore by definition, being the best agency in the world), Vin quickly signed up his first two clients and made $60,591 in his first month. Vin Clancy, agency owner and cryptocurrency marketing expert, was so energized from accomplishing this in his first 30 days that I believe he could have flown home to England without an airplane!

More important than making the money, Vin was delivering real value to his clients. With Vin's help, one of his cryptocurrency clients registered 36,000 customers for their ICO presale and raised more than $80 million in a single day. With this one case study, the World's Best Agency had proven it was true to its name.

As impressive as $60,000 a month sounds, Vin needed to grow his business by more than 50 percent immediately just to hit a million dollars in 12 months. I had faith in him, but was unsure of what obstacles lay ahead. I didn't know what to expect in the coming months, other than knowing it was going to be an amazing journey. As comedienne Lily Tomlin once joked, "The road to success is always under construction."

Notes

1. J Shah, *Heart Health: A Guide to the Tests and Treatments You Really Need* (New York: Rowman & Littlefields, 2019), 101.
2. Zig Ziglar, *Inspiration 365: Zig Ziglar's Favorite Quotes* (Naperville, IL: Sourcebooks, 2013), 149.

3

Harnessing Fear to Your Advantage

Fear is only as deep as the mind allows.

—*Japanese proverb*

IN THE MIDDLE AGES, a notorious thief was taken before the king of Lyonesse to pay for his crimes. The king had the convict taken down into the castle's musty cellar, where he offered the man a choice of two punishments. He could be swiftly hung on the gallows or face what was behind a large, foreboding rusty iron door. Without hesitation, the thief chose the rope. As the hangman placed the noose around his neck, the thief inquired, "My king I beseech you, what's behind that door?"

"I offer all the same choice," the King exclaimed with a laugh, "yet everyone chooses the rope."

With his last breath, as the hangman tightened the knot around his neck, the thief pleaded again, "Obviously, I won't tell anyone. What's behind the door?"

"Freedom," sighed the King, adding, "but it seems most people are more afraid of the unknown than death."

Truth #3 – Fear Is Good

Fear kills more dreams than failure ever will. From the parable of the talents in the New Testament, to the Cowardly Lion in the *Wizard of Oz*, we are taught that fear is a sin or, at best, a human weakness. Because of these pervasive cultural stigmas, every time we fear failure or rejection, fear public humiliation or financial ruin, we feel ashamed and unworthy. Honestly, who among us would have chosen the iron door?

As much as motivational speakers love to exclaim, "What would you do if you couldn't fail?" we know that we *can* fail. Given the real-world consequences of losing our job, our home, our family, or our life, who wouldn't be fearful? Fear is one of our most primal instincts. To varying degrees, each of us regularly experiences fear. Some are afraid to speak up in a meeting and look foolish. While others fear getting promoted and failing in the new position. Some people's anxiety level is so high that they dread whenever the telephone rings at work for fear it could be the boss calling to fire them. Fear elicits a powerful physiological response in humans that can range from heart palpitations and dizziness, to sweaty palms and dry mouths. In extreme situations, fear induced panic attacks can immobilize a person or throw them into shock. Fear can literally scare you to death. Against this litany of horrors, how can I proclaim that fear is good?

To have any chance of success in life or of *Future Proofing You*, the third of the 12 truths in this book is that you must accept that fear is good. Quite candidly, without fear, none of you would be alive. You are alive today because of the fearful actions taken by 7,000 generations of your family. Only those who ran away from sabretooth tigers, marauding hoards, failing environmental ecosystems, plagues, and evil tyrants, lived long enough to raise the next generation. Had any one of your forbearers broken this continuous chain of anxiously worrying about the world around them, you wouldn't exist. They lived in fear and survived. Fear kept you washing your hands and social distancing during the pandemic. We are all biologically programmed to be fearful.

Let's take a moment to think about our genetic history and human evolution. The oldest part of our brain, the brain stem, is commonly referred to as our lizard brain. Unlike the more advanced brain functions that regulate our emotional bonding with others or logical reasoning, the brain stem controls primitive survival instincts such as aggression and fear. The lizard brain's first response to any stimuli is to determine will this thing harm me? The brain stem is just as responsible today for keeping us safe as it was for Pleistocene cavemen 150,000 years ago. When faced with stress, the brain's way of protecting you is to produce the stress hormones cortisol and adrenaline, so that you can be ready with a fight or flight response. Before you have even a second for logical thought, the lizard brain has to decide if it should stand its ground or flee. Your higher brain functions have no choice in the matter. It is hubris to believe that you can become fearless. The fearless perish. Or as the Greek orator Demosthenes is credited with saying after fleeing the battle of Chaeronea in 338 BCE, "For he that fights and runs away may live to fight another day."

The journey from hunter-gatherer to always-connected, mobile-equipped, 24/7 entrepreneur only intensifies the societal stresses on our reptilian instincts. Entrepreneurs live with a cornucopia of persistent fears: fear of running out of money, fear of competition, and the fear of facing family and friends who trusted us with their money. Anyone seeking to change the status quo will face constant rejection and public humiliation. "Let them ridicule you, laugh at you, hurt you, and ignore you, but never let them stop you," author Apoorve Dubey wrote in her book *The Flight of Ambition*.[1] Your lizard brain feels the fear, but is ill-equipped to deal with the nuances of modern twenty-first century life. With fear so hard-wired into the very core of our being, the only way for entrepreneurs to thrive is to embrace fear. Courage is not the absence of fear, but the ability to persist in spite of it.

You will not conquer your fears because you biologically cannot. The basic building block at the center of your genetic code is a fear response system. You are hardwired to be fearful. But what you can do is learn how to channel your fears. Athletes learn how to channel and control fear as a means of motivation. They harness fear as a cognitive state, which then triggers the fight-or-flight response and gives their bodies the adrenaline needed to compete.

Psychologist Henry Murray's seminal work *Explorations in Personality*, which was published by Oxford University Press in 1938, was the

first to study how fear of failure can act as positive motivation for success. What Murray discovered was that in avoidance of fear, the mental
act of trying to avoid the fearful consequences increased students' likelihood for success. Decades of further studies on athletes have shown
that because decisions are made so quickly in sports, fear is the means
of motivation for not failing. To transform the anxiety of fear into a
positive motivational force in business, the question you need to ask
yourself is, "What should you be *more* afraid of than failing?"

Before we can learn to channel the energy of our fears into a more
useful tool, we need to identify and acknowledge the known fears
universally faced by everyone starting a business. Based on extensive
research at Harvard Business School, the seven fears plaguing today's
startup founders are financial security, ability to fund the venture,
personal ability/self-esteem, potential of the idea, threats to social
esteem, the venture's ability to execute, and lost opportunity costs. All
seven of these fears are rooted in the challenges of launching every
new business. Opening a new restaurant has the same range of fears
as designing an autonomous car. At first glance of the statistics, all of
these fears appear to be well founded and rational. According to the
US Bureau of Labor Statistics, about 20 percent of small businesses
will fail in their first year, and about half will close shop by their fifth
year.[2] So, are these fears justified?

Before answering the question, let's frame it differently: What happens if you don't try to launch your business and play it "safe"? You
most certainly won't get rich at your current job. Without earning
more money, how will you fund your children's college education, pay
off your mortgage and credit cards, or save enough to retire comfort-
ably? The longer you put off trying for a better future, the less time and
chances you will have to succeed before you die. These fears of inaction are also equally real. By recognizing the consequences of inaction,
you can heighten your awareness of one set of fears while diminishing
the power of your initial set of fears. Choose and prioritize your fears
wisely. Either you control your fear or your fear controls you.

Given how short our time on this planet actually is, it amazes me
how little time we give to thinking about our own mortality. Today at
work, you just traded a day of your life – a day you will never get back,
no matter how wealthy you become, for your company. Was it worth it?

There is nothing scary about going to a meaningless job, because you think, "It's just a day." If you're lucky, you'll probably get 29,000 of them in your lifetime. But what if you stay at a job you don't like for a year, five years, until you retire? You trade your entire life for what? Shouldn't you be more afraid of wasting the one and only life you will ever get than fearing something new that might not work out?

How many of us are living the lives we dreamt of when we were in high school or college? When did you stop dreaming? You cannot live forever, but what you create and build in your lifetime can. Immortality is making a difference with the time we have. Are you making a difference? Is your job, your career fulfilling you? And if it's not, why are you trading the only life you have for something you don't want?

And here's the real paradox – if your job isn't fulfilling, why are you so afraid of losing it?

When you leave your job to launch your business, the first fear you will face is losing financial security. In your mind, you are giving up something tangible for something ephemeral. Your spouse, parents, or friends will think you crazy, adding the fear of embarrassment to your stresses. Haven't we been taught that it is better to have the bird in the hand rather than the two in the bush? That old adage doesn't apply if the bird in hand is sick and dying. Instead of worrying about the potential financial insecurity of launching a new business, perhaps you should start worrying about the financial viability of your current employer.

Fear Inaction More than Action

The odds are, even if you didn't take the entrepreneurial leap, you won't last long at your current job. The average US worker tenure is down to only 4.2 years, down from 4.6 years in 2014 and 5.1 years in 2008. What if the company you work for goes out of business? What if it gets acquired or merges with another company? According to Thomson Reuters, 2017 set a record for the most US mergers and acquisitions in a calendar year.[3] When a $34 billion telecommunications giant like CenturyLink merges with cable company Level 3, or Disney purchases $52.4 billion worth of assets from Fox, the first action of the combined companies is to find "process and efficiency savings" (corporate consulting speak for getting rid of all employees in duplicate roles). The new entity doesn't need to maintain two human resource departments, or sales forces, or warehouses, etc. With each merger, excess offices and factories are closed, impacting the surrounding local businesses and suppliers that service these workers. America is experiencing the greatest merger and acquisition boom in history. The US has seen more than $10 trillion worth of merger activity since the 2008 recession.

More concentration equals less employment. You may excel at your job, but your office, plant, division, company, or industry could go away with the stroke of a pen. The community you live in that was sustained by one major industry could wither away like so many rustbelt towns across America's Northeast. Unless you sit on your employer's board, you really have no control over your future security. If you are still unsure, ask anyone who worked in the auto industry in the 1980s, the music industries in the 1990s, or in brick-and-mortar retail today. Century-old companies such as EMI, JC Penney, Renown, Hertz, Brooks Brothers, Neiman Marcus, and Pacific Gas & Electric have either shuttered or filed for bankruptcy in the past few years. Inaction should be the more fear-inducing choice. At least with your own startup, you can manage the risks and have greater control over your fate. So, would you rather control your own destiny or blindly accept the incompetence of others?

Overcoming the Fear of No Funding

The second most common fear with stepping out on your own is funding. How will you ever raise the capital you need? Again, try to reframe the fear into a growth mindset question: To whom should I give the opportunity of funding my company? Seriously, there are thousands of people whose full-time job is giving others money to pursue their goals.

Venture Capital firms pumped more than $136 billion into startups in 2019 – including 252 mega-deals with investments of over $100 million. When they began, most of those VC-funded startups were no different than your business. The founders had a premise, supported by a small team, and maybe a handful of customers. While the large billion-dollar deals such as Uber and Airbnb make the headlines, according to the National Venture Capital Association, startups with billion-dollar valuations accounted for less than 1 percent of all funding.

What if you don't have venture capital firms like Sequoia Capital or Greylock Partners on speed dial? How about asking your parents, aunts and uncles, or friends from college? Raising money from friends and families rivals traditional VCs in dollar amounts and dwarfs them in volume of deals. Last year, brand-new startup businesses raised more than $60 billion from the people who know them best, their friends and family. One of the added benefits of this type of funding is that when your business takes off, you've made your friends rich as well. Jeff Bezos's parents invested $250,000 in Amazon and became billionaires as a result! Best of all, friends and family aren't solely focused on tech. If you are a fan of the television show *Shark Tank*, listen carefully to the entrepreneurs' stories. Nearly all contestants have gone through a friends-and-family funding round prior to making it onto the program.

There are also strategic investors who focus on funding companies that help their own industry grow. When Ray Kroc was raising funds for his new fast-food franchise concept McDonald's, he went to meatpackers that would benefit from the increased consumption of hamburgers. Many countries, states, cities, and regions have investment funds to support local job growth. Industries ranging from farming to pharmaceuticals have strategic investment funds and the connections to help neophyte companies find customers.

Private-equity firms are a source of capital that not only invest capital, but also supply experienced management teams that can help you grow your enterprise. In 2020, private equity firms stockpiled more than $1.5 trillion in uncommitted capital.[4] As gigantic as this number appears, it only represents 2 percent of total investable capital worldwide. Initial public offerings (IPOs), private placement memorandums, reverse public shells, leveraged buyouts, initial coin offerings (ICOs), and a host of other channels are all used for funding. For US-based companies needing under $5 million, the Small Business Administration is an excellent place to start. In 2018, the SBA's average loan amount was $425,500.

For complex transactions, investment bankers can (for a percentage of the funds raised) help you get the capital you need to succeed. Investment bankers can help you determine the value of your business and can then market the investment to potential buyers with whom they have worked before. When I started my first company in my twenties, I didn't know any of this and made the costly mistake of trying to bankroll my new business with my credit cards. (Don't try this, the usurious interest rates and onerous penalties will crush you.) What I have learned from four decades of fundraising since then is that there is plenty of money out there – all you have to do is learn how to ask for it. The proof is in the results. Millions of people just like you are getting funded. According to a 2015 study, 73 percent of small business owners reported being able to access enough capital for their companies.[5]

Overcoming the Fear of Going Broke

And what if it all goes south and you have to file bankruptcy? At least five of Forbes's richest families have had to face bankruptcy at one point along their journey. The Hunt family of Texas, which inherited the fortune of oil wildcatter H.L. Hunt, saw their fortune wiped out in the 1980s and filed bankruptcy after quickly losing $7.2 billion by speculating on silver prices. Today, that same family is worth over $15 billion. Bill Gates's and Walt Disney's first companies failed. Having failed once, they had no fear of failure to overcome with their next businesses. But they didn't stop trying. They failed until they succeeded.

Instead of fearing what could go wrong. Fear what happens if you never try. For some inspiring motivation, visit an old-age home and ask the occupants their biggest regrets in life. It won't be the things they tried and failed at. It will be the things they were afraid to try. There is nothing sadder than wasted talent and a wasted life. "I coulda been a contender," Marlon Brando's character Terry Malloy laments in the film On the Waterfront. "I coulda been somebody, instead of a bum, which is what I am."

Living a life of regret is painful. Putting off your business's launch only limits the time you can dedicate to making it a success. My answer, whenever I'm asked if now is a good time to launch a business, is always the same, "The best time to launch your new company was a year ago; the second-best time is now." Instead of fearing the failure rates of new small businesses, learn how to minimize the risks and multiply your chances for success. Following the 12 truths in this book will go a long way in Future Proofing your enterprise.

The fact that 80 percent of businesses with employees survive their first year, according to the Bureau of Labor Statistics, should tell you that your fears are unfounded and blown out of proportion. Understanding why most small businesses fail demystifies your fears. With a growth mindset, you can turn each fear into an actionable obstacle to overcome. As you isolate each risk factor, you develop a plan for mitigating failure. If you can deal with it, you no longer need to fear it.

The true statistics of starting your own business should allay your fears. Small businesses employ 48 percent of all private-sector employees in the United States. Small companies account for 97.7 percent of all exporting firms and 33.6 percent of known export value. Need more proof of the power your destiny will have with a small business? Since the recession of 2008 (and in spite of all of the massive corporate mergers discussed earlier), small businesses now account for 63 percent of net new jobs created in America. To an ever-increasing percentage, the US economy and America's standing in the world rests on the innovation and grit of small business founders. You have the power to change the world, and your only fear should be wasting the opportunity while you have the time to wield it.

The most pernicious of the founders' fears is doubt. Doubt will always exist. When I launched this experiment with Vin Clancy, I had doubts that he could earn a million dollars in a year. Did I have fears of looking like a fool if he didn't achieve this seemingly Herculean goal of going from homeless to Future Proof in under a year? Of course, I did. Did I let doubt stop me in my tracks? Never. Doubt, like the fears about your business, must be reframed and examined closely. What aspects of your situation cause you to doubt and how can those specific factors be mitigated?

"Every time I was called on in class, I was sure that I was about to embarrass myself," Facebook COO Sheryl Sandberg writes in her book *Lean In*. "Every time I took a test, I was sure that it had gone badly. And every time I didn't embarrass myself – or even excelled – I believed that I had fooled everyone yet again."[6] Sandberg goes on to explain that many women harbor fears of being judged as a bad mother, wife, or daughter when they pursue their careers. These societal pressures can change the internal monologue of self-doubt from can I do it, to should I even try to do it?

Renaissance artist Michelangelo, perhaps the greatest painter in history, was plagued with doubt. When ask by Pope Julius II to paint the ceiling of the Sistine Chapel in the Vatican, he at first refused by saying that he was just a sculptor and not a painter. Artists, like successful business leaders, learn that the only way to "conquer" doubt is to push through it. So intense and persistent was post impressionist painter Vincent van Gogh's self-doubt that he sought help in mental institutions. Yet van Gogh knew the solution to his problems was the brush in his own hand. "If you hear a voice within you say you cannot paint," van Gogh said, "then by all means paint and that voice will be silenced."

"One of the ego's favorite paths of resistance is to fill you with doubt," bestselling author and clinical psychologist Ram Dass wrote. Doubt stems from self-esteem issues and a fear of not having the ability to succeed. Or as Dass put it, "Your problem is you're too busy holding onto your unworthiness."[7]

When I began my career, I didn't think I was unworthy, I knew it. I was trying to break into Hollywood any way I could think of, but I had no marketable skills and no industry connections. What I did have was a wife, two kids, college loans, credit card debt, and a mortgage to pay. My fear of letting down my sons was greater than my self-doubt. Whenever I felt the fear of failure, I looked at my small boys and focused on the life I wanted to provide for them. Fear of failing as a father propelled me forward. Fear fueled my rocket engines. Utilizing the "Fake it 'til you make it" approach to hustling, I took any and every production job I could get to pay the bills. My very first day on a movie set was as a technical advisor on a Blake Edwards picture called *Mickey and Maude*. I had talked my way into a job I was ruefully unqualified for (I truly knew nothing about the technology I was supervising). What if a piece of equipment broke and I was called on to fix it? What if I was asked a technical question and didn't know the answer. My fear was all consuming.

But I was going to get paid $1,000 a day – a fortune to a 22-year-old back in the 1980s when the average annual income in the US was just $15,239. Now Blake Edwards, while a brilliant director, had a reputation for being a tyrant on his set. Day one, I was petrified. I was so fearful that I figured if I didn't say anything all morning and could make it until lunch and then get fired; I would get fed and collect $500 dollars. That was my big showbiz career plan – don't get fired until after lunch. Frozen with fear, I spent all morning hiding in the shadows out of the director's view. I stood in the corner and didn't introduce myself to a soul. When the assistant director announced lunch, I ran to the catering truck as fast as I could. I grabbed my tray and sat at the farthest table. Unfortunately, what I didn't know about making a movie was that the cast are the first ones to get fed. Second in the chow line was the star of the film, the British comedian Dudley Moore. He got his food, followed me, and sat next to me. Now I figured I must have accidently sat at the star table and was definitely getting fired! *"Well at least I got fed,"* I thought to myself as I quickly wolfed down my steak.

What I didn't know was that Dudley, seeing me eating first, figured I was the producer's kid or related to somebody important at the studio, so he just started chatting away. Once everyone else arrived for lunch and saw me in the "inner circle," I was golden for the rest of the picture. Thirty-nine years later, I must confess here in writing that I was never asked to do a single thing on that picture. And I did nothing so flawlessly, that the production manager hired me for his next picture, *Down and Out in Beverly Hills.* Harnessing fear and overcoming doubt launched my career, just at it will yours.

Proven Technique for Tackling Doubt

Whenever you are confronted with your self-doubts or paralyzed by your fears, just ask yourself one simple question: What's the Worst Thing that Could Happen? (WTWTCH) We all have vivid imaginations and can entertain wild thoughts of unlikely scenarios, so focus on what realistically could happen if you tried and failed. There is a brilliant scene in the movie *A Beautiful Mind* where Russell Crowe's character John Nash is at a bar with his college friends trying to meet women. John, seeing that all his friends are focusing their attention on the prettiest girl, shares with them what he believes is the worst thing that can happen, "If we all go for the blonde and block each other, not a single one of us is going to get her. So, then we go for her friends, but they will all give us the cold shoulder because no one likes to be second choice. But what if none of us goes for the blonde? We won't get in each other's way and we won't insult the other girls. It's the only way to win."

Whenever I ask myself WTWTCH questions, I also must ask WTWTCH if I don't do it. As with all fears, doubt can be superseded by greater fears. I recently received an email from a reader of *Disrupt You!* who had been suicidal. A middle-aged woman with a grown daughter, she had quit her six-figure job in real estate management to pursue her passion and start a small rental business:

> *I moved to Atlanta with a small savings and I started 3 Airbnbs. I didn't have enough capital to pay the rent and maintenance for all 3 units and I ended up losing all 3 units and being evicted from my apt. And, it all happen so fast. I was devastated, depressed, and sick to my stomach. My depression and fear turned to suicide. That is – until I shared my thoughts with my daughter (thinking she would dial 911). As I laid in the bed with swollen eyes from crying, I said to my daughter, "I'm thinking about committing suicide," and she turned to me and said, "You're thinking about killing yourself over money? That's the dumbest thing I've ever heard." She said, "Mommy, entrepreneurs fail every day. Get in line if you think you did anything unusual." Well that wasn't the reaction I was looking for. I was imagining the ambulance taking me away in a straitjacket. I think I wanted the drama to distract me. But that night was the first night I got a good night's sleep. And I began to think, maybe I should keep trying.*

Her daughter was right. The worst thing that could happen in business is that you lose all your money. Felicia had survived that. She no longer had to fear going broke, and was writing to tell me that my book had helped her through the rough times. She learned that her failure wasn't due to a bad business idea, but rather, a failure in resource planning. Building on what she had learned, she was now launching another business. She had survived her worst fears and was stronger because of it.

Every experience helps you grow. With startups, you either earn or learn. Many investors even prefer entrepreneurs who have failed in the past (they learned their lessons on someone else's dollar). In fact, 80 percent of billion-dollar unicorn startups had a founder who had started a company before.[8] To every person reading this book and still having doubts, I can say with absolute certitude that up to this moment in your life, you have survived everything that you have ever feared. Think about it. As Friedrich Nietzsche so succinctly put it, "That which does not kill us, makes us stronger."

Harnessing the Three Primary Fears of Others

"Too many of us are not living our dreams because we are living our fears," motivational speaker Les Brown noted.[9] If the fear is so universal, why not harness it to help you fund your business, build your team, increase sales, and even find quality mentors? What makes fear so great is that by understanding other people's fears, you can use them to help you succeed.

Turns out, everyone you meet in your day, everyone you will interact with at work, and everyone that is key to the success of your business is also governed by fear. We all are. While the vast majority of salespeople and management professionals would tell you to focus on building a bond and being likable to a prospective client, the truth is that being liked or loved is not within your control. Planting the seeds of fear, however, can be. "It is better to be feared than loved," sixteenth-century philosopher Niccolò Machiavelli observed, "if you cannot be both."

I am not suggesting that you use Mafia scare tactics to intimidate prospects, but rather you consider the other person's primal motivation in crafting your approach to working together. You know what you want to get out of a meeting, but did you ever think about what motivates the person sitting across the table?

Imagine for a moment that you have a new product that is perfect for a large corporation. The company could save vast amounts of money using your product over its existing supplier. In fact, the company could end up buying millions of dollars' worth of goods from you over the next few years. For you, this may be the most important meeting of your entire career. For the corporate executive sitting across the desk, this meeting is the only thing preventing him from leaving for lunch. In such a situation, it doesn't matter how likeable and charming of a salesperson you are, or how salient your pitch is, your prospect is thinking about his lunch. Having surmised that you are not a physical threat, the man's lizard brain has focused on the third of the primal four Fs: feeding.

"This filtering system of the crocodile brain has a very shortsighted view of the world," Oren Klaff explains in his book *Pitch Anything*. "Since this is not an emergency, how can I ignore this or spend the least amount of time possible on it?"[10]

But what happens if you mention to the executive that his competition has just started using your product to increase their margins, or that your boss is meeting with his boss later in the week to discuss this same topic, or that you have some inside information on which divisions are being shuttered after the recently announced merger? Competition, embarrassment, and changing circumstances all instantly elicit the fear response. Any of the aforementioned statements will make the executive fearful and force his brain to release adrenaline and cortisol and light up his synaptic nerves like the siren on a firetruck. No caveman thought about his hunger when he was about to become a sabretooth tiger's lunch. In the mind of the executive, feeding will now take a backseat to the defense instincts of fighting or fleeing.

The truth is that there are three primary fears that can be your greatest ally in business: fear of unemployment, fear of missing out (FOMO), and fear of public humiliation. Each is a tool that, if properly used, you can leverage to achieve your goals.

Even though the US economy has sharply rebounded since the 2008 recession, employees' psyches can take an entire generation to recover. My parents were children of the Great Depression, which conservatively skewed their views on job security, money, and debt for the rest of their lives. In a recent NHP Foundation study, 75 percent of Americans are still worried they could lose their homes and 40 percent of respondents feared that job loss could trigger the loss of their homes. Fear of job loss is so profound that more than half of Americans have not taken more than a week of vacation in the past year according to the Department of Labor for fear of appearing dispensable. Knowing that this is the mindset of the majority of people you will interact with in your career, how can you make meeting you or doing business with you a priority? How can not working with you cost that person their job or their promotion? Self-preservation is to most corporate executives their paramount driving force. Self-preservation is so top of mind that many executives "duck-and-cover" during mergers for fear that any decision they make could get them noticed or fired. If you can put this arrow in your quiver, it's the most versatile weapon in the fear arsenal. By framing the opportunity you are presenting as an existential threat, fearful executives will have to pay attention and find a way to resolve the fearful situation you created. Your goal is to make working with you the most logical solution.

FOMO, fear of missing out, is a complex fear. This second fear is a powerful cocktail made up of equal shots of fear, greed, and ego. The FOMO fear is that inaction will mean missing their chance. Greed is triggered because the opportunity in front of them could have been theirs for the taking. Ego comes into play because their pride will be hurt by being so stupid as to miss out. The entirety of social media, who has the coolest life and the most followers culture, is built on manipulating our FOMO. When all you see online is the greatest hits reel of everyone else's lives, the fear of missing out can become all consuming. In business, FOMO is best leveraged whenever there is a herd mentality. The larger the company or the industry, the less likely that anyone in management wants to be the outlier. There is a reason the big three automakers always get into financial trouble at the same time – they think and act as a herd. Too many managers fear that sticking their neck out with an original idea can get their head chopped off. In today's nervous corporate culture, most executives are lemmings – they want to be the first to go second.

My best use of FOMO in sales involved four US presidential candidates and control of the White House. Given the recent events with Russia and Facebook, it is hard to imagine that just one election prior, no one in Washington was thinking about using social media to elect a president of the United States. Four years before Russian trolls figured out how to influence the 2016 US presidential election, I published a whitepaper titled, *All Politics Is Social: Social Media Engagement Will Decide Election 2012*. My assertion as to the importance of social media as a communications channel was provocative at the time, as none of the major presidential candidates were spending any of their vast campaign war chests on Facebook or Twitter advertising. My whitepaper was also self-serving. In 2011, I was CEO of a social media advertising startup in desperate search of clients and ad revenue. Recognizing that US presidential candidates would be spending $7 billion that year, I was determined to get a piece of the action. At the time, campaign managers spent the vast majority of their ad budgets on television and radio. After my first meeting with one of the candidates' campaign managers, I quickly realized that with all the pressures they were under 24 hours a day, the last thing they had any time for was learning about a new medium. The last time any of them ran a presidential race was in 2007, when Facebook had less than 20 million users (and most of those weren't voters). As I saw it, I had three challenges: no one understood what I was selling, no one was interested in what I was selling, and therefore, no one was buying what I was selling. And even if I solved those three issues, most campaigns demanded exclusivity from their vendors, which would have precluded me from signing up more than one presidential candidate. So, I flipped the script.

First, I met with the technical staffs of both the Democratic National Committee and the Republican National Committee. I hired a lobbyist to get me in front of anyone on Capitol Hill who understood anything about the internet. I let it be known that we considered our SocialVibe Network to be the equivalent of broadcast television networks such as ABC, CBS, and NBC. I wanted to be fair and let both sides of the aisle know that we would not be giving any candidate exclusive access to the more than 100 million US registered voters we reached daily online. I then let Governor Mitt Romney's campaign know the only days I could meet with them in Boston to answer questions, because I had to be in Washington, DC, Georgia, and Texas. I used the same tactics with the campaigns of Texas Governor Rick Perry, Georgia Tea Party Activist Herman Cain, and of sitting President Barack Obama.

Each campaign manager assumed his competition was using us. I had no presidential campaign experience, but these managers couldn't take the career-ending risk of being the only campaign manager not using social media. I never did get to explain social media to any of these four candidates' campaign managers, but all of them became pay-ing clients. FOMO is a powerful fear. From that day on, every new campaign manager was afraid to be the only one not using social media and today, it is the most powerful driving force in American politics. This example also leads us to the last of our great three fear tools: fear of public humiliation.

No one likes to look stupid. Late-night comedian Jimmy Kimmel regularly makes a bit out of asking random people on the street what they thought of a certain new movie or band. The joke is that Kimmel makes up these nonexistent films, and with the cameras rolling, watches as people talk glowingly about how great the movie was and how they are planning to see it again that weekend. These people are not chronic liars, but the fear of looking stupid on national television is so strong that the average person would rather pretend that they know what's going on than admit their ignorance. If you can plant the seed, as I did with the presidential campaign managers, that they have more to risk *personally* by not doing something and looking stupid, you'll close the deal.

You don't have to be a trained psychologist to realize that constantly dwelling in the past and focusing on prior mistakes robs you of today's time and energy to move forward. But ignoring past lessons that you can learn from is not how we progress. Babies learn to walk by not being afraid to fall down. They keep on trying what doesn't work until they discover what does work. This one simple learning-to-walk paradigm is how mankind went from dwelling in caves to taking one small step on the moon. Entrepreneurs must be forward-focused and harness their fears. We are dreamers who translate our visions of tomorrow into actionable goals.

There was much for Vin to be fearful of in launching the World's Best Agency. Would he get clients? Could he help them achieve success? Would the ICO market evaporate as quickly as it materialized? To Vin's credit, all of these fears would be supplanted by his greater fear: would he disappoint his mentor and lose this one opportunity for success?

During our mentoring sessions, I never had to call out Vin's fears. Vin had already told his family and friends about our experiment. His strong British fear of public humiliation was greater than his private doubts. Vin's confidence was also bolstered by his first month's success. By the close of month two, Vin had exceeded his expectations by earning another $80,026 and increased his year-to-date total revenue to $140,617. I was

(continued)

(continued)

hopeful that with two successful months under his belt, Vin would have the mental skills to tackle whatever setbacks might be ahead. What I wasn't anticipating is how quickly failure would strike.

Notes

1. Apoorve Dubey, *The Flight of Ambition* (Basingstoke, UK: Macmillan Publishers India Limited, 2009), 64.
2. Katherine Gustafson, "What Percentage of Businesses Fail and How to Improve Your Chances of Success," Lending Tree (August 7, 2020), www.lendingtree.com/business/small/failure-rate/.
3. Dan Primack, "2017 Was a Record Year for Mergers and Acquisitions," *Axios* (January 3, 2018), www.axios.com/2017-was-a-record-year-for-mergers-and-acquisitions-2522131994.html www.axios.com/2017-was-a-record-year-for-mergers-and-acquisitions-2522131994.html.
4. Kate Rooney, "Private Equity's Record $1.5 Trillion Cash Pile Comes with a New Set of Challenges," CNBC January 3, 2020.
5. Georgia McIntyre, "What Percentage of Small Businesses Fail? (And Other Need-to-Know Stats)," *Fundera* (September 14, 2020), https://www.fundera.com/blog/what-percentage-of-small-businesses-fail.
6. Sheryl Sandberg, *Lean In: Women, Work, and the Will to Lead* (New York: Knopf Double Day, 2013), 28.
7. Ram Dass, *Journey of Awakening: A Meditator's Guidebook* (New York: Random House, 2012), 177.
8. Andrew Vasylyk, "Why VCs 'almost blindly' Invest in Founders with Previous Exits," Medium.com (August 28, 2018), medium.com/startupsoft/why-vcs-almost-blindly-invest-in-founders-with-previous-exits-23824334a260.
9. M.D. Sharma, *Top Inspiring Thoughts of Les Brown* (New York: Prabhat Prakashan, 2020), 89.
10. Oren Klaff, *Pitch Anything: An Innovative Method for Presenting, Persuading and Winning the Deal* (New York: McGraw-Hill Education, 2011), 11.

4

Embracing Failure as Part of the Journey

She was unstoppable. Not because she did not have failures or doubts, but because she continued on despite them.

—*Beau Taplin*

VACUUM CLEANERS SUCK. At least that's what they are supposed to do. In 1979, when a young boat designer purchased what claimed to be the most powerful vacuum cleaner in the world, he was frustrated. Rather than sucking up the dirt, it mostly just pushed it around his workshop floor. Having once visited a sawmill that used a cyclonic separator to remove sawdust from the air, he wondered why the same technology couldn't be used in a home vacuum cleaner? Anticipating instant wealth, he quit his job and quickly built a working prototype. But the prototype needed improving. He spent the next five years, and every penny of savings, trying to build prototype after prototype of his bagless vacuum cleaner. While his wife worked to support his obsession, everyone else laughed at him. After his first 5,126 prototypes failed, James Dyson's 5,127th prototype made him a $5 billion fortune. Best of all, he did it without any investors or shareholders. The Dyson Cyclone may suck, but James Dyson's Future Proof life certainly doesn't.

Truth #4 – Failure Is Great

The Japanese have a proverb 七転び八起き (Nana korobi ya oki), which is loosely translated as "Fall down seven times and get up eight." This concept of resilience is so ingrained into Japanese culture that they don't think of themselves as being resilient, but rather assume that all cultures think this way. Unfortunately, the concept isn't embraced in Japanese corporate culture. When companies have a failure, CEOs are expected to publicly apologize for letting investors and employees down and often have a hard time finding a new job. "It is a social expectation in Japan that, if you've slipped up, your immediate responsibility is to apologize," says Luke Nottage, professor of comparative and transnational business law at Sydney Law School, whose work focuses on Japan and the Asia Pacific region. Failure is so institutionalized in corporate Japan that the CEOs hold carefully scripted apology press conferences for failing complete with deep bows and crying.

Possibly the most risk-averse culture in Europe is Germany. Efficiency is rewarded while risk-taking is often thought of as foolish and wasteful. "In Germany, failing is a stigma," says Berlin startup founder Lukas Kampfmann. "It's hugely problematic since it discourages people from starting a company."[1] To overcome this anti-entrepreneurial bias, Kampfmann invited visiting entrepreneurs from Dublin to throw an Irish Startup Wake. After signing the condolence book on entry, Berliners drank whiskey, mourned the deceased companies, and learned from founders who had previously failed.

One of the countries that is working at the highest levels of government to change attitudes toward risk and failure is Mexico. The federal government, with the support of universities and the business community, launched an annual event called *Semana Nacional del Emprendedor*, or National Entrepreneur's Week. Much like *Shark Week* on the Discovery Channel, for one week each October, the entire nation celebrates startups. When the president of Mexico and I spoke at the conference, it became the most streamed event in the country's history. Awards are given out and startups get to meet investors and other entrepreneurs. To get over the stigma of having a failure, a group of friends in Mexico City, whose startups had failed, created Fuckup

Nights (F.U.N.) with the motto "We Live Life Without Filter." Much like an open-mic night at a comedy club, anyone can get up and tell the tragically funny story of how they failed. Since 2012, F.U.N. has expanded to over 320 cities in more than 90 countries with more than 100,000 people attending each year. (These events are also a great place to recruit talent for your own startup.) "Fuckup helped us to break free from prejudices about failure and accelerate the learning it brings," according to one startup founder, adding. "The events have been a great impact to our teams and leaders, and allowed us to set the right tone to important conversations inside the company."

One country with a healthy attitude toward failure is Israel. Nicknamed "Startup Nation," this tiny country of only 8.5 million people has the most startups per capita of any country in the world. With approximately one startup per 1,400 people, it feels like everyone you meet there is either working for a startup or has a close friend that does. Yoel Naor, CEO of startup Silentium, credits Israel's attitude with being in the middle of the desert. "It all begins with a need or lack of a resource, and sometimes a difficulty to cope."[2]

One of the ways Israeli startups overcome failure is by focusing on local successes. Tel-Aviv startup Waze was acquired by Google for $1.3 billion and NVIDIA purchased Mellanox for a massive $15.3 billion. Many Israeli startups when they reach a certain size move to the US to grow. Taboola and Outbrain moved to America in preparation for a US IPO. Wix shareholders earned a 650 percent return when it went public in 2013. According to Barclays, Israeli companies have raised over $10 billion on Nasdaq and the New York Stock Exchange (NYSE).[3] Instead of going public, the vast majority of successful Israeli startups are acquired. Companies as diverse as McDonald's and Nike have acquired small Israeli companies. Once a community overcomes the stigma of failure, risk taking creates a virtuous cycle were one generation of founders share knowledge with the next.

"You always pass failure on the way to success," actor Mickey Rooney wisely assessed. So, in order to have success, you must overcome your failures. The following four tips will help you embrace failure and propel yourself forward.

Four Approaches to Embrace Failure

1. *To be happy and successful, you need to love what you do.* Don't regret any experience in which you learned something new. Given that failures are inevitable, and an important part of the process of discovering success, you need to learn to love failure. Before you find success, you are going to experience a lot of failure. This is a hard truth for many to wrap their heads around. Just as you cannot appreciate the majestic beauty of a sunrise without first experiencing the darkness, one will never truly enjoy success without experiencing the satisfaction of overcoming obstacles. The second and third generations of billionaire families are some of the most miserable people I know because they have never achieved on their own. Success is about the journey, not the destination. Failure is a frequent stop on the road to success. Learn to embrace it and recognize its role in the process.

2. *Stay confident.* An extraordinary attitude will take you farther than extraordinary talents. You aren't a failure; you just failed at this one approach to success. Your next attempt can have the desired outcome. People who maintained their self-confidence are the same people whether they are on top, on the bottom, or moving between the two. Don't get me wrong. You are going to feel bad. But acknowledge your emotions. As the Irish Startup Wake taught the German attendees, you can grieve for your loss. Feeling bad is part of the healing process. According to a 2017 study in the *Journal of Behavioral Decision Making*, researchers discovered that embracing your emotions can help you work harder to find better solutions in the future.[4]

3. *Learn coping techniques for moving on.* When failure stresses you out, there is a natural tendency to binge junk food or get mind-numbingly drunk. Instead, make a list of healthy coping skills and keep them prominently posted on your desk or wall. Taking a warm bubble bath, practicing deep breathing yoga, playing with your dog or talking it out with a friend are all great tools for coping. The key to getting over failure is to get it out of your system and move on. My go-to technique for letting go of stress is long walks on the beach. In addition to the sunshine and exercise,

ocean air is abundant with negative ions, which have been proven to neutralize free radicals, revitalize cell metabolism, enhance the immune system, and even balance the nervous system.[5] One of the joys of living in Los Angeles is that the soothing sound of the surf clears my head and is my proverbial happy place.

4. *Don't give up because you failed.* You may be just one little step away from success. When you fail, even if you lose all your money, you are not "starting from scratch." While failing, you have gained invaluable skills and knowledge that will make you more prepared the next time. Think, for a moment, about the strategy you use to master a video game and rise through all the levels. Each time you "die" in the game, you've learned how to face and overcome the obstacle that ended your last game. Eventually, after trying again and again, you fail yourself to victory.

Before founding Alibaba and amassing a personal fortune of over $46 billion, Jack Ma failed his college entrance exams for three years and was even turned down for a job at a local Kentucky Fried Chicken restaurant. When I first met Ma at a Digital Music conference in Hong Kong in 2000, he had already spent five years building websites for Chinese companies and had just launched Alibaba. China didn't have broadband, but Ma had a vision for the future of ecommerce. Ma is not an engineer. He glows with the kind of energy that can't be stopped or even slowed by failure. By the time he took Alibaba public on the New York Stock exchange in 2014, it was the largest initial public offering (IPO) in US history.[6] Ma truly loves what he does and embraces his failures wholeheartedly.

Larry Ellison, now the tenth-richest person on the planet, had to mortgage his home to keep Oracle afloat when no one believed in his vision. Even Arianna Huffington, who sold the *Huffington Post* for more than $300 million, couldn't make it as a writer. In her twenties, Arianna was rejected by 36 publishers and nearly gave up on her profession. Only going into debt with a bank loan enabled her to hold on. Walt Disney, Bill Gates, Abraham Lincoln, Lady Gaga, George Foreman, and Henry Ford all went broke before achieving greatness. I could fill an entire encyclopedia with stories of famous people who bounced back from bankruptcy, debt, and failure.

Reducing Your Chances of Failing

While you can overcome failure, you can also reduce your chances of failing in the first place – 42 percent of small businesses fail because there is no market need for their service or product. Surely you can avoid this pitfall by testing the market before you spend your time or resources launching something no one wants or needs. Identify your customer. Speak with them. Find out why they do, or do not, like your product. Customer feedback saves you time and money. You will never have a successful business if you don't know what people are willing to pay for. "It takes humility to seek feedback," writes Stephen Covey in *The 7 Habits of Highly Effective People*. "It takes wisdom to understand it, analyze it, and appropriately act on it."[7]

Another 29 percent of small businesses fail because they run out of cash. Again, plan for your burn rate. How much money does your company consume each month? If you simply divide the amount of money you have raised by your business's monthly burn, you will know how many months of *runway* you have left before you must take off or crash. Be realistic and not overly optimistic with your assumptions. Most people believe that entrepreneurs are crazy, wide-eyed optimists. On the contrary, in my experience the most successful ones are pessimists who embrace their fears in order to prosper. They plan for the worst and are then seldom disappointed. Go to startup events and meetups. Talk to other founders. Learn from the mistakes of those who went before you. The more iterations of your business you can do in your mind, the less money you will squander waiting for the market to tell you what you should have already known.

The next most common reasons for failing according to Harvard Business School (HBS) are all avoidable mistakes. Underestimating the competition, setting the wrong price, or having poor marketing are rookie mistakes that won't happen with proper planning. The one set of statistics that should embolden you is the impact small businesses have on the US economy. At $19.42 trillion, the US economy is 25 percent of the entire planet's gross world product. And what is driving this massive financial superpower? Entrepreneurs like you starting a small business.

The one last remaining causes of failure that completely baffles me is those founders who start spending money while lacking a business model. Siri was acquired by Apple for $200 million without any way of earning money. Facebook acquired Instagram for a billion even though it didn't have a business model. In certain venture circles, VCs will invest in a startup concept that doesn't have a clue as to how they will make money. I am not of that camp. Siri and Instagram are black swan exceptions. These were tools needed by a larger company that can be monetized by the acquirer's existing business. There will be more exceptions in the future, but I wouldn't bet my future on a non-revenue-producing business that just burns cash. If you don't know how you are going to make money, that's a charity, not a business. Go file your 501(c)(3) nonprofit status with the Internal Revenue Service and raise donations.

You don't have to know how soon you'll be profitable when first starting out, but you should at least have a path you are aiming toward. Jeff Bezos knew what Amazon's business model was when the company was just him and his desktop computer. Jeff Bezos knew Amazon had to invest heavily in infrastructure to dominate ecommerce and his investors gave him the time and capital to build a trillion-dollar empire. Bezos wasn't profitable for nearly a decade, but by the time he had proven his business model, he was the richest person in the world. Put another way, Bezos kept losing money until he was the richest man in the world. His is the ultimate *Future Proofing You* story as Amazon's success came from utilizing all 12 of the truths outlined in this book.

As long as you can communicate a viable plan of action, investors will be patient and won't let you fail. But spending all your money before you have a business model makes about as much sense as drinking all your water before you hike across a desert so that you won't have to carry the canteen.

Vin's road to success had its share of failures. The World's Best Agency was approached with a very lucrative offer from a company in the protein shake business. The shake maker claimed to have a huge social media following and was looking to grow its audience and online subscription sales. In mentoring Vin, I told him to be on the lookout for opportunities where you can take financial risks if they had the potential to deliver big rewards. In Vin's mind, the direct sales shake manufacture was the perfect opportunity.

Vin wisely recognized that selling protein shakes directly to the end user was a very-high-margin business for his client. So, instead of the World's Best Agency charging its normal retail rate for its services, Vin was willing to do the marketing work for a percentage of the gross sales his agency generated. To his client, this was a win–win offer. Vin would be 100 percent committed to making the product a success and therefore the two companies' goals would be in perfect alignment. Since Vin was in control of the sales figures, he knew he couldn't be cheated or underpaid by his client. What could possibly go wrong?

Vin did a fantastic job of targeting the right audience online and driving high click-through rates on his ads. But the clicks weren't converting into sales. Vin continued to refine his targeting and adjust the sales funnel. While his fine-tuning continued to increase the click-rate, it had no impact on the conversion rate. People were stopping and looking at the eye-catching ads as Vin wanted them to – they just weren't buying the product. Vin poured more and more of his profits from other clients into solving the problem. Turns out, the one step that Vin had skipped in building his sales funnel was actually tasting the product. It wasn't the marketing. The product was awful (and the company didn't have the customer base it claimed when Vin had negotiated the deal).

When we talked about the fiasco, I reminded him again that you either earn or learn. What did he learn from this failure? His insightful response was brilliant. Because he was so financially invested in the shake's success, he spent more time perfecting the sales funnel than he had ever spent on a campaign in the past. He had mastered the holy grail of online ecommerce: amazing click-rates. How could Vin apply the lessons of this failure into an opportunity? Vin's insight was that he could take what he had learned marketing flavorless shakes and make more money selling his own product. He had the formula for success. Vin was going to package his growth-hacking expertise into a webinar, course, and ebook titled *Ace the Game*. This would be his second revenue stream. Vin could sell a product he created and controlled the quality of, directly to the end consumer and capture 100 percent of the revenue. (Spoiler alert: his eBook generated $45,800 in sales in its first two weeks.)

In his exuberance for *Ace the Game*, Vin wanted to immediately abandon World's Best Agency and just focus on his new publishing business. Dealing with clients, and not having a social life, was exhausting him. From where he sat, being a publisher looked like a fun picnic. No clients, no sales calls, no pitch presentations, just a money-printing sales funnel. I cautioned that until the direct sales came in from his new course, he still needed his agency to pay the bills. In less than 100 days' time, Vin had gone from unfocused and unemployed to running two businesses of his own.

Even with the time-consuming setbacks from the protein shake client, Vin's crypto marketing business continued to grow. He was so busy working on the Agency, tinkering with the shake campaign, and planning for his growth-hacking course that it wasn't until we had our end-of-the-month mentoring that he had the time to do his monthly accounting. The night before our last meeting of the month, Vin tallied the month's results and nearly fainted. With only three months into our challenge, Vin smashed through the mental barrier of earning six figures in a month and created $103,494 in sales. To put that amazing accomplishment in perspective, Vin had earned in just that one month enough income to be in the top 10 percent of annual earnings for all Americans. He was becoming Future Proof.

Notes

1. Lindsay Gellman, "German Start-ups Learn to Fail," *New York Magazine* (October 29, 2018).
2. Jordan Yerman, "A Startup Nation: Why Israel Has Become the New Silicon Valley," *Apex Experience* (May 22, 2019), apex.aero/articles/startup-nation-israel-become-silicon-valley/.

3. Sophie Shulman, *Israelis Dream of Big U.S. IPOs, but Are Swallowed by M&As Instead*, CTech (January 30, 2020), www.calcalistech.com/ctech/articles/0,7340,L-3784912,00.html.

4. Amy Morin, "10 Healthy Ways to Cope with Failure," *Very Well Mind* (November 12, 2019), www.verywellmind.com/healthy-ways-to-cope-with-failure-4163968.

5. Troy Anderson, *Why Negative Ions Have a Positive Effect on the Human Body*, AirTamer.com (November 15, 2014), www.airtamer.com/negative-ions-positive-effect-human-body/.

6. Aimee Picchi, "Alibaba Launches Biggest IPO in US History," CBS News (September 19, 2014), https://www.cbsnews.com/news/alibaba-ipo-trading-to-start-after-22-billion-sale/.

7. Thomas Nelson, *Big Book (Little Book): 1,001 Proverbs, Adages, and Precepts to Help You Live a Better Life* (United States: Thomas Nelson, 2005), 196.

5

Igniting Your Superpower by Applying What Makes You Unique

Mutation: it is the key to our evolution. It has enabled us to evolve from a single-celled organism into the dominant species on the planet. This process is slow, and normally taking thousands and thousands of years. But every few hundred millennia, evolution leaps forward.

—*Professor Charles Francis Xavier, X-Men*

AT AGE NINE, MICHAEL was diagnosed with attention deficit hyperactivity disorder (ADHD). For the next two years, he took the drug Ritalin. But as an 11-year-old, he felt stigmatize by needing the medication and figured out he could manage his attention deficit symptoms by getting out his excess energy swimming. His mother and doctor agreed to take him off the meds if he would continue to focus on spending time in the pool. Just four years later, Michael Phelps was an Olympic athlete. The most decorated Olympian of all time, Phelps has won 28 Olympic medals (including 23 gold). If you are thinking swimming is Phelps's superpower, you'd be wrong. He worked really hard training day in and day out for years to earn his swimming victories. Michael Phelps's superpower is ADHD. "I could go fast in the pool," Phelps recalled. "It turned out, in part, because being in the pool slowed down my mind. In the water, I felt, for the first time, in control."

Phelps isn't alone in harnessing the power of ADHD for success. Poor concentration, a lack of self-regulation, and hyperactivity – the classic symptoms of ADHD – are positive tools for innovation and entrepreneurship according to a 2017 study by researchers at the University of Munich in Germany. "People with ADHD are more likely to be sensation seekers, so uncertainty does not scare them but attracts them," says Dr. Johan Wiklund, a co-author of the study, adding, "They also tend to not premeditate, so they throw themselves into action without considering the consequences."[1]

Truth #5 – Your Unique Superpower Makes You Successful

Each one of us is unique. If we are all the culmination of a unique series of genetic mutations taking place over millions of years, then each of us must possess a unique superpower. The fifth truth you must accept in order to achieve is the belief that you have a superpower. You have something inside you that makes you so different that it is your competitive secret weapon. Tap your superpower and you'll be as unbeatable as Michael Phelps. The challenge is identifying your unique genius early enough in life to harness it.

> "Everybody is a genius. But if you judge a *fish* by its ability to climb a *tree*, it will live its whole life believing that it is stupid."
>
> A fabricated quote popularly attributed to Albert Einstein.

Superpowers aren't about walking through walls or having telepathy; superpowers are natural talents that we all have from birth. For some it may be persuasiveness or super confidence, for others it can be organizational skills or an exceptional memory. Consensus building, likeability, self-confidence, altruism, and optimism are all powerful attributes that some people possess at extraordinary levels. The more you understand what makes you unique, the greater your chances of using it to created opportunities and wealth.

Every successful leader I know drew success from tapping their superpower. LinkedIn co-founder Reid Hoffman has super vision. Reid can, from a business perspective, see farther into the future than anyone I have ever met. As a founder and an investor, Reid's super vision propelled him to be a powerful force behind PayPal, Facebook, Airbnb, and LinkedIn.

Can you imagine how impossible it would be to single-handily transform an 818-page historical biography of an eighteenth-century politician (who had never even run for office) into a singing and rapping musical? "Making words rhyme for a living is one of the great joys of my life," says composer and lyricist Lin-Manuel Miranda. "That's a superpower I've been very conscious of developing. I started at the same level as everybody else, and then I just listened to more music and talked to myself until it was an actual superpower I could pull out on special occasions."[2] Honing his superpower was one of the reasons the Broadway sensation *Hamilton* went on to garner a Pulitzer Prize, a Grammy, and 11 Tony awards. Talk about power, Miranda's *Hamilton* set box office records and led Broadway to its highest grossing season with a whopping $1.45 billion in ticket sales.

We are all born with superpowers. While I've never met anyone who can leap tall buildings in a single bound like Superman or control the weather like Storm, every successful person I do know has learned to harness their superpower to stand out, attract business, and be memorable. My friend Dr. Mark Goulston is a super-listener. Goulston honed this talent into training FBI hostage negotiators and being a therapist who specializes in suicidal patients. As proof of his superpower, over the course of his long career treating people who had tried to take their own lives, Dr. Goulston never lost a patient. Ken Rutkowski, the founder of METal International, is a super-connector who is able to match people with ideas, to people who can bring them to fruition. Doesn't sound like a superpower? Ken's connections have created over $3 billion in business deals and enabled him to never need a regular job. Anyone who has ever met or worked with Bill Clinton will tell you his superpower is charisma. The president can win over people with just a smile and a handshake. "I found that with a little creativity, and a lot of dedication, any difference can be turned into something amazing," writes deaf author Cece Bell. "Our differences are our superpowers."[3]

If you are identifiably unique, you can control your destiny. People will seek you out with opportunities if they understand what you have to offer. Your superpower could be organizational skills, or an exceptional memory. You may be amazing at trendspotting or the best at pitching. "Enthusiasm is my superpower," states Swiss designer Tina Roth-Eisenberg. "One might say that confidence yields the same result. I disagree. Confidence is about yourself; enthusiasm is about something else. Confidence is impressive, but enthusiasm is infectious. Confidence is serious, enthusiasm is fun."[4]

Every successful entrepreneur learned to master their power. Richard Branson's is intuitively understanding what the average consumer thinks, while billionaire Mark Cuban's super strength is thinking unconventionally. The truth that you need to recognize is that harnessing your natural superpower is the foundation of all your future success and a key to maximizing wealth. Even if your superpower is being an introvert, recognize and develop your difference into your greatest strength. "Solitude is one of our great superpowers," writes bestselling author of *Quiet: The Power of Introverts in a World That Can't Stop Talking*, Susan Cain. "Solitude is the key to being able to make effective decisions and then having the courage of convictions to stand behind those decisions."[5]

Superpowers define us and guide us. They are the talent that strengthens everything we do in life and frame our personal brand. The sooner you can identify and grow your superpower, the further your career will go. "Knowing your superpower changes everything," says blogger and life coach Nadalie Bardo. The challenge then is to identify your superpower and use it as a foundation for *Future Proofing You*. Here are five probing questions designed to help you find your true superpower.

What Comes Naturally to You?

As obvious as this may seem, your superpower has been with you since childhood. List the traits and attributes others would use to describe you. List the things that come naturally to you. "When you are born," Kahlil Gibran writes, "your work is placed in your heart."[6]

If you are having a hard time identifying your natural skills, then work backwards; what are you subpar at? "I discovered that my insecurities and my flaws were things that I actually need to embrace," singer-songwriter Skylar Grey discovered. "I let them become my super-powers." By sharing her insecurities in her lyrics, Grey helped make Eminem's *Love the Way You Lie* into a hit. Since 2010, she has become one of Eminem's most frequent collaborators. Analyze what aspects of work you can't stand and the reason might be because it goes against your natural strength. I recognized early on that I hate following rules and being told how to do a job. Structure goes against every creative bone in my body. The result of knowing this is that I realized that I make a much better boss than I do an employee. Controlling your destiny starts with self-awareness.

What Do You Do Better Than Anyone You've Ever Met?

No false modesty here. You know what you are good at. "It's interesting that you put me in the league with those illustrious fighters [Muhammad Ali, Joe Louis, Jack Johnson], but I've proved since my career I've surpassed them as far my popularity," boasts Mike Tyson. "I'm the biggest fighter in the history of the sport. If you don't believe it, check the cash register."[7] You better believe you're the best boxer if you are about to step in the ring and risk your life against the best of the best. But spending your life working in jobs that don't challenge or fulfill you is also risking your life. A job that doesn't utilize your gifts, doesn't let you grow. Slowly, over time, it will drain you of your ambition and rob you of your dreams. The goal is to hone your natural gifts and, with hard work, take them to the next level. What did your teachers reward you for doing? What underlying skill did you bring to bear to attain achievement? Knowing your superpower will encourage you to train harder at developing it to its full potential. Identifying it will also improve how you present yourself and market your business.

John Livesay had a very successful career selling advertising for trade publications until the web came along and people stopped reading trade news in print. Even though he was an award-winning sales executive at Conde Nast, when an entire industry collapses, jobs become scarce for everyone. Trying to find a new career, John looked inwardly to identify why he had been successful at sales. He realized it wasn't his subject matter expertise on women's fashion, but his uncanny ability to communicate through storytelling. His unique superpower is finding an emotional connection in every sales story. John's book *Better Selling Through Storytelling* has given him his second successful career as a sales keynote speaker. By knowing his superpower, Livesay could market his sales storytelling skills and be unique among motivational speakers.

Retired convenience store owner Jerry Selbee had been a bit of a math whiz when he was young and got an undergraduate degree in mathematics from Western Michigan University. With not much use for a mathematician in his hometown of Evart, population 1,900, he and his wife ran a real mom-and-pop store on Main Street for 17 years. In 2003, the retiree went back to his old store and noticed a brochure for Michigan's new lottery game called Winfall. Unlike Mega Millions, which rolls up the lottery money into the next game any time there is no winner, Winfall rolled the money down. If no one picked all six numbers, then the lower-tier prize winners would earn higher payouts. It took Jerry just three minutes to realize a flaw in the state's math. "I said, if I played $1,100, mathematically I'd have one four-number winner; that's 1,000 bucks," Jerry explained using the example of purchasing every possible four-number combination. " I divided 1,100 by six instead of 57 because I did a mental quick dirty and I come up with 18. So, I knew I'd have either 18 or 19 three-number winners, and that's 50 bucks each. At 18, I got $1,000 for a four-number winner, and I got 18 three-number winners worth $50 each, so that's 900 bucks. So, I got $1,100 invested and I've got a $1,900 return." Mathematically, he couldn't lose money. After winning week after week, he invited friends to invest with him so that everyone could benefit. He continued this for every game for six years. In total, he grossed over $26 million in winning tickets.

What Makes Time Disappear for You?

Being able to control time is a pretty amazing superpower, and yet we all do it now and again. I am sure we have all daydreamed about having the Flash's chronokinetic ability to manipulate time. Making time disappear is a completely different concept. When you hear yourself apologizing to someone, *"I'm sorry but I lost track of time,"* what were you doing that made the hours fly past? For some, it may be a hobby such as painting or songwriting. But if time truly disappears, you might want to recognize that your superpower should be your vocation, not your avocation. Martha Stewart worked on Wall Street until she was 41, but she so loved hosting dinner parties for colleagues and friends that she started a catering business on the side for fun. Then Stewart wrote her first book *Entertaining* about the subject she so loved and enjoyed. Stewart was so passionate about throwing the perfect event that she amassed a $600 million fortune by focusing on her superpower. "You can tell what's important to people by looking in two places: their calendars and their checkbooks," writes leadership consultant David Dye. Scroll through your past few year's calendars and a pattern will emerge of how and where you enjoy spending your time. Go with the natural flow of your movements if you want to create lasting wealth.[8]

When Craig Newmark was laid off from his programmer job at Charles Schwab, he still loved spending time writing code on his computer. In fact, it was his favorite way to spend time. Wanting to keep in touch with his coder buddies from work, Newmark created a basic message board where he listed local events that might interest his friends. As more people started using it, Newmark added more billboard topics, including new job listings. Today, Craigslist has 50 billion pageviews per month and more than a million job listings. His time-stopping hobby also made Craig a billionaire.

When Friends Ask Your Advice, Why Are They Coming to You?

This may surprise you, but the people you interact with most – your friends, family, and coworkers – already know your superpower. They seek your wisdom every time they have a problem in your area of strength. Investment Banker Oren Klaff spent over a decade helping businesses get funding, but realized that more than the capital, entrepreneurs were constantly seeking his advice on how to pitch prospective investors and customers. "You only have five minutes," warns Klaff, "before your pitch wanders into a mental no-man's land."[9] Klaff's superpower is pitching. For him it is both a skill and a science. His book, *Pitch Anything,* is a gold medal winner and one of the top sales books on the market today.

Kansas City residents James and Susan Feess could only cope with their mundane 9-to-5 jobs by focusing their minds on researching their next European backpacking adventure. "My biggest 'aha!' moments occurred when I received emails from people asking my advice," recalls James, and *The Savvy Backpacker* blog became their full-time job. Today, the husband and wife travel enthusiasts write a successful blog and publish budget guides for various European destinations. Not sure why your friends seek your advice? Just ask them.

What Would You Do If Money Didn't Matter?

Nothing identifies your superpower better than removing money from the equation. Too many people believe that they have to wait until they are wealthy to follow their passion, when in fact, it will be their passion that will make them wealthy (more on this in the next chapter). During my years as a record company executive, I had the good fortune to work with some of the most famous and talented musicians on Earth. After a while, I noticed that artists fell into two very distinct categories: those who went into the business for fame and fortune and those whose souls had to create music even if no one ever paid them. The first group didn't last long, while the second have enriched our world. "Music is so therapeutic for me that if I can't get it out," explains Eminem, "I start feeling bad about myself – a lot of self-loathing."[10]

Painter Pablo Picasso spent his entire career trying to be true to the artist he was as a child. "Every child is an artist," Picasso noted. "The problem is to remain an artist once they grew up." He didn't paint to become wealthy; the wealth came to him when he immersed himself in his art. While I am no Picasso, I have loved to paint water-colors since I was a child. For me, time truly stands still and I just focus on the painting in front of me. Because watercolors are a medium where the split-second timing of the wetness of the paper and the flu-idity of the paint can be unforgiving, it takes absolute concentration. My entire world for 6, 8, 10 hours straight is reduced to one sheet of cold-pressed cotton paper. As a busy entrepreneur, my time painting is a respite from the world and a chance for my mind to rest.

When the Covid-19 pandemic struck, I was forced to stay in my home for months on end. All of my international speaking engagements had been canceled and all my meetings were replaced with virtual Zoom calls. While losing substantial income, I was determined to have a growth mindset and find the positive in my new reality. I chose to look at sheltering-in-place as a gift of time. So, to help inspire others, I announced that I would post a new watercolor painting every day on social media. I kept up the challenging pace for 100 straight days. The focus and practice improved my skills with the brush and I enjoyed the daily feedback from followers. But just like those rock stars who made music because they had a need to express themselves, what happened next surprised me. As my artwork spread around the world, I heard from gallery owners and artist agents. I was offered commissions from collectors and even a solo show at the prestigious Richard Taittinger Gallery in New York. I had created a new revenue stream by unleashing a superpower I had kept dormant since childhood. I have created art my entire life, but would have never had the courage to pursue it as a career if not for Covid-19's forced sequestration.

Bill Gates's superpower is problem solving. It drove him to create Microsoft and amass incredible wealth. But after becoming the richest man in the world, when making more money clearly didn't matter, Bill's superpower drove him to solve bigger problems, such as curing polio and ending poverty with the Bill and Melinda Gates Foundation. Sure, he could have just written a check like so many other philanthropists, but that would have denied him and the world of utilizing his superpower. How else can you explain one of the world's richest men spending his time focused on building a waterless toilet to help bring sanitation to the millions without access to clean water. "Progress in fighting polio might be one of the world's best-kept secrets in global health," Gates wrote in 2017, after spending $3 billion trying to eradicate the disease. "If things stay stable in the conflicted areas, humanity will see its last case of polio this year."[11]

"Better to have a short life that is full of what you like doing than a long life spent in a miserable way," suggests American philosopher Alan Watts. "But it's absolutely stupid to spend your time doing things you don't like, in order to go on spending things you don't like, doing things you don't like and to teach our children to follow in the same track."[12]

Having the determination and resilience to become Future Proof is much easier when you believe in your superpower. Instead of operating from a place of unsubstantiated optimism, which can fold like a house of cards when faced with setbacks, knowing that you have a special competitive advantage will bolster your resolve to see past any obstacle and metaphorically leap tall buildings in a single bound.

Identifying Your Kryptonite

Now that you have discovered your superpower, you must also identify your kryptonite. Superman has nearly limitless strength, except for his one ultimate weakness, which is kryptonite. None of us are all powerful and omnipotent. We all have blind spots and weaknesses that are the antithesis of our strengths. "Often, what we struggle with becomes the foundation of our greatest success," James Woosley writes in *Conquer the Entrepreneur's Kryptonite: Simple Strategic Planning for You and Your Business.* "You can either learn to live with your kryptonite or you can conquer it. Do what others don't and you will have a distinct strategic advantage."[13]

Facing my kryptonite took me years to acknowledge. While I pride myself on being a big-picture thinker, I am not one to get into the nitty-gritty details. The process and paperwork that makes large institutions function efficiently stops me in my tracks. I can structure the most complex of business transactions in my head, but don't ever leave an original contract that needs to be signed on my desk because I'll never find it. I've diffused the power of my chaos-kryptonite by always having a highly organized teammate at my side. Too many founders make the mistake of hiring junior versions of themselves because they are the kind of people they prefer to hang around with. Identify your weaknesses and build a team that makes you indestructible. Batman had Robin – even superheroes can benefit from a sidekick who helps them turn their greatest weakness into their greatest strength.

Nothing will make you feel like you can conquer the world more than conquering yourself. "The first and best victory," as Plato taught Aristotle, "is to conquer self." By facing your internal weaknesses head on, you recognize that everything in your life is malleable. You will gain strength and confidence to tackle new and greater challenges. You will overcome doubts, remove limitations, and no longer fear that which had previously seemed insurmountable. Throughout his entire childhood, actor Bruce Willis struggled with stuttering. "I could hardly talk. It took me three minutes to complete a sentence. It was crushing for anyone who wanted to express themselves, who wanted to be heard and couldn't. It was frightening," Willis recalls. "Yet, when I became another character, in a play, I lost the stutter. It was phenomenal."[14] Willis faced his kryptonite by performing in front of his classmates. In college, a drama professor encouraged the future *Die Hard* star to see a speech therapist, which enabled him to go on to conquer Hollywood with $3.2 billion in lifetime box office grosses.

At the start of our year of mentoring, Vin and I butted heads on virtually every topic. From what business to start and how to brand it, to the need for multiple revenue streams and the constant requirement of prospecting for more clients, Vin's life experience pointed him in a different direction than the one I was suggesting. But Vin doesn't possess the stubborn ego that plagues many entrepreneurs. It is hard for most people, especially successful ones, to accept that whatever knowledge got them to that point of their lives won't allow them to progress any further. Vin's superpower was being prescient enough to get out of his own way. Vin was adaptable.

"Getting out of my own way allowed me to progress fast," Vin reflected that this was his superpower. "Learning to trust the process, even when I didn't think it was right; everything from what business endeavors to work on to cutting my hair." (When I met Vin, his hair was down to his shoulders and I suggested he try to look and dress more like the people he was trying to get as clients. He adapted and grew his customer base.) As a mentor, I have to agree with Vin's assessment. Had he not possessed his superpower, I would have grown tired of arguing a point or making suggestions on how he should change. But by being able and willing to accept that his instincts for survival are not necessarily the instincts needed for thriving, Vin acquiesced. Controlling your own destiny often means walking away from habits that make you comfortable.

"It takes a lot less mental load to listen to the smart people around you and focus on doing rather than making things perfect," Vin said. Vin's superpower allowed him to recognize the moment he was disagreeing with something and pause internally, to see the source of his opposition. If Vin didn't have the facts to support his point of view, he listened to those around him. As the months went on, Vin developed this skill further. He found himself learning from clients and subcontractors. Vin knew that all his future success would require committing to be a lifelong learner. Most people and companies crumble when faced with rapid cycles of change. But Vin spent a year working outside his comfort zone adapting to a very dynamic crypto market and it was working. Being open-minded doesn't mean being empty-minded. Where Vin did have the expertise, he was confident in standing his ground because he knew his decision was built on experience, not ego. Vin's superpower enables him to quickly adapt to any changing business condition. Adaptability is the core skill to becoming Future Proof. It is a Darwinian truth of business that it is not the most intellectual or the strongest that survives, but the person that survives is the one that is able to adapt to or adjust best to the changing environment in which it finds itself.

With the actions of four months writing proposals and servicing clients settling into a manageable rhythm, Vin focuses on boosting his margins. Vin starts bartering his services for the services of other vendors to reduce his costs. He starts mentoring two protégés in marketing in exchange for them working for reduced compensation. And he adds a third revenue stream, affiliate sales. Just as Amazon commissions those who drive traffic to their site, Vin reaches out to his network of friends and associates with the opportunity for them to make money off of any leads they send his way. With big-ticket clients taking up more and more of Vin's time, he starts farming out smaller projects, which he otherwise would have had to turn down, to his associates and starts making a commission on their work. Just like Amazon, his network becomes his net worth. Affiliate sales takes some time to setup and to check on the progress and quality of the vendors he is referring, but he knows it will pay out over the course of the

(continued)

(*continued*)

year. Though month four is not a record setter, Vin still achieves $96,978 in sales. Being slightly ahead of the curve feels good. For the remaining eight months of the year, Vin only needs to have average revenue of $82,364 per month.

Notes

1. Crystal Ponti, *The Innovating, Creative Superpowers of ADHD*, Yes! Solutions Journalism (April 13, 2017), https://www.alternet.org/2017/04/innovating-creative-superpowers-adhd/.

2. Celia Fernandez, *10 Things to Know About Lin-Manuel Miranda*, Latina .com. Posted February 17, 2016.

3. "Cece Bell Quotes," Good Reads (August 31 2020), www.goodreads.com/quotes/8499991-and-being-different-that-turned-out-to-the-best-part.

4. "Tina Roth-Eisenberg Quotes," Accessed August 31, 2020. https://www.quotemaster.org/q6eabe85518ec2ea8e643d333c51d6f7a.

5. "Susan Cain Quotations," Quotetab. Accessed August 31, 2020. www.quotetab.com/quotes/by-susan-cain.

6. Sheryn Yeo, and Shan Lim, *The Audacity to Dream* (New York: Candid Creation, 2013), 10.

7. Ted Kluck, *Facing Tyson* (New York: Lyons Press, 2006), 199.

8. Gwen Moran, "The Importance of Finding (and Facing) Your Weaknesses," *Fast Company* (February 10, 2014), www.fastcompany.com/3026105/the-importance-of-finding-and-facing-your-weaknesses?position=12&campaign_date=11032020.

9. Oren Klaff, *Pitch Anything: An Innovative Method for Presenting, Persuading and Winning the Deal.* (New York: McGraw-Hill Education, 2011), 11.

10. "Eminem Quotes," Accessed August 31, 2020. www.brainyquote.com/quotes/eminem_446841.

11. Ray Sipherd, "Bill Gates: For Polio the Endgame Is Near," CNBC (October 24, 2017), https://www.cnbc.com/2017/10/24/bill-gates-humanity-will-see-its-last-case-of-polio-this-year.html.

12. Alan Watts, "What If Money Was No Object," Genius.com. Accessed August 31, 2020. https://genius.com/Alan-watts-what-if-money-was-no-object-annotated.

13. "James Woosley Quotes," Good Reads. Accessed August 31 2020. https://www.goodreads.com/quotes/7112806-often-what-we-struggle-with-becomes-the-foundation-of-our.

14. John Parker, *Bruce Willis: The Unauthorized Biography* (London: Virgin, 1997), 8.

6

Turning Perseverance into Passion

A river cuts through rock, not because of its power, but because of its persistence.
James N. Watkins

ANYONE WITH A NEW IDEA at a company knows how difficult it can be to get management to change. "They just don't get it" is the constant refrain of frustrated employees everywhere. When a 32-year-old director of operations and marketing couldn't convince his bosses to try his new idea, he quit to start his own company. Unfortunately, he didn't have funds that he needed to open his first location and he spent the entire next year knocking on doors around Seattle, Washington, pitching potential investors to try and raise the $400,000 he needed to start his business. For months, every potential investor said no, but he was persistent. With no job, and his wife pregnant with their first child, Howard refused to give up. Having grown up in Brooklyn's Canarsie public housing projects, and having made it to the West Coast all on his own, Howard knew he wasn't a quitter. Of the 242 people he pitched, 217 turned him down, even though his business idea was already popular in Europe. Having seen the popularity of espresso machines in Italian coffee shops, he thought Americans would enjoy these aromatic beverages as well. Turns out, he was right. Today, Howard Schultz's Starbucks has over 28,000 locations, employing more than 290,000 partners. The rich taste of espressos didn't make Howard Schultz a multibillionaire, his perseverance did.

"Can I make it as an entrepreneur?" the 17-year-old student thought to himself. A bright voracious reader, he had grown tired of the structure of school and wanted to know if he had what it takes to make it on his own as an entrepreneur. An immigrant, the teenager thought it wouldn't take much to keep himself alive in America. "So, my threshold for existing is pretty low," he figured. "I could be in some dingy apartment with my computer and be okay and not starve."

To prove to himself that he had the perseverance to do whatever it takes to succeed, he challenged himself to live for a month on just $30. "So, it's like, 'Oh, okay, if I can live for a dollar a day, then at least from a food cost standpoint, well it's pretty easy to earn like $30 in a month anyway, so I'll probably be okay," the now-successful entrepreneur recalled. He survived the month living on pasta, hot dogs, oranges, and pizza. By focusing on his goals, he learned to live without things today, in order to pursue his dreams for the future. When he launched his first company with his brother a few years later, they slept in their office at night to save money on an apartment and showered at the local YMCA. "We were so hard up, we had just one computer so the website was up during the day and I was coding at night ... Seven days a week."[1] That sacrifice of living on pizza and persistence paid off. Today, Elon Musk, the CEO of both SpaceX and Tesla, is worth more than $142 billion. He eats better now, too.

Truth #6 – Passion Makes You Unstoppable

Like Musk, Vin Clancy was an immigrant with something to prove to himself and the world. Coming to America fueled their passion for success. As outsiders, their dreams about America were different from those born here. I knew he had the raw talent to become a millionaire, but I wondered if Vin would tap out midyear and force me to start the *Future Proofing You* experiment over. To ensure Vin completed the year-long quest, he needed to turn his persistence into passion.

"Nothing in this world can take the place of persistence," President Calvin Coolidge wrote. "Talent will not; nothing is more common than unsuccessful men with talent. Genius will not; unrewarded genius is almost a proverb. Education will not; the world is full of educated derelicts. Persistence and determination alone are omnipotent."[2]

"I never took a day off in my twenties," Microsoft founder and world's richest man for nearly 20 years, Bill Gates, proudly proclaims. "Not one."[3] One of the most persistent founders in the world, Bill Gates wasn't motivated by the money (or he would have stopped working by 30). Gates had a higher purpose. He had a vision for there to one day be a computer in every home and the good that it could accomplish. The universality of computers, and the positive impact they would have, became his personal passion.

Since Atkinson and Birch first published *Dynamics of Action* in 1970, scores of researchers have tried to understand the factors that make some people more persistent than others. Educators, employers, and even the military have tried to build predictive models for measuring the likelihood of achievement. Are some people just born with persistent traits or was persistence a skill set that could be developed over time? Most recently, MacArthur Fellow Angela Duckworth published the pop psychology book *Grit: The Power of Passion and Perseverance*, which spent 20 weeks on the *New York Times* bestseller list. While the scientific community debates the validity – or lack thereof – of her findings, one key determinant of passion did stand out in her book. "Why were the highly accomplished so dogged in their pursuits?" Duckworth writes. "For most, there was no realistic expectation of ever catching up to their ambitions. In their own eyes, they were never good enough. They were the opposite of complacent. And yet, in a very real sense, they were satisfied being unsatisfied. Each was chasing something of unparalleled interest and importance, and it was the chase – as much as the capture – that was gratifying. Even if some of the things they had to do were boring, or frustrating, or even painful, they wouldn't dream of giving up. Their passion was enduring."[4]

In other words, passion with purpose fortifies persistence. The greater the purpose that can be assigned to the task, the more persistent we will be in reaching our goals. How many of us, after working a long, grueling week, can't find the energy to finish the project we have been working on for months in the backyard or garage? You tell yourself that you can always finish building the deck or painting the guest room next weekend. But when you volunteer with Habit for Humanity to build a new home for a deserving family, you'll continue hammering long after the last ray of sunlight has left the sky. Duckworth explains this phenomenon with a simple parable:

"Three bricklayers are asked: 'What are you doing?' The first says, 'I am laying bricks.' The second says, 'I am building a church.' And the third says, 'I am building the house of God.' The first bricklayer has a job. The second has a career. The third has a calling."

I ascribe to the belief that the purpose of life is to live a life of purpose. The more meaning we can put into our work, the more fulfillment we will feel. Having a purpose puts you in control of your destiny. You are not creating wealth to be rich, but rather, to enrich the world by fulfilling your purpose. The endorphins released by our brains when we experience purposeful moments are the positive reinforcement we need to push on. Our biology chemically rewards us for achievement. Our quest to experience fulfillment is what drives persistence. "In anything we do, any endeavor," Starbuck's former Chairman Howard Shultz is fond of saying, "it's not what you do; it's why you do it."[5] When you have a driving purpose, persistence can be cultivated.

Successful people weren't born persistent. It is not an innate gift. Persistence is a learned skill that grows out of having an openness for new experiences, which in turn, raise the conscientiousness of your actions. Vin wasn't working his butt off because he craved the money – riches were merely by-products of his pursuit. He was fulfilling a deeper need to test his mettle and prove to himself that he was good enough to succeed. Being raised in the British class system where working-class children were actually told to respect their upper-class betters, Vin's persistence is the quintessential story of the American Dream. Immigrants come to work in this country with a higher purpose than the mundane tasks they appear to be doing on a daily basis. Much like the aforementioned bricklayer building a house of God, in their eyes, immigrants are not just picking crops in a field, toiling away on a construction site, or stocking shelves in a convenience store – they are working towards a defined goal. Even when the goal is beyond reach, their persistence is a beacon for their children to follow. This definition of passion explains why, according to a 2014 study of US Census Bureau data by the nonpartisan Kauffman Foundation, immigrants are nearly twice as likely to start a new business as native-born

Americans. The Foundation also discovered that 24 of the top 50 venture-backed businesses also had at least one foreign-born founder. Even more impressive, according to a report from the Partnership for a New American Economy, 40 percent of Fortune 500 companies were founded by an immigrant or the child of an immigrant.[6] So, for many, persistence is determined by their environmental background, not some innate biological trait.

For those lucky enough to find their purpose early in life, they set their goals while still young and spend the rest of their days living a purposeful life. My friend Dr. Martha Missirlian had her teeth knocked out by a swing as a child. From the moment her dentist made a dental bridge that brought back her smile, she knew her purpose in life was to be a dentist. She wanted to be that hero who could change people's lives. For those of us not lucky enough to be immigrants or have our front teeth knocked out, how do we find our purpose?

Both Martha and Vin found their purpose through life experiences. The more you interact with the world, the more injustices you witness, the more life you live – instead of just gliding through it on auto-pilot – the more likely you are to discover your passion. Participation is the key factor to developing passion. Get involved. Travel. Try to get out of your comfortable bubble and start feeling the world around you. Start by being more mindful of what moves you and why.

It's never too late to start being purposeful. Walmart, Intel, Ford Motor Company, and Lululemon were all started be people in their forties. Home Depot and McDonald's were started by men in their fifties. And Charles Ranlett Flint did not establish IBM until he was in his sixties. All of these founders were driven by a mission and the money followed.

Some people never give up. At age 65 and living off a $99 a month Social Security check, most people figured the old man had retired and given up on his dream. Knowing how much his family and friends raved about his fried chicken recipe, he hopped in his old car and drove all over America peddling his recipe. The first 1,009 restaurants he pitched turned him down and told him to give it up and head back to Kentucky. When he was told yes at the 1,010th restaurant, that one sale propelled Colonel Harland Sanders's Kentucky Fried Chicken on to becoming the second largest restaurant chain in the world with over 22,000 locations and $23 billion in annual revenue.

For some, persistence drives them in their twenties. When I started mentoring Vin, I was reminded of another passionate young man who lived in a small 400-square-foot apartment a few blocks away from Vin's flat in Venice, California. Decades before, Tony was stuck in much the same place in life as Vin. He was jobless, broke, and spent his days watching soap operas. When he hit rock bottom, and was tired of being fat and broke, he committed himself to spend every waking hour on transforming his life. By his mid-twenties, with no formal education or training, Tony Robbins was making over a hundred thousand dollars a year as a human development trainer. As an author and life coach, Robbins would go on to work with some of the most successful people on Earth, including Oprah Winfrey, Andre Agassi, and President Bill Clinton. Decades later, his *Unleash the Power Within* life mastery course is still attended by thousands each year and has helped him amass a $500 million fortune. "The path to success is to take massive, determined action," Robbins writes. "A real decision is measured by the fact that you've taken a new action. If there's no action, you haven't truly decided."[7]

Unless they inherited their wealth, virtually every successful person has a personal story about perseverance and finding their passion. The one that personally inspires me the most is the story of a 13-year-old named Bethany Hamilton. A typical happy Hawaiian teen, Bethany loved to surf. On the morning of October 13, 2003, Bethany experienced every surfer's greatest fear: she came face-to-face with a 14-foot-long tiger shark. The shark bit off her left arm, severing it just inches below her shoulder. By the time she made it to the hospital, young Bethany had lost 60 percent of her blood and was in hypovolemic shock.

But Bethany was unstoppable. Within a few weeks, she was back in the water surfing. Needing to relearn the sport as a one-armed athlete, she started using a custom board that was a little longer and thicker and designed with a handle for her right arm. Within a month of her accident, Bethany entered her first major surfing competition. In two years, she was the overall winner in the Explorer Women's Division in the NSSA National competition. Still surfing today, Hamilton has competed in events in Australia, Fiji, Indonesia, and

Brazil. "Courage doesn't mean you don't get afraid," Hamilton wrote in her 2004 autobiography. "Courage means you don't let fear stop you."[8] A true inspiration to young and old alike, her story was made into the movie *Soul Surfer*.

Four Questions for Cultivating Passion

To help you get in the mindset for a journey of personal self-exploration to cultivate your own passion, here are four reflective questions you should ask yourself:

Would Your Fourth-Grade Self Be Proud of Who You Are Today?

Think back to your youth. What moved you? What did you once enjoy that you don't spend any time doing today? When and why did you stop?

When I was five years old, I saw my first magician perform at a birthday party. I loved how he was able to get adults and children alike to forget for a moment everything they knew about the world and believe that anything was possible. I wanted to be able to do that for people and have been obsessed with magic ever since. I would spend hours rehearsing one card move or sleight of hand. Although I paid my way through college performing as a magician, I didn't pursue it as a vocation because I was afraid I wouldn't be good enough to support my family. Even when my first software company became a financial success, I didn't feel the passion from tech that I felt as a magician. So, I brought magic back into my life. I have been fortunate to have many achievements in my life, but none has compared to when I successfully auditioned before the late magician Dai Vernon, known around the world as "The Man Who Fooled Houdini," and became a performing member of the Academy of Magical Arts at the Magic Castle in Hollywood. Discovering your passion is truly magical.

What Makes Time Stand Still for You?

In explaining relativity, Albert Einstein wrote, "Put your hand on a hot stove for a minute, and it seems like an hour. Sit with a pretty girl for an hour, and it seems like a minute." The great Greek mathematician Archimedes, who was the first to approximate π, would get so engrossed in his work he would forget to eat for days. Rolling Stone guitarist Keith Richards's passion in the studio is legendary. Richards stayed awake for five days straight without a minute sleeping to record "Before They Make Me Run" for the *Some Girls* album.

> Catch your dreams before they slip away
> Dying all the time
> Lose your dreams
> And you will lose your mind.
>> "Ruby Tuesday" by Mick Jagger and Keith Richards

Everyone gets lost in their own world at times where clocks make no sense and hours fly by in an instant. Buried in those moments is the source of your passion. It may not even be the activity itself, but, rather, the sensation the action elicits in you. For an artist, it can be the act of creation or the thrill of performing. For the scientist, the challenge of discovery or the momentary mastery of the forces of the universe. For coaches, passion can be the expertise they can share or the impact they can make in other people's lives. Next time you get lost in thought, pay attention to where you went for therein lies your inner passion.

If You Were Billionaire Bruce Wayne (aka Batman), How Would You Save the World?

Of all the superheroes in the DC Comics Universe (Aquaman, Superman, Wonder Woman, Green Lantern, etc.), only Batman is a career choice. Bruce Wayne was born with no more superpowers than you or I. But when his parents were murdered in front of him as a small boy, it ignited a passion in him to seek vengeance against criminals. You too were born into an imperfect world. How are you going to fix it?

Climate change. Malnutrition. Poverty. Human rights. Universal education. Clean energy. Violence. Our world is facing a litany of existential issues and injustices that desperately need someone to step up and take action. No one can solve these crises on their own, but as anthropologist Margaret Mead pointed out, "Never doubt that a small group of thoughtful, committed citizens can change the world; indeed, it's the only thing that ever has."[9]

Find a cause and run with it. If nine-year-old Milo Cress can start a global movement to ban plastic straws, or 15-year-old Greta Thunberg can address the United Nations Climate Change Conference, what's stopping you? Creating opportunities for positive change puts you in control of your destiny, regardless what obstacles stand in your way. With the limited time each of us has on this planet, the real challenge for each of us is to determine where we feel we can make the most impact. With such a grand purpose to your life, every day you spend on your business is now imbued with a divine purpose. You are no longer making money for money's sake, but rather for the good that those resources will enable you to achieve. Dr. Bill Dorfman took the mundane task of going to the dentist to get your teeth whitened and elevated the experience into the Smiles for Life campaign, an annual charity drive that has raised more than $40 million for children's charities around the world. Actor Paul Newman, along with his friend A.E. Hotchner, started Newman's Own food company to raise money for charity. Still going even after the actor died in 2008, the company has donated more than $500 million to charitable causes. Long after he stopped starring in movies, comedian Jerry Lewis dedicated his life to helping those with muscular dystrophy and raised $2.45 billion for the nonprofit MDA. When asked how he achieved so much in life, Jerry replied, "Nothing can stop anyone who has a love and passion about their work."[10]

If You Only Had a Year to Live, How Would You Spend It?

This last question speaks to the fragility of life that the pandemic brought to the forefront of our minds. None of us know how long we will live. When John Lennon recorded the song *Borrowed Time*, he couldn't have known that he would soon be murdered and the tune would be released posthumously. If you really want to create wealth and develop persistence in all you do, find a purpose bigger than yourself.

For years, raising my children was my purpose. It drove me to work harder and achieve more than I thought I was capable of doing.

The fear of letting them down and wanting a better life for them was the fuel to my fire. They inspired me to keep going through every obstacle in my path as I figured out how the business world worked. Once they were grown and out of the house, I felt lost and abandoned. I uncovered a new purpose when I was writing my first book *Disrupt You!* I realized that I had the ability to share with people the skills needed to change their lives. After interacting with thousands of readers around the world, my purpose became preserving democracy by expanding the global middle class. I am passionate about teaching people how to become entrepreneurs. A stable middle class is the backbone of a free society, and entrepreneurs are the true job creators that power our world. Once I realized I had a skill set to share, I found an energy that had been lacking in my prior corporate career. I was now on a mission, traversing the planet teaching, lecturing, and writing. I have had the privilege to work with government leaders and educators to develop curriculums to inspire our youth, and I am humbled by the impact these programs are having. After a half a century of chasing a profit, I find greater satisfaction in looking beyond the bottom line.

But just having a purpose will not make you persistent overnight. Now that you have the *why* in your life. Here are the six proven techniques for staying on course.

Six Techniques for Maintaining Passion

1. *Build a support network of other persistent people.* It is much easier to overcome failures and setbacks if you have people who can encourage you. From a psychological perspective, you will work harder to achieve something if you believe that you would be letting others' down than if you are just doing the action for yourself. Any Army staff sergeant will tell you that the secret to building an effective platoon is to get the soldiers to care about the men and women in their squad. Tapping into the energy of others becomes infectious and can grow a passion into a movement.

   "When you do what you love, people rally round you. Enthusiasm is contagious and you attract other people who are passionate too," Ventureneer founder Geri Stengel says. "However, what I've found most interesting is that those very people are not just there to cheer you on during good times, they stick around for you to lean on when times are tough. They support you inevitably. That's the magic of passion."[11]

2. *Set tangible goals and outline all the micro-steps needed to achieve them.* Very early on in our year, Vin became overwhelmed by everything coming at him on a daily basis. We've all been there. By the time we respond to hundreds of emails, voicemails, text messages, WeChats, WhatsApps, Skypes, Snaps, and Instagrams, our day is gone. The first thing Vin wrote in big letters across his whiteboard was: *ONE YEAR TO ONE MILLION DOLLARS.* "God or bad," Vin wrote me, "it stares you in the face, which is a good idea for any goal you have in your life."

Vin got in the habit of mapping out his day the night before. Make a list of what you must accomplish tomorrow and tape it to the wall next to your desk as a constant reminder of your priorities. Focus on the big things first and cross them off. You'll be amazed how motivating a list with 8 out of 10 items crossed off can be! As simple as writing down your goals and tasks appears, it has been scientifically proven to be very powerful.

The Harvard MBA program only takes the best of the best and accepts less than 15 percent of applicants. Harvard MBAs are so sought after by corporations that the median graduate's annual salary 10 years after graduating is $204,800 (and many employers are also willing to pay off a graduate student's school loans). As good as that sounds, a 10-year Harvard study showed that 3 percent of their MBA graduates earn 10 times as much as the other 97 percent combined.[12] What differentiated the 3 percent from their classmates? Written goals. Turns out that 84 percent of MBA students have no specific career goals and another 13 percent had some goals in their heads, but never committed them to paper. Only the 3 percent with the super earning power had written down clear goals and mapped out an action plan of how they were going to accomplish them.

Self-made millionaire and bestselling author Grant Cardone takes goal writing to the next level, setting and writing his goals twice a day. First thing when he starts his day and the last thing he does before bed. "I want to wake up to it. I want to go to sleep to it and I want to dream with it," Cardone exclaims. "I want to write my goals down before I go to sleep at night because they are important to me, they are valuable to me and I get to wake up to them again tomorrow."[13]

In 1969, a young Wing Chung martial artist read Napoleon Hill's self-help book *Think and Grow Rich*. Following an idea in the book, the 29-year-old wrote a letter to himself:

My Definite Chief Aim,

I, Bruce Lee, will be the first highest paid Oriental super star in the United States. In return I will give the most exciting performances and render the best of quality in the capacity of an actor. Starting 1970 I will achieve world fame and from then onward till the end of 1980 I will have in my possession $10,000,000. I will live the way I please and achieve inner harmony and happiness.

Bruce Lee[14]

Lee's career took off shortly thereafter with his performance in Lo Wei's *The Big Boss* in 1971. Lee made only five films before his untimely death in 1973 at age 32 and yet is still considered the most influential martial artist of all time. For his influence on martial arts and popular culture, *Time* magazine named Lee as one of the 100 most important people of the twentieth century.

3. *Beyond writing down your goals, you must devote a set time of each day to working on them.* Make that time sacred without exceptions. If you are consistent, you will be persistent. Bestselling author Stephen King, whose more than 50 novels have sold over 350 million copies, writes six pages every day. King has followed the same routine nearly every day for over 40 years. "I have a glass of water or a cup of tea," King explains. "There's a certain time I sit down, from 8:00 to 8:30, somewhere within that half hour every morning. I have my vitamin pill and my music, sit in the same seat, and the papers are all arranged in the same places... The cumulative purpose of doing these things the same way every day seems to be a way of saying to the mind, you're going to be dreaming soon."

4. *Develop your own reward system to keep things fun and exciting.* Gamification, which has proven effective for customer engagement

and education, is just as useful a tool maintaining motivation even if you are the only player. Gamification utilizes your own natural inclination for achievement and pairs it with your internal need to be rewarded or attain status. It is not the size of the reward that matters, but the mere act of earning it. For years, whenever I achieved a goal, I would buy myself a magic trick. Sure, I could have afforded to get one at any time, but by making it my reward system, I could only get something new for my hobby if I earned it. When Sir Paul Nurse was awarded the Nobel Prize for Medicine for his work discovering the key regulators cell cycles, he fittingly bought himself a new motorcycle as a tangible reward. Set up your own rules and decide on a prize.

5. *Make sure your goals are your goals.* You can't fake passion. Just because your parents or spouse or friends have a passion for something, doesn't mean it will motivate you. Not wanting to disappoint others will only get you so far and then persistence starts to wane. Controlling your destiny is about being honest with yourself and those around you.

6. *Don't assume money will motivate you.* If your goal is just amassing money, then there is no milestone for success. More houses and more cars are just more things. Maximizing your wealth is nice, but is unfulfilling as a passion. As Henry David Thoreau wrote, "Wealth is the ability to fully experience life" and only true passion makes that possible.[15]

"When people would ask me what I did for a living," Vin said, "I would tell them 'Every month I wake up with zero and I have to make $100,000 by the end of the month.' It's really difficult." The stress of working six and seven days a week was starting to show on Vin's face. Lack of exercise coupled with a lack of a social life was pushing him to his breaking point. Vin's passion wasn't the money, but the achievement of becoming a millionaire. Perhaps I should have told him to find a balance before he worked himself to exhaustion, but much like West Point's intensive Beast (Cadet Basic Training), I wanted him to know what he was truly capable of doing and not set limits. Every time Vin came to me with his fears of burning out, my answer to him was always the same: "Work through it."

In spite of the setbacks and exhaustion, the extra hours of writing proposals for new clients paid off. He was burning the candle at both ends: working with clients all day and prospecting for new ones each night. Try as he could, his month was coming up short.

Miraculously, just before Vin closes the books on the month a new client sends in his retainer deposit. Once again, Vin clears the $100K hurdle with $110,558 and brings his year-to-date earnings up to $451,647. With five months under his belt, he now had the wind on his back. The recent strong months meant that he *only* has to average $78,336 per month for the remainder of the year. Little did he know that two of the most powerful tech companies in the world, Google and Facebook, were about to pull the rug out from under him and destroy his business.

Notes

1. Chelsea Greenwood, "6 people Who became Millionaires by 30 reveal their Keys to Success," *Business Insider* (June 20, 2018).
2. Dave Kerpen, "These 17 Quotes Will Inspire You to Be More Persistent," *Inc.* (November 6, 2017).
3. Sheila McClear, "Bill Gates Doesn't Recommend his Method of Getting Ahead: "Most People wouldn't Enjoy It" *The Ladders* (June 27, 2019).
4. Angela Duckworth, *Grit: The Power of Passion and Perseverance* (New York: Scribner, 2016), 127.
5. Riz Pasha, "75 Howard Schultz Quotes on Business, Leadership & Success," Succeedfeed.com (July 7, 2018), https://succeedfeed.com/howard-schultz-quotes/.
6. Partnership for a New American Economy, *The "New American" Fortune 500* (June 2011), http://www.nyc.gov/html/om/pdf/2011/partnership_for_a_new_american_economy_fortune_500.pdf.
7. Martin Meadow, *Simple Self-Discipline Box Set* (Schaumburg, IL: Meadows Publishing, 2019), 256.
8. Bethany Hamilton, *Soul Surfer: A True Story of Faith, Family and Fighting to Get Back on the Board* (London: Simon & Schuster UK, 2012), 44.

9. Nancy Lutkehaus, *Margaret Mead: The Making of an American Icon* (Princeton, NJ: Princeton University Press, 2008), 261.

10. "Jerry Lewis Quotes," Brainyquote.com. Accessed August 31, 2020. https://www.brainyquote.com/quotes/jerry_lewis_846267

11. RebeKah Iliff, "7 Tips for Loving Your Career and Working with Passion," *Entrepreneur* (June 9, 2015).

12. Annabel Acton, "How to Set Goals (and Why You Should Write Them Down)," *Forbes* (November 3, 2015).

13. Ibid.

14. Arman Suleimenov, "The Bruce Lee's Definite Chief Aim in Life," *Medium* (October 24, 2013).

15. Larry Chang, *Wisdom for the Soul* (Washington, DC: Gnosophia Publishers, 2006), 746.

7

Don't Fly Solo: Finding the Right Mentor for Each Phase of Your Career

Had there not been you, there never would have been me.
—*Oprah Winfrey speaking to her mentor Barbara Walters*

AT 14, HE AND HIS SINGLE mom got evicted from their apartment. By 16, the directionless high school student had multiple arrests on his record and was a loner with no friends or girlfriends. At 220 pounds, he was a tough teen with a chip on his shoulder and no future. One day at school, knowing he was too big for anyone to stop, the troublemaker decided he was going to use the teachers' bathroom. "I'm washing my hands, a guy walks in, and he goes, 'Hey, you can't be in here,' very stern. I was a punk at that time, I looked at him like, 'Yeah, alright in a second.' He screams, 'Hey, you get the fuck outta here!' He was bright red, veins everywhere. I kind of walked by him, brushed my shoulder by him."

"That night I went home, I felt bad, I knew I acted like a punk," the former high school punk continued. "I went to find him the next day and said, 'Hey, I just want to apologize to you, I'm sorry for being so rude,' and I just apologized and I stuck my hand out to him. He grabbed

111

my hand, he shook it, he held onto it, he said, 'I appreciate your apology, I want you to play football for me,' and I went, 'OK.'"

Freedom High football coach Jodi Swick continued to mentor the young man all the way to being one of the most sought-after and recruited players in the history of the school. Thanks to Swick's guidance, Dwayne "The Rock" Johnson not only was awarded a full scholarship to the University of Miami, he would go on to play in the NFL, wrestle professionally, and become one of the highest-paid actors in the history of Hollywood, earning over $300 million. Having a mentor at such a low-point in his life changed the trajectory of The Rock's entire future and catapulted him to heights he could have never imagined for himself. "It changed my life," Johnson recalled years later. "I am here, I believe, in large part due to that man, his name is Jodie Swick, he has since passed away and I (thank him)."[1]

Truth #7 – You Can't Go It Alone

With a little push, a stone can conquer the world, too. From the time that humans first started living as large communities, around 4500 BCE in Uruk, Mesopotamia, people built walled cities as impenetrable fortresses to maintain the power of those ruling within the walls and keep out those wanting to change the status quo. This defense mechanism worked reliably until the introduction of the catapult. A catapult is an ingenious and powerful device that harnesses three properties of physics to transform otherwise inert stones into unstoppable wall-busting weapons capable of overthrowing the mightiest of kingdoms. First, tension, the state of being stretched, is applied to the catapult's arm as it is ratcheted tighter and tighter lifting the rock, until it is pushed to near its breaking point. When the arm is released, torque comes into play. Torque is a twisting force that causes rotation and propels objects quickly forward. Then gravity, a force that attracts a body toward the center of the Earth, takes over the projectile's trajectory until the stone reaches its target. Entering the business world can appear as impenetrable as the walled cities of ancient times. Having a mentor push you beyond your self-limiting boundaries is your catapult for breaking down internal and external walls.

At the beginning of your career, your value and ability to succeed is limited by your lack of experience. You sit there with lots of ideas swirling around in your head but you lack the inertia to move them forward. Mentoring is all about finding a direction in which to focus your energy and build your inertia. A good mentor will challenge you to stretch your goals. *What are you truly capable of achieving? What is holding you back from achieving your goals?* Through constant dialogue, going round and round evaluating your progress and mistakes, the mentor raises your trajectory and propels your career farther than you first thought possible. Lastly, a mentor centers you and keeps you on target so you can smash through barriers and reach your goals. Like The Rock and the stone, you can't achieve success on your own.

There is a modern myth perpetuated by Hollywood and Silicon Valley that the successful entrepreneur is a solitary figure who makes it on his or her own: the self-made man. One-man armies like Rambo don't exist in the real world. Even action stars need mentors. "It's important to recognize that at every step of the way, I had help. It's important to acknowledge that," Arnold Schwarzenegger told University of Houston graduates in a 2017 commencement speech, adding, "As soon as you understand that you are here because you had a lot of help, you realize you need to help others."

Many of us dream of being the lone innovator who, while mocked by those around him, single-handedly topples giant corporations and becomes fabulously wealthy. I can assure you that is not how anyone became successful. We've all heard Mahatma Gandhi's famous quote, "First they ignore you, then they laugh at you, then they fight you, and then you win." Turns out, like so many quotes on the internet, Gandhi never said it. Like the myth of the lone entrepreneur, the idea of going it alone has become enshrined in our culture as the only true way to rise to the top. Keeping that myth alive used to be my job when I worked with a different kind of rock.

During my years of working at record labels, part of my job was to perpetuate this myth on behalf of our artists. Fans want to feel close to their favorite rock stars and connect with the music that flows straight from a musician's heart to their own. That fantasy would be broken if people were aware of the hundreds of professionals (agents, producers, arrangers, chorus masters, composers, engineers, sound technicians, A&R administrators, tour managers, roadies, assistants, tour coordinators, drivers, stage managers, creative directors, videographers, photographers, record executives, promoters, set builders, songwriters, vocal coaches, backing vocalists, conductors, studio musicians, editors, program directors, choreographers, publicists, makeup artists, and wardrobe stylists) working anonymously behind the scenes to foster that intimate connection. I remember being backstage at the original Wembley stadium in London watching the assistant wardrobe stylist steaming the wrinkles out of a famous rocker's T-shirt before he went on to sing by himself in front of 120,000 adoring fans. We want to believe that our favorite musician made it all alone because too often, we feel all alone.

> A coach is someone who tells you what you don't want to hear, who has you see what you don't want to see, so you can be who you have always known you could be.
>
> — *Dallas Cowboys coach Tom Landry*

Drake had rapper Lil Wayne. Kareem Abdul Jabbar had UCLA basketball coach John Wooden. Vincent Van Gogh had post impressionist painter Paul Gauguin. Mark Zuckerberg had Apple co-founder Steve Jobs. Actress Lena Dunham had filmmaker Nora Ephron. Frank Sinatra had crooner Bing Crosby. Salesforce founder Marc Benioff had Oracle CEO Larry Ellison. Even Mother Teresa credits the mentorship of Father Michael van der Peet, whom she met in Rome while waiting for a bus, for giving direction to her life. After meeting Father Michael, her mission became mentoring others. "Never worry about numbers," Mother Teresa taught, "Help one person at a time, and always start with the person nearest you."[2]

The mythology of being self-made is so strong in our culture that too many people perceive themselves as weak or incapable if they ask for help. Nothing could be farther from the truth. Success is a team sport. No one ever built a billion-dollar company without employees, investors, business partners, and customers. Consider, for a moment, how many people it takes to make a smartphone. We all rely on our phones every day to run our lives, and yet, there is not a single person on the planet who can make an iPhone from scratch: from mining to swiping. Knowing how to mine yttrium, terbium, lithium, and gadolinium from the earth is a vastly different field of knowledge than knowing how to manufacture a silicon chip or program in Swift or Objective-C. It takes thousands of discrete knowledge sets to make the phone and thousands more to create the network infrastructure that makes it useful. No one person possesses all of the knowledge and skillsets to do what it takes to succeed. And even if you could learn how to do it all yourself, wouldn't you want to accelerate the process by learning from those who have done it before? Sir Isaac Newton, who many consider one of the most influential scientists of all time, admitted, "If I have seen further, it is by standing on the shoulders of giants."

"Wherever you are in life right now, and whatever you know, is a result of the ideas, experiences, and people you have interacted with in your life, whether in person, through books and music, email, or culture. There is no score to keep when abundance leads to even more abundance. So make a decision that from this day forward, you will start making the contacts and accumulating the knowledge, experiences, and people to help you achieve your goals," Keith Ferrazzi writes in his book *Never Eat Alone*. "But first be honest with yourself. How much time are you ready to spend on reaching out and giving before you get? How many mentors do you have?"[3]

The first step of solving any problem is recognizing that you have a problem. If you are afraid to ask for help, ask yourself why. Most likely, what you are afraid of is not receiving the help, but the rejection of getting turned down. Successful people hate being rejected just like everyone else, but they overcame their fear by looking past the moment. Just as you won't close every sale, you won't find that every person you reach out to is open to mentoring. "I take rejection as someone blowing a bugle in my ear to wake me up and get going, rather than retreat," declares superstar Sylvester Stallone.[4]

If fear isn't holding you back from finding a mentor, then perhaps your ego is the culprit. If you were the only person on the planet to have the idea for your new business, how could anyone not as smart as you possibly help? "Understandably, there's a lot of ego, nervous energy, and parental pride involved, especially with one- or two-person start-ups – factors that tend to manifest themselves in a cocoon-like state of mind where, 'Only I/we get it and nobody else can possibly help make this thing work.' Trust me: they can and they will," billion-aire serial entrepreneur Sir Richard Branson advises, adding. "Going it alone is an admirable but foolhardy and highly flawed approach to taking on the world." I feel so fortunate to have had one of Branson's original partners, Ken Berry, as my mentor. He saw something in me that I didn't know was there and inspired me to achieve more than I had ever thought was possible.

Three Ways to Find a Mentor Using LinkedIn

The best way to control your destiny in an uncertain world is to have a guide who can steer you toward opportunities and away from pitfalls. The process for finding great mentors begins with finding someone you would like to emulate in your life. *Whose career inspires you? Whose work in your field do you admire?* While we would all like to be mentored by a famous billionaire (and it may happen someday), at the start of your career look for people who are one or two rungs up the ladder from where you are.

LinkedIn is a great place to research potential mentors. Not only can you see who is making a difference in your field, but you can study their trajectory and look for things that you share in common. *Did they also come from a small town or a farm? Did they go to the same college as you? Was their first job similar to the one you hold now?* Understanding a potential mentor's path to success will increase the likelihood that their advice will be applicable to your future. When I was still in college and writing for the *UCLA Daily Bruin* student newspaper, I was obsessed with asking celebrity speakers who came to campus how they made it to the top of their fields. At one point, the stars I interviewed (Bob Hope, Doug Henning, Gene Wilder, and others) had all been students like me. I was convinced there must be a secret ladder to the top that they had taken. What I discovered was that the ladder they used is available to everyone, but the super successful people had someone holding it steady for them as they climbed the rungs. LinkedIn can help you find your support system.

LinkedIn offers several clues to how open a person would be to being a mentor. There are three items to look for in a potential mentor's profile: articles, endorsements, and volunteer experience.

1. *Look at who writes and posts articles on LinkedIn.* Any person who regularly writes articles in their field is clearly a leader looking to make more connections in their industry. Just as they are seeking to expand their relationships, they understand your desire to do the same thing. I can't tell you how many times after writing a column for *Fortune* or posting on LinkedIn, I've heard from people passionate about the same topic. By following what people are posting, you also have a jumping-off point to start your dialogue. Instead of emailing out of the blue, "Will you be my mentor?" you can offer your perspective on their article. Start by posting well-thought-out comments. See how they respond. That exchange of ideas is the beginning of a relationship. You can seek advice on a topic, rather than on your career. Mentorships, like all meaningful relationships, evolve over time. Don't rush the process. Just as you wouldn't propose marriage on a first date, don't pop the "will you mentor me" question too soon. Let mentorship grow organically out of your conversations and you may never even have to use the "M-word."

2. *The second part of the LinkedIn profile to give insight into a person's character is their endorsements.* Reading through a potential mentor's endorsements may show examples of how they mentored other people in the past and the influence they have had on others' careers. A person who wrote a heartfelt endorsement about benefiting from mentorship might also be the perfect mentor for you. Especially keep an eye out for anyone who helps people at the start of their journey. Odds are, they enjoy helping others and have done it time and again. Search for role models you can look up to and people who take an interest in your career. But here's an important insight: "You don't have to have mentors who look like you," suggests former US Secretary of State Condoleezza Rice. "Had I been waiting for a black, female Soviet specialist mentor, I would still be waiting. Most of my mentors have been old white men, because they were the ones who dominated my field."[5]

3. *Listed volunteer experience in the LinkedIn profile is a valuable clue.*
Does the person have a charitable heart? The more involved successful people are with their community, the better a mentor they
will be for you. Not only does volunteering shed light on the quality of their character but it also shows that the person has a wide
network of contacts outside of their workplace. Conversely, you
don't have to find successful people who are involved in charity
work on LinkedIn. Go volunteer and personally get active in community organizations. Your hard work and positive attitude won't
go unnoticed by the more senior executives volunteering alongside you. "Stop the 'will you be my mentor?' emails and start being
present to embrace the learning opportunities all around you," recommends *Shark Tank's* Robert Herjavec.[6]

Going beyond LinkedIn, Herjavec suggests that the best way
to find a mentor is by paying attention to those who are giving you
advice every day. At the start of his career when he was working at
Avis Rent a Car, Herjavec was chatting with the company's founder
Warner Avis. Mr. Avis pointed out the office window to a hot dog
vendor at the edge of the parking lot and told Robert that he "was
acting like the vendor – pushing product, and doing all the work
to make a living. He followed that statement with, 'You need to be
the guy supplying the dogs to all the vendors if you ever want to
scale.'" Herjavec writes in one of his LinkedIn posts, "That day was
a turning point in my professional career. I realized that I couldn't
do it alone."

Building a Network of Mentors

"So, it's not one mentor. It's a constellation, a network of mentors who
really amplify my abilities and knowledge in particular vectors," asserts
LinkedIn co-founder Reid Hoffman, adding. "The fastest way to change
yourself is to hang out with the people who are already the way you
want to be."[7]

Harvard University research supports Hoffman's assertion. Social
psychologist Dr. David McClelland concluded that the people with
whom you hang out, what he refers to as your "reference group," determine as much as 95 percent of your success or failure in life. If you

hang out with gangsters, you'll end up in prison, but if you hang out with rising stars, your star will rise also. Or as motivational speaker Jim Rohn keenly notes, "You are the average of the five people you spend the most time with."[8]

Mary Barra is the first female executive to lead a major automaker. When asked who was the one mentor that aided her the most, the General Motor CEO said that her career hadn't been shaped by just one or two mentors; instead, it's been influenced by a network of them. "Different people see different aspects of us as we progress in our careers and handle the opportunities and challenges along the way," Barra noted.[9] She learned early on in her career the importance of being more vocal and assertive in meetings. Another mentor instilled in her the importance of integrity and honoring one's commitments. These lessons and skills helped Barra shatter the glass ceiling and rise to the very top of her profession.

Are your inner circle of friends and business associates achievers? One of the reasons groups such as Young Presidents' Organization (YPO) are so successful is that they habituate prosperity. There is no better way to maximize your wealth than by surrounding yourself with successful people. With over 24,000 members in more than 130 countries, YPO creates success for young CEOs and founders through peer mentorship. What could you achieve by hanging out with members such as Facebook COO Sheryl Sandberg or Motorola founder Bob Galvin?

Another great group to join is Entrepreneurs' Organization (EO). With more than 14,000 members around the world, EO focuses on entrepreneurs who have built their business to at least $1 million in annual revenue. When I keynoted the 2019 EO global gathering in Lisbon, I was impressed with the comradery and energy of the 1,000 attendees. People came from across the globe to share their knowledge and help others grow their businesses. From Chamber of Commerce meetings, to organizations such as Founder Institute, Toastmasters, Provisors, and Vistage, every city has local groups for founders and startup entrepreneurs to support each other. And if your community doesn't have any, what better way to build your mentor network than starting your own monthly meetup?

When social media marketer Harrison Painter decided to move back to his hometown of Indianapolis, Indiana, after working in California for several years, he missed the vibrant support system that Los Angeles had for startup entrepreneurs. So, taking what he learned in LA, Harrison founded Amplify Indy to assist nonprofit and social entrepreneurs in networking and collaboration. "Our focus is to create massive positive social impact in central Indiana," says Painter. Now Amplify Indy is changing the trajectory of the entire state.

Another great resource for connecting with mentors is SCORE (score.org). SCORE's mission is to foster vibrant small business communities through mentoring and education. Its website connects mentors and mentees in an effort to give every entrepreneur the support necessary to thrive. SCORE believes, as I do, that small business is the engine driving the US economy, and these companies are critical to our communities. Annually, SCORE volunteers conducted over 295,000 mentoring sessions and 147,000 online educational workshops, and had more than 250,000 people attend local community workshops. In 2019 alone, SCORE mentors helped start 29,681 new businesses and create 97,387 new jobs. In the same year, they also helped 67 percent of their clients to increase their revenue.

SCORE mentors are available in 62 different industries, ensuring mentees can find the partners they need to be successful. According to US Small Business Administration statistics, SCORE works. Small business clients who receive three or more hours of mentoring report higher revenues than those who don't. With more than 11,000 mentors, SCORE set the goal of helping a million entrepreneurs in 2020.

Finding a Partner

As we stated at the beginning of this chapter, the seventh truth is that you can't go it alone. While having mentors to guide you will hasten your journey to success, having a partner to share the burden with is indispensable. All of the aforementioned techniques for securing a mentor also work for finding a business partner. Building anything new is an arduous task, so having someone to share the load with you is preferable to going it alone. When you are in it together, you can keep each other's spirits high. You'll find that you have more tenacity when you don't want to let your partner down.

Find a partner with complementary skills to yours. We all have blind spots, and finding someone with the skillsets to complement yours makes you both unstoppable. Steve Wozniak, perhaps the foremost coder in the world at the time, couldn't sell water in the desert; but partnered with Steve Jobs's business savvy, they changed the world. Bill Gates couldn't have created Microsoft without Paul Allen. Google required the genius of both Larry Page and Sergey Brin. Would you be able to fly around the world if Orville Wright didn't have his brother, Wilbur, by his side? How different would banking be if Henry Wells hadn't partnered with William Fargo? How would you ever get 99 $^{44}/_{100}$% pure Ivory Soap clean if brothers-in-law William Procter and James Gamble hadn't partnered? And, would you have ever tasted the rich creamy goodness of Chocolate Fudge Brownie ice cream if Ben Cohen and Jerry Greenfield hadn't opened their first ice cream shop in 1977? "We measured our success not just by how much money we made," Jerry recalled, "but by how much we contributed to the community. It was a two-part bottom line."[10]

Using Mentorship to Build Your Team

"First he told me it was a stupid idea," eBay founder Pierre Omidyar said about meeting the company's future first employee and president Jeff Skoll, "and then he agreed to come on board."[11] Getting people to join your company is only half the battle. Job satisfaction is not tied to salary. A good paycheck may lure them in the door, but unless they feel their career is moving forward, they won't stay. Now that you have been mentored and are building a team for your new startup, the roles reverse. If you want to keep the best and the brightest, whether in your corporate department or at your fledgling startup, you need to provide mentorship to the team.

According to Leigh Branham, author of *The 7 Hidden Reasons Employees Leave*, 89 percent of managers believe that employees quit to earn more money. The truth is that only 12 percent quit over salary; the vast majority (79 percent) cite "lack of appreciation" as the motivating factor to move on.[12] By including mentorship in your company culture from day one, people will feel not just a connection to the company but to their peers and mentors. There are two types of internal mentorship programs every company needs to implement from day one:

1. *Peer mentors are a great way to onboard new employees and help them build friends and support within the organization.* To help onboard new talent at Google, Nooglers (new employees) wear a propeller beanie cap so everyone knows to reach out and be helpful. I'm not saying that you have to go to such extremes, but by pairing each new hire with someone who knows the ropes, they will get up to speed faster, find a group of friends to bond with, and learn the unwritten rules of office politics.

2. *As your company grows larger, the second type of mentorship comes into play.* Career mentors are a combination coach and internal advocate. By giving someone a connection higher up in the organization, it gives that employee an outlet other than their immediate supervisor. Sun Microsystems did an in-depth study of its mentorship programs and was amazed by the findings because of the effect on both the mentee and mentor's career path within the company. Worried about turnover? Mentee retention rates were 72 percent higher than those who didn't participate in the program. Best of all, mentees saw more increases in pay and were promoted five times more than those not in the program. As far as the mentors, they were promoted six times more than other employees.

   Company mentoring programs are also a key tool in promoting diversity in the workplace. According to Cornell University's School of Industrial and Labor Relations, mentoring programs boost minority representation in management anywhere from 9 to 24 percent. Mentorship programs also increased retention rates for women as much as 38 percent. "I think the greatest thing we give each other is encouragement ... knowing that I'm talking to someone in this mentoring relationship who's interested in the big idea here is very, very important to me," former Disney/ABC Television Group President Anne Sweeney said. "I think if it were just about helping me get to the next step, it would be a heck of a lot less interesting."[13]

When I ran very large organizations with employees spread out around the globe, I used a third type of mentoring program: distance mentoring. As the name implies, it helps people who may not be at headquarters build relationships with peers in other locations and divisions within the company. (We will analyze the advantages of remote working in Chapter 12.) I couldn't have made the jump from startup founder to corporate executive without company mentorship programs. The most effective program I was ever a part of was Universal Studios' Cross-Business Asset Management team. CBAM was made up of representatives from film, television, theme parks, digital, music, consumer products, and senior management. The net result of CBAM was more internal deals being done within the company. Why license a song for your movie from another company when you know someone from your own music division? As the new kid on the block, CBAM was invaluable for me getting my new digital projects funded and endorsed by other divisions.

"If I hadn't had mentors, I wouldn't be here today. I'm a product of great mentoring, great coaching ... Coaches or mentors are very important. They could be anyone – your husband, other family members, or your boss," PepsiCo Indra Nooyi noted.[14] But what happens if you invest all of this energy into upgrading the quality of your team and they leave? *Imagine what happens to your company if you don't improve the quality of your team, and they don't leave.*

Upscaling Your Team

The last part of team building that is the hardest for many first-time entrepreneurs to face is recognizing when your company has grown beyond the skills of the team that built it. As companies grow and mature from a handful of people in one room to thousands of employees around the world, the skills needed to manage and maintain that growth may be out of reach for your current team members. Put another way, when you first start out, there was no way for you to attract the best, most experienced talent to fill all the slots in your startup. Now that you can attract more senior-level talent, how do you upgrade your organization?

The first step is to identify where your company isn't executing. Once you know the source of the problem, the next step is to decide whether underperformers can raise their game or if it is too big of a leap to handle internally. When Walmart, America's largest brick-and-mortar retailer, wanted to up its online game, management knew that Walmart's current employees didn't have the e-commerce expertise to compete with Amazon, so they grabbed Amazon's vice president of retail systems and retail services Suresh Kumar and made him Walmart's global chief technology officer and chief development officer.

Luring away top talent is very expensive, and there will always be a bigger company that can offer them more money. With 53 percent of workers dissatisfied with their current job, the culture you created at your company may be a bigger draw than the biggest paycheck. The trick to getting the best talent is to not wait until you need them. A founder always needs to be networking for possible employees. Long before you have any head count to fill, make sure that you are reaching out and interviewing two or three potential new hires per month. By developing a deep bench, you will be able to fill future openings faster and have a better chance of discovering talent with one foot out the door somewhere else. Decades ago, when a startup named WhoWhere had a team come in and pitch me for some business, I was so impressed with their VP of Corporate Development, Ellen Levy, that I asked her to wait a moment after the rest of her team had left. All I said to her was, "What would it take for you to quit your current job and come work for me?" I never did get to lure her away, but years later, she reversed the conversation and got me to join a new startup she was on the advisory board of, called LinkedIn.

"One thing I never thought about in my big-company job? Cash flow. When your business has billions of dollars in revenue, you can make a lot of mistakes and still have a viable business," CEO and Ellevest co-founder Sallie Kracheck warns. "But in a startup, make a few hiring mistakes and you can find yourself in real jeopardy fast."

Your idea is only as good as its execution, and it will take a team of people to get you to your goal. The encouragement and support that mentors and partners gave you on your journey need to be paid forward to those you hire. Company culture is not a motto on the wall or a mission statement in an employee handbook. It starts from how you recruit, retain, and encourage those within your organization. Hopefully, my mentoring sessions with Vin would give him a framework for mentoring others. With several employees recently hired and on the hunt for several more, it had taken Vin Clancy less than six months to transition from mentee to mentor, and from employee to management.

> As Vin now has some part-time freelancers helping him with his workload, he must deal with the one problem that vexes most founders: when to delegate. Vin was disappointed with the quality of his freelancers and frustrated by the time wasted having to redo their work. By bringing the talent in house, Vin is able to mentor and delegate better. More people doing the work freed Vin to squeeze out enough time to craft 10 new client proposals. With much of the mundane tasks now done by others, Vin spends his time following up on the proposals and closes four of his new prospects.
>
> Fighting off the flu all month and not getting enough sleep, his herculean efforts pay off. Vin again earns six figures for the month. Now halfway through the year, the $109,439 in sales for month six puts Vin 56 percent of the way to his goal of becoming a millionaire.

Notes

1. "Dwayne Johnson Thanks High School Coach for Hollywood Success," Hollywood.com (June 10, 2016), www.hollywood.com/general/dwayne-johnson-thanks-high-school-coach-for-hollywood-success-60592220/.
2. Adam S. McHugh, *The Listening Life* (New York: InterVarsity Press, 2015), 212.
3. Keith Ferrazzi and Tahl Raz, *Never Eat Alone* (New York: Crown, 2014), 366.
4. Harvey MacKay, *Use Your Head to Get Your Foot in the Door* (New York: Penguin, 2010), 135.

5. Caroline Castrillon, "5 Mistakes to Avoid When Seeking a Mentor," *Forbes* (November 26, 2019).

6. Jonathan Chan, "How to Find a Mentor Who Can Unlock Your Potential," Foundr (August 8, 2016), https://foundr.com/find-a-mentor.

7. Nicole Perlroth, "15 Minutes with: Reid Hoffman, the Guru," *Forbes* (April 6, 2011).

8. Jim Rohn, *Jim Rohn's 8 Best Success Lessons* (Issaquah, Washington: Made for Success Incorporated, 2014).

9. Mary Barra, "My Mentors Told Me to Take an HR Role Even Though I Was an Engineer. They Were Right," Linkedin.com (August 3, 2015), www.linkedin.com/pulse/mentor-who-shaped-me-my-mentors-told-take-hr-role-even-mary-barra/.

10. Chuck Kocher, "Profile of a Successful Company: Ben and Jerry's," *The Transformation Company* (August 14, 2012), https://the#transformation.company/profile-of-a-successful-company-ben-and-jerrys/.

11. Alyson Shontell, "10 Super Successful Cofounders and Why Their Partnerships Worked," *Business Insider* (June 4, 2011), www.business#insider.com.au/10-super-successful-cofounders-and-why-their-partnerships-worked-2011-6#larry-page-and-sergey-brin-1.

12. David Sturt and Todd Nordstrom, "10 Shocking Workplace Stats You Need to Know," *Forbes* (March 8, 2018), www.forbes.com/sites/davidsturt/2018/03/08/10-shocking-workplace-stats-you-need-to-know/?sh=27f8194cf3af.

13. Neil Ball, "Top 15 Mentoring Quotes," *Mentoring Magazine* (May 5, 2019).

14. Snigdha Majumder, "If I Hadn't Had Mentors, I Wouldn't Be Here Today," *Medium* (September 25, 2019), https://snigdham.medium.com/if-i-hadnt-had-mentors-i-wouldn-t-be-here-today-d3619c59ab6e.

8

Everything Is a Tech Startup. Yes, Everything!

What new technology does is create new opportunities to do a job that customers want done.

—Tim O'Reilly

IF YOU COULD TIME travel in your flying DeLorean, like *Back to the Future*'s Marty McFly, to the year 2010, with all of the knowledge you have from living in the twenty-first century, what tech stock would you tell your younger self to buy? Think how rich you would be if you had purchased Facebook, Amazon, Netflix, or Google years ago. But, none of those companies were the best-performing technology company of the decade. Should you have selected a hardware company like Tesla or Apple? Those aren't the biggest winners, either. Or perhaps you should have chosen Baidu, Alibaba, Tencent, Xiaomi, or one of the other massively successful Asian technology unicorns? Those wouldn't have been your best investment, either. Had you invested in any of the aforementioned billion-dollar successes, you wouldn't have made nearly as much money as if you had just purchased stock in Domino's Pizza.

That's right, Domino's Pizza is a technology company. More than half of Domino's revenues come from digital platforms. Wisely realizing how much time today's consumers spend on their mobile phones daily, Domino's management invested heavily in being an app-centric company. Today, Domino's has more people working in its IT department than any other part of the company. Domino's is a tech startup whose stock has appreciated more than 2,000 percent since 2010. You could say that an investment in Domino's Pizza couldn't be topped!

Your business isn't just about what product you sell or service you offer, it is about how you engage with your customer and every function that those customers never see. Yes, Domino's creates tasty pizzas, but they also create marketing to reach consumers, they design social media content to engage with customers, they construct apps to make ordering easier, they originate research to discover new consumer tastes and trends, they recruit new franchise owners and employees, and they manage a vast digital supply chain to reduce costs associated with servicing 17,000 stores in more than 90 countries around the world. Making pizza is actually the easiest and smallest part of the business.

"At least 40 percent of all businesses will die in the next 10 years if they don't figure out how to change their entire company to accommodate new technologies," predicts Cisco Executive Chairman John Chambers.[1] In fact, Cisco's $50 billion a year business is solely focused on the back-office networking hardware and software that keeps other businesses functioning.

Truth #8 – Everything Is a Tech Startup

The eighth truth you must embrace for *Future Proofing You* is that every business is a tech startup. If you are serious about maximizing wealth, harnessing technology is the only way you can scale. Think about your own life for a moment. What is the first thing you do in the morning, even before your feet touch the ground? You check your phone. And for most of us, it's the last thing that tucks us into bed each night. The average American now spends five hours a day interacting with their phones. That translates to 76 full days taken out of your 365-day year. Each minute, of every day, people watch 4.7 million YouTube videos, send 19 million texts, scroll through 700,000 Instagram pictures, share 2.5 million Snaps, query Google 4.1 million times, send 59 million messages, and send 190 million emails.[2] If that's where people are focusing their time and energy, isn't that the place your new business should be?

Now think about how you spend your money. We all earn different incomes, but on a percentage basis, how much of your monthly income do you spend on digital goods? This is my favorite question to ask audiences when I keynote conferences or speak at college campuses. Most people's initial reaction is 2–3 percent. When I remind them of Netflix and their mobile bill, some will shout out 10 percent. If I was standing in the room in front of you at this very moment, I would wager a hundred dollars that you spend more than half of your income on digital goods. Wanna bet?

Before I relieve you of your crisp Benjamin, allow me to define *digital goods*. In the modern economy, digital goods are anything that are not physical. Your rent or mortgage are digital goods. Same definition works for your student loans, credit card debt, payroll taxes, and social security contribution. But we haven't even started to scratch the surface. Your mobile, cable, and internet services are digital. Same goes for your utilities, auto payments, auto insurance, health insurance, and life insurance. Streaming entertainment services such as Disney+, Hulu, Netflix, and Spotify are all digital (going to the movie theater is a digital good as well). Don't forget the Kindle e-Book some of you are reading this on. Do you pay membership dues for a union or a club? After paying for all those digital goods, it is amazing that you still have food in your belly and a shirt on your back (though you most likely purchased the shirt digitally at Amazon, which has now eclipsed Walmart as the number one apparel retailer in the United States).

During the pandemic, we also learned that many more things could be virtualized and made digital. Distanced learning online replaced sitting in a classroom. Business conferences didn't have to require airplane flights or hotel ballrooms when conducted virtually on Zoom or Google Hangouts. With online delivery services and collaboration software tools such as Slack or Microsoft Teams, the company you worked for didn't even need to have a physical headquarters as people continued to do their jobs remotely. If you survived Covid-19 by not leaving your home for weeks or months, then every aspect of how you worked, played, and socialized relied on being digital. And now that people have adapted to working from home, that genie is not going back into the bottle. The revolutionary data speeds of 5G will only increase everyone's engagement in the virtual world of tomorrow.

If you are spending most of your time and money in the digital world today, why not build your career and business there. Unilever, the giant conglomerate that produces everything from Dove soap and Lipton Tea, to Axe body spray and Best Foods mayonnaise, recognizes that even tangible consumer goods must focus on the digital world. "We should no longer be talking about *digital marketing*," Unilever's Chief Marketing and Communications Officer Keith Weed announced, "but marketing in a digital world."

Perhaps venture capitalist and web pioneer Marc Andreessen said it most succinctly. "Software is eating the world." With more than 6 billion customers just one click away, there is no better location to make your first million. For nearly every product and service you can think of, Google, Facebook, and Yelp are more important to brick-and-mortar retailers than the old adage of *location, location, location*. If Google can't find you, how will your customers?

The biggest excuse I hear from those afraid of tech and still mentally operating in the twentieth century is that they are not engineers. Steve Jobs wasn't an engineer and he built a trillion-dollar company without ever learning to code. The same is true of Alibaba founder Jack Ma, who didn't even own a computer until he was in his thirties and still found time to make a $44 billion fortune online. You don't have to understand how to rebuild a transmission to use a car. An automobile is just an indispensable tool to get you where you want to go. Social media and digital marketing are no different.

Rick Steele is a nontechie who embraced the internet and made millions without inventing anything. In 1999, when everyone was launching a website, he and his partner created Lowest Mortgage, a lead generation site for real estate brokers across the country. Steele learned the ropes with that business, but when he saw the looming subprime loan disaster emerging, he needed to find something else to sell online. Having just purchased a new house, Steele was annoyed at the cost of window coverings. Rick assumed that selling any product online would be easier than using search engines to sell mortgage leads. With that one insight, selectblinds.com was born in 2003. His business of reselling someone else's product online grew quickly, from

$855,000 the first year to over $65 million a year in 2013; a 7,600 percent increase in just 10 years.

Not ready to jump in and build your own app or website? Why not sell products on eBay? In the UK alone, the e-commerce site created over 1,000 new eBay millionaires in just 2017. Janine Dutton, a mother of three, started by selling underwear from her kitchen table and grew her eBay business into a $3 million a year online retailer of lingerie and swimwear. From your same kitchen table, you can sell merchandise on Walmart, Facebook, Craigslist, Offer Up, and Amazon. According to a recent survey by Feedvisor, approximately one fifth of all Amazon merchants sell more than $1 million a year, and that number keeps growing.

But what if you are in the service business? Are you just relying on word-of-mouth referrals to grow your business? If you are, then ask yourself this question: When you needed a glass window replaced or wanted to find a good restaurant in a new town, did you ask around or check your phone? Shockingly, according to a 2017 CNBC/SurveyMonkey Small Business survey, only 36 percent of small businesses have a website, and just 40 percent post on social media. That is why so many small businesses fail. They are living in an analog past and not accepting the true digital nature of all twenty-first century commerce.

Best of all, the digital world has leveled the playing field for small businesses to compete with multinational industrial giants. Tinder earns more than $1.2 billion a year from its 5 million members, but that didn't stop Laurie Davis from launching her dating website eFlirt .com for just $50 and a Twitter account. Consumer products giant Procter & Gamble sells more than $7.2 billion of Gillette razors each year, but that didn't stop millennials Michael Dubin and Mark Levine from starting Dollar Shave Club in 2011. Five years later, Dubin and Levine sold their tech startup for $1 billion to Procter & Gamble's largest competitor Unilever. The reason why Laurie Davis, Michael Dubin, and Mark Levine could compete so effectively is that they are accessing consumers using the same internet and mobile networks as the multinational corporations, but with a greatly reduced overhead.

With a shared global technology infrastructure, giant corporation's scale has lost most of its advantages. "We know that power is shifting from brawn to brains, from north to south and west to east, from old corporate behemoths to agile start-ups, from entrenched dictators to people in town squares and cyberspace," author Moisés Naím explains in *The End of Power*.[3] The only advantage that multinationals still have is more hours in the day. Without hundreds of employees working 40 hours a week, you need to make the most of every minute you have. Converting opportunity into wealth becomes a matter of time management.

Time Management Is a Competitive Edge

Most people fail at time management because they don't realize how much time they waste. The typical smartphone user checks his or her phone 2,617 times every day, according to a study by research firm Dscout. That eats up 90 minutes a day wasted with their phones (or 23 full days per year). Next, unplug the television. The average American fritters away another 33 hours a week in front of the TV. According to Nielsen, the average American spends more than 11 hours per day watching or interacting with media. If you are wasting the majority of your waking hours, is it any wonder why you haven't succeeded yet?

While the software at the end of the chapter will empower you to get the most productivity out of every day, tools are only as good as the blueprint you lay out for their use. The secret to maintaining focus and getting the most out of each day is planning. As I've already stated in earlier chapters, your day actually begins the night before. By writing down the things that would have kept you up worrying, you are actually closing all the open tabs in your brain. Unfinished or unresolved issues make you feel stressed and anxious. Make a list of the five things you absolutely must accomplish tomorrow, and then cross out everything else. Be surgical in what you must accomplish and cut out the unessential. Then number them in order of priority. Studies show that people who write down their lists are 90 percent more likely to complete their list than those who do not. If you have a team to manage, require the same list from then. The following are my three best tips for increasing your productivity.

Three Tips for Increasing Productivity in a Digital World

1. *Use the morning scrum.* One of the most efficient practices I have learned from running software development is the morning scrum. Instead of kicking off the day with a leisurely roundtable meeting with coffee and donuts, a scrum has everyone standing in a circle for no more than 15 minutes. No one gives progress reports or status updates. Instead, they announce what they need help on for that day. In 15 minutes, bottlenecks are resolved companywide.

2. *Break up the time.* I've met very few people who can maintain SAT-test-taking levels of concentration for an entire workday. Your brain is attached to a living, breathing organism that gets fatigued. Focus and concentration have biological limits, and results will diminish the more you test those boundaries. Close your office door and work uninterrupted for 50-minute chunks of time and then get up to stretch for 10 minutes. Grab a snack. Stay hydrated, and you can repeat this for 12 hours without any loss of focus.

3. *Do not leave your email tab open.* Same for any messaging apps and most importantly: silence your phone. You can set a time after your top five tasks are completed to quickly respond to people. Handling all of the incoming distractions at once will help you prioritize who is important and who is a time-suck. "Not everything matters equally, and success isn't a game won by whoever does the most," warns Gary Keller, author of *The One Thing*. "Yet that is exactly how most play it on a daily basis."[4]

For complex tasks (writing a proposal, building a budget, or brainstorming), be realistic about how long it really takes to get things done. Block out a reasonable amount of time on your calendar. For meetings outside of the office, don't forget to factor in drive time. Rushing to a meeting because you are late causes your adrenal glands to produce cortisol. Excess cortisol causes stress, anxiety, depression, headaches, and even memory problems.

If you are the kind of person who says yes to every request, learn to say no. "People think focus means saying yes to the thing you've got to focus on," Steve Jobs was fond of saying. "But that's not what it means at all. It means saying no to the hundred other good ideas that there are."[5]

The biggest stumbling block for time management is not delegating. The longer that you've been a one-person-band, the harder it gets to let go. I explained to Vin why you have to get used to hiring C students in growing a company. Founders are the top of the class when it comes to their own businesses. They are highly motivated to do any task perfectly, or else the new enterprise fails. Continuing the school metaphor, founders can get a perfect 100 percent on a test, while a C student only scores a 70. But if you hire two C students, their cumulative output is 140; and three students equals 210. If you accept this math, you will recognize that hiring one employee won't double your output or efficiency. No one has built a billion-dollar company without learning to delegate.

Whenever you delegate, the burden of communication is on you. Be very specific when defining the project and give feedback whenever possible along the way. Let your people show their creativity in getting things done their way. Try whenever possible to match the task to the motivation and talents of the person. Always show appreciation and provide incentives for going above and beyond.

The tasks I would recommend never delegating are those things you really enjoy. If you are a creative director who founded her own advertising agency, you didn't get into the business to manage personnel and budgets. You enjoy being creative. Keeping your job fun will keep you motivated and make working for you more enjoyable. This explains why celebrity chefs Michael Voltaggio, Susan Feniger, and Mary Sue Milliken can still be found cooking in their restaurants.

Once you remove the clutter from your day, you'll find your purpose for starting the business reemerge front and center. The happiness that comes from fulfilling your purpose will make you a more inspiring leader to work for and will increase everyone's productivity.

With your day organized, the next step of running a tech-centric company is using digital tools to replace much of your back-office work. Nearly all of the functions performed by scores of employees at major corporations are now available for free, as open source software or apps that can be leveraged when needed and abandoned when obsolete. Big corporations can't be as nimble to respond to new opportunities because they are mired in annual planning cycles and entrenched hierarchical structures. "To put it another way, in the old economy managers played chess. You succeeded by seeing a move or two further than your opponent," DigitalTonto's Greg Satell explains. "However, the new game of strategy is more like an online role-playing game. You go on missions, earn new skills and artifacts, but you are continually looking for new quests."[6]

Vin's Top 22 Growth-Hacking Tools

Vin built the World's Greatest Agency by taking advantage of this new approach to business, and so can you. Growth-hacking tools can help you scale your reach, reduce your customer acquisition costs, provide instant market feedback, and help you build a virtual workforce of freelancers and specialists. Hacking together a digital business with little or no capital is Vin Clancy's specialty. Vin keeps tabs on hundreds of online resources for underfunded entrepreneurs. With new products emerging all the time, here are Vin's top 22 tools for getting started:

1. *Slack*. Now that you have assembled your team, you need to be able to manage them. In the beginning, renting suitable office space may be prohibitively expensive and the best people may not live in the same geography as you. Slack is a virtual office hub that brings all your communication channels, tools, and files together so you can collaborate online. If you are managing multiple teams and projects, Slack can be divvied up to help everyone save both time and money.

2. *WordPress*. A decade ago, creating a quality business website was a time-consuming, complicated, and costly task. Web designers could charge tens of thousands of dollars for the most basic site capable of customer personalization, e-commerce, and content publishing. Worst of all, you would need to keep an engineer webmaster on retainer to deal with ever-changing technical issues caused by new browsers, operating systems, hardware, and viruses.

WordPress is a simple-to-use templated tool that allows anyone to build and manage their site. Today, WordPress powers 31 percent of the internet. For as little as $4 per month, WordPress takes care of all the technical backend complexities and even provides live chat customer support. (WordPress has powered my own site, jaysamit.com, from the start, and I couldn't be happier.)

3. *Pexels.* Now that you are building your website and marketing materials, you'll need professional quality images to bring your message to life. Pexels provides designers, writers, artists, programmers, and entrepreneurs access to hundreds of thousands of beautiful photographs that they can use for free. Pexels users can modify the photos any way they wish and use them in any medium, royalty free.

4. *Canva.* Stock photography will only take you so far. If you don't have the design chops to transform your photos into eye-catching social media posts, or are too lazy to learn Photoshop, Canva's drag and drop tools will create professional layouts with consistently stunning graphics. With its huge stock image library, photo filters, icons, shapes, and free fonts, Canva has helped over 10 million users create over 100 million designs. "A monkey with arthritis in his thumbs," claims Vin, "could make a beautiful event invite using Canva."

5. *Portent's Content Idea Generator.* Having pictures on your site and in your emails is not enough. You are going to have to create some clickbait marketing copy. Writing catchy article headlines or email subject lines is both an art and science. Using the Portent Agency's SEO algorithms, the Content Idea Generator quickly spits out highly clickable Buzzfeed-worthy ideas. I typed the heading "tips for first-time entrepreneurs" into https://www.portent.com/tools/title-maker and it spat out "19 Reasons First Time Entrepreneurs and James Franco Are the Weakest Links." Admit it, you'd definitely click on that headline.

6. *Reddit.* Even the best content is only effective if you can target the right audience in a timely fashion. Not sure who your target market is, or what topics your audience is interested in right now? Reddit is your solution. Reddit is a web content and social news aggregation site whose 234 million unique monthly visitors vote content up and down. With such a broad reach and unequaled user engagement,

Reddit is a treasure trove of up-to-the-minute information you can use to keep the content for your social media channels relevant.

7. *Rebump.* No matter how powerful your subject line might be, some days people are just too busy to open your email. So Rebump is a free automated tool that sends friendly reminder follow-up messages to your recipients that appear as if you resent the email yourself. Rebump users claim an average 30 percent response rate to their emails. If you are going to set Rebump to keep sending the same message 10 times, however, Vin strongly suggests using humor so as not to alienate your prospect.

8. *Ninja Outreach.* You'll need more than just great social media marketing to conquer the world – you'll need an army. Ninja Outreach instantly gives you hassle-free access to over 25 million bloggers and social media influencers. This one simple app saves leads, sets up influencer marketing and outreach campaigns for link building, and handles guest posting, content promotion, and digital PR. On the back end, Ninja Outreach tracks all your campaigns and conversations without the need to create cumbersome spreadsheets or hire an SEO team. Ninja Outreach even has a feature that allows you to find anyone's email address just by giving a search for the specific domain.

9. *Stripe.* Congratulations! Your marketing and army of influencers have thousands of new customers clambering to spend money with you. Stripe is an extremely easy-to-use payment processor that allows individuals and businesses to receive payments online. Taking very little time to set up, Stripe requires no minimum monthly fee and only charges a tiny per-transaction fee for handling all of the technical, fraud prevention, and banking infrastructure requirements needed to handle e-commerce. With over a million businesses utilizing Stripe, it's no wonder that the San Francisco startup is now worth more than $9 billion.

10. Indeed.com. You are not going to conquer the world or build a million-dollar business all on your own. With over 200 million unique monthly visitors, Indeed.com is the number-one job site in the world. In addition to having over 100 million resumes, it is a good resource for market-setting salaries. Best of all, you can post your job listings for free.

11. *Phantom Buster* is a "Swiss army knife" collection of different marketing tools you can use to grow your business. It includes these *phantoms*, as well as many others:
    o *Professional Email Finder* locates email addresses for anyone at any company.
    o *LinkedIn Network Booster* will automatically send invitations and a personalized message to a list of LinkedIn users.
    o *LinkedIn Message Sender* will automatically send personalized messages to your LinkedIn connections.
    o *Craigslist Global Search* enables a worldwide single search of every Craigslist site.
    o *Craigslist Page Scraper* enables you to extract every information out of a Craigslist page and the email address of the person posting.
12. *Dux Soup*. Similar to the LinkedIn part of the above, Dux Soup enables you to create smart LinkedIn automations such as direct message campaigns that drip messages every few days into potential leads' inboxes.
13. *Crystal Knows* is a tool that helps you understand other peoples' personalities better. Based on their social profile, Crystal gives you a personality profile and tips on how to best interact with this person. For instance, are they more driven by emotions or numbers? Do they prefer a formal or informal tone in their emails? Amazing information and largely free to use.
14. *HotJar* is an invisible piece of software that analyzes the way people use your website, enabling you to optimize it better to convert your traffic or improve the way people interact with your website. HotJar creates a "heat map" of where people scroll to, what they click on, and what they ignore. Great insights.
15. *PushCrew* allows you to send notifications without people having to download your app. Installing PushCrew on your website enables you to send notifications to site visitors about new offers or new blog posts or to keep people informed about their order even if they're not in their browser. This helps to improve click-through rates better than email, and it has high visibility. Great for one-click subscription (i.e., no need to send them an email).

16. *FOMO* is designed to create scarcity in ecommerce. When consumers see "Only 3 rooms left in this hotel," "85 others are looking at this hotel right now," and "Someone from London has just booked this room," it increases the chances that they will book. This marketing technique is known as the "fear of missing out," and that is exactly what this software does for you: it sends pop-up notifications and FOMO-statements on your website as someone is browsing.

17. *Optimizely* is a tool for running what's known as a "split test" or an A/B-testing tool. Visitors to your website randomly see one of two different variants of the site, and this tool measures which one converts better. There are various alternatives to Optimizely, such as Google Optimize, Visual Website Optimizer, and Convert.

18. *Leadfeeder* shows you the companies visiting your website, how they found you, and what they're interested in. You can then find their emails and create a campaign to win back visitors.

19. *Buffer*. What good is creating great social media content if you are too busy hustling to be bothered posting all day? *Buffer* makes it simple to schedule posts, analyze performance, and manage all your social media accounts in once place from the convenience of your desktop or mobile device. Buffer supports text, images, videos, and even gifs. To maximize follower engagement, they also have an automated tool for replying to your audience.

20. *Sumo* allows you to place banners and other objects on your website to get more email subscribers. Simple to set up (no coding required) and will help you grow your email subscribers on your website.

21. *Viral Loops*. One great marketing strategy is creating a referral program whereby your current customers act as ambassadors and bring in their friends as new users. Paypal and Dropbox did this very successfully to grow their businesses. Viral Loops gives you everything you need to set up your very own referral program. This works particularly well in Facebook messenger.

22. *MixMax* is a Gmail extension that shows you if people you emailed have opened the email, how many times, and whether they have viewed the attachment/clicked the link. This comprehensive tool even tracks whether your email was forwarded. These are great insights for making your emails look better, scheduling them to send them later, and for using templates.

From the start, Vin and I developed a very direct, check all egos at the door, method of communicating. Both of us were too busy to spend time figuring out how to sugarcoat criticism or mask frustrations. For mentoring to be truly effective, both sides have to be honest and transparent. The learning also needs to be mutually beneficial. I enjoyed learning about new tools and hacks from Vin. He, in turn, appreciated being shown ways to be more efficient with his time.

With so many digital channels vying for consumer's attention, Vin's major challenge at the start of this experiment was time management. If you've never had more opportunity than you can handle, you probably haven't developed time-optimization behaviors. My first maxim, "Daylight is for selling," strikes a chord with Vin, who, while staying positive, teeters on burnout. People who try to keep up with the pace of inbound emails and calls end up squandering their days playing a frustrating version of whack-a-mole. "Either you run your day or your day runs you," entrepreneur and motivational speaker Jim Rohn cautions.[7]

Notes

1. Frank Brienzi, "Allegro Development Continues to Revolutionize Commodity Management," *World Finance* (September 26, 2018), www.worldfinance.com/markets/allegro-development-continues-to-revolutionise-commodity-management.

2. Lori Lewis, "2020 This Is What Happens in an Internet Minute," Visual.ly. Accessed August 31, 2020. visual.ly/community/Infographics/other/what-happens-internet-minute-2020.

3. Moisés Naím, *The End of Power: From Boardrooms to Battlefields and Churches to States, Why Being in Charge Isn't What It Used to Be* (New York: Basic Books, 2014), 36.

4. Gary Keller and Jay Papasan, *The One Thing* (New York: Bard Press, 2013), 67.

5. Carmine Gallo, "Steve Jobs: Get Rid of the Crappy Stuff," *Forbes* (May 16, 2011), https://www.forbes.com/sites/carminegallo/2011/05/16/steve-jobs-get-rid-of-the-crappy-stuff/?sh=699b8c0f7145.

6. Greg Satell, "Why Bigger Is No Longer Better," *Forbes* (September 7, 2013), www.forbes.com/sites/gregsatell/2013/09/07/why-bigger-is-no-longer-better/?sh=75cc54b678a0.

7. Lisa Thal, *Three Word Meetings* (Austin, Texas: River Grove Books, 2016), 77.

9

Filling the Void

If you look long enough into the void, the void begins to look back through you.
—Friedrich Nietzsche

THE LAUNCH OF A new iPhone is always a spectacle. But the launch of the iPhone X was one of the biggest of all time. Thousands of Apple super fans were camping out in the streets to be one of the first to own this tenth anniversary phone. As you are nearing the front of the line, eager with anticipation, a man comes out of the flagship Apple Store. He puts his $1,000 prized-possession into an iPhone case and asks you to smash it on the ground with all of your strength. Thinking him mad, you try to refuse. With a crowd of fanboys and television press staring at you, you finally relent. You grab the shiny new phone that you have been craving to hold in your hand all night and hurl it onto the concrete sidewalk. Nothing happens. Not even a scratch. As amazing as the Mous Limitless case is, what is even more impressive is how the team behind it became millionaires before their very first phone case had even shipped.

Every successful new product or technology creates new adjacent markets. Before Henry Ford mass-produced the Model T, there were no car washes or gas stations. Before George Beauchamp invented the electric guitar, there were no amplifiers, mixing consoles, tremolos, or heavy metal rock and roll. Before Mark Zuckerberg launched

141

Facebook, there were no social media experts or influencers. When Apple introduced the iPhone in 2007, it also created a void for a $68 billion a year mobile phone accessory market. Even after 10 years of iPhones and Androids, there were still voids needing to be filled. People were tired of dropping and cracking their expensive smartphones. No one had yet created a small, attractive iPhone case that would really protect a dropped phone from serious harm. Phone screens shatter if only protected by a slim case, and the bulky protective military-style cases were impractically huge to lug around. Seeing a void in the market, five nearly bankrupt millennials from Ipswich, England, made a slick YouTube video showing how their new Limitless case could be dropped from a 45-foot crane and absorb the shock. Their Indiegogo crowdfunding campaign raised an astounding $2,469,907 from over 50,000 new customers. Another void was profitably filled.

Truth #9 – You Must Fill a Void

"The characteristic of great innovators and great companies is they see a space that others do not," says former Google Executive Chairman Eric Schmidt. "They don't just listen to what people tell them; they actually invent something new, something that you didn't know you needed, but the moment you see it, you say, 'I must have it.' "[1]

Too many entrepreneurs struggle and fail because they try to create an entirely new industry. Developing disruptive world-changing products such as the iPhone can take years to achieve and is really, really hard to do. Making money by filling a void that disruptive world-changing products create is, by contrast, much easier. If you want to become Future Proof, the truth that must become your guiding mantra is: *fill the void.*

Seeing that millions of people post pictures of their dogs on Instagram, the team at Paw Champs recognized a void in the $66 billion pet industry market. Getting your pet to look at your phone was a challenge. So, they created Flexy Paw; a simple plastic phone attachment that holds a dog treat on the edge of your phone to help you grab your pets' full attention for the "PAWfect" picture. The Instagram pet phone accessory void was filled.

In this era of endless innovation, the world's largest corporations are constantly spending billions of dollars creating new categories of "must have" products. Apple, Samsung, and other manufacturers can't survive financially off of legacy products. (Have you purchased a Sony Walkman lately?) Each January, more than 175,000 attendees pack the Las Vegas Convention Center in search of the next big thing at the Consumer Electronics Show. Every year, another new category emerges with the promise to change the world and sell billions of dollars of product. Think of all the new product categories that didn't exist just a few years ago: 3D printers, smart speakers, video doorbells, Internet of Things (IoT) appliances, Wi-Fi mesh networks, drones, virtual reality, and augmented reality glasses. Each of these new product introductions creates two voids for the savvy entrepreneur.

Mortar and Use Case Voids

The first void that needs filling is what I refer to as *mortar* products. If the big multinational corporations are making the bricks, you can make millions supplying the mortar that holds their market together. Because of the substantial investment these titans of industry are making in their new products, they need to focus on the large, primary uses of their devices where they can grab the biggest bite of consumer spending. Multinational corporations act like carnivorous sharks in the water chasing the largest fish they can eat. You, being much smaller, need to think and act like the clever remora. The remora is a small fish whose suction-cup dorsal fin allows it to latch onto the underside of sharks and feed off of the scraps dropped by the larger predators as they devour their prey. It is a symbiotic relationship that serves the needs of both the sharks and the remora. Apple was too busy selling $738 billion worth of iPhones to focus on the iPhone case market. Similarly, automakers let others develop the $300 billion US aftermarket for vehicle customization. Best of all, if you grow your niche big enough, the market creator may even decide to buy your startup for a substantial premium, giving you two bites at the apple.

When surfer Nick Woodman pioneered the action video camera market with his revolutionary GoPro, the company knew that it would soon face stiff competition from other video camera manufacturers.

Facing that real threat, the fast-growing company had to focus all of its resources on new iterations of its signature camera. Mounting cameras on surfboards and motorcycle helmets created a new void for apps that could quickly and easily edit these videos into compelling social media content. The Replay and Splice apps quickly filled the void and became the must-have software for GoPro users. Needing to stay ahead of other camera makers, GoPro decided to vertically integrate the video editing apps into their business. In 2016, GoPro acquired Stupeflix and Vemory, the startups who created the two apps, for $105 million. Historically, the most likely acquirer of *mortar* companies are the brick makers themselves. By acquiring a chunk of the new ecosystem, companies make it harder for new market entrants to displace them.

In 2001, Apple created the market for digital music with its revolutionary iPod and iTunes ecosystem. The software and hardware worked so seamlessly together that Apple assumed they controlled the entire market. As vertically integrated as those two products were, Apple still left a huge void: headphones. The more people used their iPods, the more they wanted to improve the quality of the cheap earbuds that Apple provided. Beats Electronics was so effective at filling this void with their Beats by Dre headphones that in 2013 Apple made its largest acquisition ever when it acquired the company for $3 billion. Enormous new categories create enormous voids to fill.

The second void created by new products is demonstration use cases. Large company marketers need to be able to immediately explain their products by showing them in use. When Apple created the iPad, the company needed a simple way to explain the new concept of swiping the screen to consumers. As hard as it is to believe, swiping left and right didn't exist prior to March 2012. Scouring the world for a game developer willing to make a swipe-centric game, Apple found the nearly bankrupt Rovio Entertainment in Finland. Apple marketers included clips of Jaakko Iisalo's new game in nearly every television commercial it ran for the iPad launch. With over $100 million worth of free marketing support, Rovio's Angry Birds quickly became one of the most successful mobile games in history. Not only have there been more than 3 billion downloads of the game (across all platforms), but Angry Birds spawned a multibillion-dollar licensing empire that includes feature films, animated television series, books, comics, toys, clothing, music, and even Angry Bird carbonated soft drinks.

Videogame platforms are a great example of how manufacturers are willing to spend millions of dollars seeding their nascent market. Who would buy a PlayStation or Xbox if there weren't videogames to play on them? Every new product category requires a symbiotic ecosystem to survive. Filling the void fills the vacuum created by their introduction. Once a gaming platform catches on, every developer flocks to where the players are and pays those same manufacturers a royalty per game unit sold, for the privilege of running on their hardware. But in order to prime the pump, whenever a new platform is being introduced, manufacturers will actually pay companies to develop new software titles that highlight their hardware's latest competitive features. In the 1990s, when I was designing CD-ROM videogames for the PC, Atari approached me about developing a game for their new Atari Jaguar CD platform. No video gaming system had ever incorporated compact disc technology, and Atari was hoping to launch a new ecosystem to capture the market. The Jaguar CD was a complete financial flop for Atari and forced the company to permanently exit the gaming console market. But since Atari had committed in advance to purchasing tens of thousands of units of my Vid Grid game, it was one of the most profitable games of my career (even though only a handful of gamers ever got the opportunity to play it).

With the virtual reality and augmented reality markets estimated to be selling over $200 billion worth of hardware by the year 2022, major technology companies are funding millions of dollars of software demo titles. The stakes for companies such as Apple, Google, and Facebook have never been higher. If consumers start spending the kind of time in spatial reality that they spend on mobile today, the advertising and e-commerce opportunities could exceed a trillion dollars. (This void is such a huge opportunity, most of Chapter 10 is dedicated to exploring its potential.)

Cross-Pollination

Another good place to look for voids is anywhere that has cross-pollination taking place. In nature, cross-pollination is when a bee or the wind transfer pollen from the anthers of one flower to the stigma of another flower. While the flowers are each just sitting there, the bee gets all the honey. Be the bee. When John von Neumann cross-pollinated the fields of mathematics with human strategy, game theory was born. Later, when he mixed physics and engineering, von Neumann hatched both the atomic bomb–making Manhattan Project and the field of computer science. American architect Buckminster Fuller cross-pollinated engineering with biology to create solutions for transportation, architecture, and urban design. The entire field of biotech grew out of the supposition that it doesn't matter if it operates a living thing or a computer, "code is code." With that as a starting point, the combination of biology and digital computer science has created bioinformatics, computational genomics, synthetic biology, etc. "The technology we use to manipulate biological systems is now experiencing the same rapid improvement that has produced today's computers, cars, and airplanes," explains Biodesic founder Rob Carlson.[2]

If you look around for the new areas of cross-pollination, you are bound to find opportunities for the bee. With Tesla, Elon Musk was cross-pollinating an automobile with an iPhone to create an app on wheels. Both industries focused on mobility, so why not combine them. With so much cross-pollination taking place today, it can be difficult to differentiate between the next void to fill and hype that isn't going anywhere. To help sort out future trends and opportunities, the global research firm Gartner annually publishes the Gartner Hype Cycle curve. For two decades, by tracking how much hype there is in the press about any new technology, Gartner has been able to map out with reasonable accuracy which innovations are catching on and which are flaming out. The curve postulates that every innovation goes through five phases. First, the *Technology Trigger* is some splashy new breakthrough in a lab or a university. The trigger is far too unproven to be commercialized by companies. There is so much excitement for the Trigger's potential that a crescendo builds in the media, creating a *Peak of Inflated Expectations*. When nothing real materializes in people's lives, the new technology languishes in the *Trough of Disillusionment*. Many startups fail at this stage of the curve, as early investors in the sector are nursing their wounds waiting for sales to develop. As real products slowly come to market, the tech rises up the *Slope of Enlightenment* until finally, they become mainstream and broadly accepted on the *Plateau of Productivity*.

I've watched as everything from Internet of Things and cryptocurrencies, to quantum computing and augmented reality, move along this curve. A decade ago, artificial intelligence (AI) speech recognition was a far-fetched dream. Today, AI bots account for 85 percent of all consumer interactions. Unfortunately for science-fiction fans, flying cars are still stuck in the Technology Trigger stage, but light cargo drone delivery systems are just entering the Plateau of Productivity as Alibaba, Amazon, and even Domino's Pizza are rolling out drone delivery.

By applying an eye toward cross-pollination of the Gartner curve's new trends, and their related voids, new opportunities emerge. As of the writing of this book, I am most excited by the combination of 5G, cloud computing, wearables, AI, and spatial reality to create an always-on, always-connected, augmented reality world.

30-Day Challenge Revisited

How do you find a niche to exploit in this new 5G-enabled world? Go back to your *3 Problems a Day 30-Day Challenge* chart from Chapter 2. Look at the ideas and opportunities you identified as problems and see if a new technological void could be the answer. Could augmented reality or virtual reality be the solution you are looking for? What about a 3D-printed solution? What problems could you solve with a drone? Maybe Luke Skywalker was wrong and these are the droids you are looking for.

Void-filling entrepreneurs have started drone businesses to measure farmers' crops, predict commodities markets by flying over Florida orange groves, sell real estate, aid in search-and-rescue operations, and even provide shopping malls with security. None of these startup companies invented drones; they just applied the flying technology to underserved niche markets. They filled voids that existing solutions couldn't feasibly or cost-effectively service.

As the aforementioned drone examples illustrate, you can make millions filling the void with service businesses. Not every solution has to be a physical product. Prior to drones, companies needed to do aerial infrastructure inspections, ranging from oil pipelines to powerlines. These companies needed to hire pilots and charter costly airplanes or helicopters. Rooftop or bridge inspections, for example, could be dangerous work with inspectors dangling from cables in all types of hazardous weather conditions. The global market for intelligent inspections for the power, rail, and energy industries exceeds $27 billion annually (not including the $20 billion spent analyzing the collected data sets). Drones not only filled the existing void by being 75 percent cheaper than airplanes, they expanded the entire market by being more affordable to potential users that had previously considered airplanes prohibitively expensive.

New Technology Solves Old Problems

For each idea on your *3 Problems a Day 30-Day Challenge* chart, ask yourself this basic question: Why hasn't someone done this before? If the answer is that the technology wasn't available or affordable to match the problem it was solving, then that is the void to focus on. The Fitbit wasn't invented in the 1990s because the weight of all the components back then would have been over 100 pounds! Try getting in your daily 10,000 steps carrying the equivalent of five cases of soda. As core technologies evolve, they get smaller, cheaper, and faster. This evolution creates new use cases. Light Detection and Ranging (LiDAR) is a very expensive laser measuring system that was used by weather services to accurately map topology of land masses from space. In 2017, Waymo engineers were able to reduce the cost of a LiDAR system from $75,000 to $7,500, making it practical for a wide range of new business uses. Following Moore's law, within this decade, LiDAR sensors could be the size and cost of a computer chip. Voids are not just limited to the real world.

Voids exist in the digital world as well. The creation of LinkedIn fundamentally changed the global workplace. Having a great resume was no longer the tool by which corporate recruiters would discover you; everyone now needed a LinkedIn profile to get hired. With job opportunities and entire careers hanging in the balance, the professional LinkedIn profile creator was born. "Helping them land a job and, in turn, more money," says profile copywriter Sean Meyer, means "then they're going to pay you a good chunk of change for it."[3]

If you are using an app daily, odds are, it created a multimillion-dollar void. Social media "experts" run the Twitter, Instagram, and Facebook accounts of celebrities and major brands. SEO experts handle Google AdSense for small business owners. There are even dating site experts who, for a price, will increase your chances of finding everlasting love by optimizing your profile. With people now spending more time on their phones than any other activity, digital freelancing has grown into a multibillion-dollar niche market.

Upwork identified this void and now is the largest online site for digital freelancers. Grossing more than $1 billion a year, the service connects 12 million freelancers to more than 5 million businesses needing help with everything from website development and social media marketing to graphic design and project management. With more than 3 million opportunities posted each year, Upwork filled the void created by downsized corporations looking for freelance talent. "Initially, I let the clients' budgets guide my pricing strategy," advises Danny Margulies, who earns a six-figure income from the site, "but over the next few months I became more aggressive, increasing my hourly rate to $75, $100, and even $125 per hour."[4]

Find Voids Others Are Too Busy to Fill

Sometimes the biggest voids can materialize from just the spark of an idea. When billionaire visionary Elon Musk announces a new technology, the entire business world notices. In 2012, Musk spoke for the first time about a proposed very-high-speed vacuum-tube train in which passengers sitting in pressurized capsules would glide on air bearings. According to Musk, travelers could go from Washington, DC, to New York City in 29 minutes (Amtrak's high-speed Acela train presently takes 2 hours and 45 minutes) or from Los Angeles to San Francisco in 35 minutes (half the time of flying on commercial jets). This futuristic form of mass transportation, which Musk dubbed Hyperloop, captured the imagination of scientists, journalists, engineers, investors, travelers, and government officials around the globe. Thousands of articles were published and millions viewed his concept video on YouTube. When

Musk announced that he wasn't planning on launching a commercial Hyperloop and would allow the technology to be open sourced, a massive void was created in the market.

Within weeks of Musk's pronouncement, teams of entrepreneurs across the globe started raising money to build Hyperloop systems. Hyperloop One raised over $160 million and began working with governments on feasibility studies in Finland, Sweden, Russia, Dubai, and the Netherlands. Bibop Gresta and Dirk Ahlborn's Hyperloop Transportation Technologies (HTT) quickly ran a crowdfunding campaign on Jumpstarter for funding. HTT crowdsourced its engineering and began discussions with governments in France, Austria, Slovakia, Hungary, India, and China. Startup Transpod raised $15 million to study routes in Canada, while Startup Zeleros focused on Spain. Dutch startup Hardt Global Mobility focused on Rotterdam's busy freight port. As if Hyperloop technology wasn't buzzworthy enough, rloop is a new company striving to bring Hyperloop technology to the Blockchain. (Even though no one has ever proven the feasibility or safety of putting humans in a vacuum tube traveling at speeds of 760 mph (1,200 km/h), every vacuum (void) gets filled. At the time of this writing, eight years and hundreds of millions of dollars later, no human has yet to travel any distance in a Hyperloop. Regardless, the media *hype* was enough to launch an entire new transportation industry.)

The rloop Hyperloop coin was just one of over a thousand cryptocurrencies launching in 2018. The void that Vin's World's Best Agency was filling, the sudden massive demand for marketing initial coin offerings (ICOs), was created when Bitcoin's value skyrocketed tenfold in a matter of months. It seemed for a moment, that everyone wanted to become a crypto-millionaire. In February of 2018, *Forbes* published its first list of cryptocurrency's richest, with the headline: Meet the Secretive Freaks, Geeks and Visionaries Minting Billions from Bitcoin Mania. "In the world of cryptocurrency," *Forbes* proclaimed, "billion-dollar fortunes can be made overnight, speed is everything."[5]

Vin's Void Vanishes

A perceived speed to market was the advantage the World's Best Agency was providing its clients. Vin had the only agency focused exclusively on this new industry. For the thousands of entrepreneurs eager to launch their own alternative coins, the success of Vin's first crypto-client raising $68 million in a couple of days was all the track record they needed to hire him. With so many alt coins competing to get noticed by consumers, Vin could raise his rate to whatever the market would bear. In the course of just a few months, ICOs raised over $3.5 billion in cash for alt coins promising to use the Blockchain to revolutionize everything from secure messaging to Blockchain-based smartphones. With thousands of alt coins stampeding their way to an ICO, entrepreneurs knew the gravy train of quick cash couldn't last forever. Speed to market was the difference between having your new coin being worth billions of dollars or nothing at all!

With such astronomically high stakes, Vin's expertise and services were in high demand. The same skills and free tools that used to earn him just a few hundred dollars a month now had clients paying Vin $5,000, $10,000, and even $50,000 per month. Vin could see his entire future mapped out ahead of him. He would spend the rest of his life being the ICO expert and make millions upon millions of dollars. Just like the alt coin creators, Vin too hoped the gravy train would never stop. But it all came to a crashing halt on January 30, 2018, when Facebook announced a broad advertising ban on Bitcoin, ICOs, and everything associated with cryptocurrency. It seemed too many fraudulent scammers had also jumped into the crypto market, and government regulators across the globe were voicing concerns about the public getting fleeced. By March, Google also announced that it would no longer allow ads about cryptocurrency-related content, including initial coin offerings (ICOs), wallets, and trading advice across any of its advertising platforms.

That's the problem with highly concentrated markets such as digital advertising. The 800-pound gorillas who dominate a market can crush the little guy any time they want. If you ever find that the majority of your business is coming from only one or two sources, beware: you are one customer away from going under. Of the more than $88 billion spent in digital advertising in 2017, over 90 percent was gobbled up by Google and Facebook.

If Vin could no longer reach an audience for his clients, he would be out of business and have to find a new direction for his fledgling agency. While nearly all of Vin's competition had to close up shop, the advertising ban didn't stop Vin. It was just a jarring bump in the road. Vin had already proven to himself that he could build a business from scratch and overcome obstacles. Maintaining a positive mindset, Vin had his plan B at the ready.

From our very first meeting, I had stressed to Vin that he needed multiple streams of revenue. The more sources of revenue you have from different channels, the more one income stream can compensate for a dip in another stream. At the height of the crypto insanity, Vin was too busy with high-value crypto clients to make time for any other business that came his way. Rather than miss out completely on these smaller opportunities, Vin was making referral fees from farming out projects that he was too busy to handle. Vin was also busy preparing to launch his third revenue stream: selling his digital marketing product *Ace the Game* online. When there was downtime at the World's Best Agency, Vin was working feverishly on the materials for his *Ace the Game* growth-hacking eBook. He so believed in the success his sales funnel would generate that he didn't want to delay its launch. Vin was days away from marketing his course when Google and Facebook sucker-punched him in the gut by banning crypto advertising. Vin got lucky.

"Luck is what happens when preparation meets opportunity," Roman philosopher Seneca wrote in the first century. Never were those words truer. Having spent all of his spare time during the past few months researching the latest and greatest free online marketing tools for *Ace the Game*, Vin surmised that he could use these same tools to reach the crypto enthusiast without having to rely on marketing through the now-banned channels of Facebook, Instagram, Google AdSense, or YouTube. It would be a lot more work, but he was prepared. Best of all, Vin's success in using his course materials for the Agency would be a case study that proved the value of *Ace the Game* to perspective growth-hacking customers. A real win—win. Despite facing an advertising ban that neither Vin nor I could have predicted, Vin's two revenue streams were working together to forge a mighty flow of income into the World's Best Agency.

Vin just missed hitting triple-digit revenue in month seven, but given the obstacles he had to overcome, $95,504 was a fantastic accomplishment. I found it interesting that as exhausted as Vin had been at the beginning of the month, after grinding it out for 180 days, the intellectual challenge of outmaneuvering Google and Facebook reinvigorated him. The welfare child from England had slayed mighty multinational goliaths. For the first time all year, he felt invincible. Revenues of $95,504 in the seventh month brought his year to date total to $656,590. So far, Vin's sales for the first seven months had averaged $93,798 per month. From here on out, he only has to earn $68,682 for the remaining five months to achieve his million-dollar goal. The goal of making $1 million in a year that he had scrawled on his whiteboard 212 days ago now felt within reach. His spirits were higher than ever. Pressure, he learned, is what makes diamonds.

Notes

1. Drake Baer, "Eric Schmidt: Do What Computers Aren't Good At," *Fast Company* (July 10, 2013).
2. Robert H. Carlson, *Biology Is Technology* (London: Harvard University Press, 2010), 3.
3. Sean Meyer, "7 Little-Known Niches that Could Make You a Boatload of Money," *Medium* (March 10, 2018).
4. Danny Margulies, "How I Broke into Freelance Copy Writing Online and Started Earning over $100,000 a Year," *Business Insider* (April 14, 2015).
5. Jeff Kauflin, "Forbes' First List of Cryptocurrency's Richest: Meet the Secretive Freaks, Geeks and Visionaries Minting Billions from Bitcoin Mania," *Forbes* (February 7, 2018).

10

The Trillion-Dollar Opportunity

The trend has been mobile was winning. It's now won.
—Eric Schmidt, former executive chairman of Google

AMERICA'S FEET ARE HURTING. According to a survey by the American Podiatric Medical Association, nearly 8 out of 10 people experience foot pain. The source of much of this chronic foot pain is wearing the wrong-size shoes. If your shoes are too big, you develop blisters. If they are too tight, bunions and crossed toes. Corns, calluses, and hammer toes are all foot deformities that develop from wearing ill-fitting shoes. Now foot pain, or more accurately the alleviation of foot pain, has gone mobile. With 60 percent of people wearing the wrong-size shoe, there has to be a better way to measure feet than the metal Brannock device shoe store salespeople have been sliding under customers' feet since 1925. Thanks to mobile phones, there is an app for that. In 2019, Nike introduced an app that quickly scans your feet and collects 13 data points with hyper-accuracy. By combining computer vision, machine learning, and recommendation algorithms, Nike created an app that enhances the customer experience while increasing brand loyalty. Happy feet make happy customers. Feet are mobile.

Returned merchandise quickly eats away at a retailer's profit margins. When IKEA realized that 14 percent of its returns were because consumers purchased furniture too large for their homes, they turned to mobile for a solution. While it wasn't IKEA's fault that many consumers are spatially challenged, it was affecting the bottom line. The IKEA Place app enables customers test out real-world sized virtual furniture in their homes using spatial reality with 98 percent accuracy before making a purchase. Sofas are mobile.

Don't want to wait in line at Disney World for a chili cheese dog? Now there's an app so you can preorder food. Need to change your flight while your Uber has you stuck in traffic? There's an app for that. Want to find a night when five friends can meet for dinner and automatically make the reservation and add it to everyone's calendar? There's an app for that. By leveraging the devices consumers already have on them, businesses from every industry have spent the past decade creating app-based solutions. But the era of the smartphone app is coming to an end.

Mobile Is Going Spatial

Every aspect of business, from sales and marketing to delivery, from back office to supply chain management, is now mobile. The most obvious truth in this entire book is that the world has gone mobile. The economy is mobile. Your life is mobile. You must accept that no matter what you are working on, you are running a mobile business. Our reliance on mobile is only going to increase as smart cities roll out 5G, edge computing, and Internet of Things (IoT) sensors. According to IDC, by 2025 there will be 41.6 billion IoT sensors having us all living in a data-rich new virtualized world known a spatial computing. We will go from constantly searching for information, people, and things to living in an environment that anticipates our needs and responds to our every action. Mobile centricity will expand into a graphical and data overlay of our cities and homes. Spatial reality will be as vital to the success of a two-person startup as it is to the largest multinational conglomerate. If I was building a company today, the biggest opportunity I see for maximizing wealth is spatial reality. All of the truths we have so far explored can now coalesce around grabbing a piece of this trillion-dollar opportunity. The easiest way I know of future proofing you is to grab some of the billion-dollar opportunities this technological revolution is unleashing. A thousand old problems will be solved and a myriad of new voids will be created.

There are over 14 billion mobile phones and tablets in use today, and that number is forecasted to grow to 16.8 billion by 2023. The average US consumer now spends 5.4 hours a day on their smartphone. From a business perspective, the foundation of mobile's importance is data. This year, people will create more data than all the prior years of history combined. (And that fact will be true whether you are reading this in 2021 or 2031!) Because each mobile device automatically identifies each user's location, mobile marketing is the most targeted and cost-efficient tool for any entrepreneur regardless of product or service. By layering location with intent (as determined from the 15 exabytes of personal information within Google's data centers), companies can save a fortune in advertising spend while consumers are swiftly connected to the products and services they need.

Truth #10 – Spatial Reality Is a Trillion-Dollar Opportunity

Within the next three years, your phone will stay in your pocket and your smart glasses or smart contact lenses will provide a heads-up display overlaid onto the real world. Can't read the Chinese menu when traveling in Beijing? Your glasses will automatically translate it into the language of your choice. Can't find your way back to your hotel? A blue line will appear on the sidewalk, creating a path across the city for you to follow. Gone are the days of wandering the aisles of the supermarket searching for a few items from the 40,000 products on the shelves. With augmented reality, a shopper can state something as simple as, "Show me the foods I can eat on a Keto diet," and every other product in the store will literally vanish from sight. No need to remember a wallet or photo ID when going to the store or airport, because your biometrics will be scanned by sensors enabling seamless purchases and ease of travel.

We are heralding in the fourth transformation of computing. The first transformation was the development of the personal computer, which connected people to intelligent machines. Next came the internet, linking people with vast stores of knowledge. The third transformation was mobile computing. Mobile connected people to other people and information and untethered everyone from their desks. As transformational as these three technologies were in changing how we live, they all were still restricted to functioning in a two-dimensional digital plane. Spatial computing is the next step, connecting people to their environment, with real-time data.

The catalyst for this brave new world is a confluence of "exponential" technologies working together. Mobile delivery of data will grow exponentially, with 5G providing searches at 1.4 gigabits per second (23 times the speed of today's fastest 4G networks so that you can download a two-hour movie in just 3.6 seconds). The trillion Internet-of-Things sensors will provide the cloud with a constant stream of data about our environment, supply chain availability, proximity options, social life, and health. Artificial intelligence will interpret specific data sets from the cloud in real-time, sending information to a wide range of augmented wearables that communicate with us through sight, sound, touch, and biofeedback. Smartphone viewing, which will most likely peak at six hours per day in 2022, will be replaced with omnipresent heads up displays. All our waking hours will be data enhanced. The physical and the virtual will seamlessly meld before our very eyes creating an augmented life called spatial reality.

Just as the internet's increasing presence disrupted virtually every business at the beginning of this century, spatial computing will cause seismic realignments in both the public and the private sector. Apple, Facebook, Google, Netflix, and Amazon's business models will all be disrupted. If information is provided when needed, what happens to search? If every location and moment has selling potential, what happens to ecommerce and advertising? What new forms of entertainment, esports, and interactions will smart glasses enable for social networks? How will personal data and privacy be protected – or exploited – by governments and corporations? How many businesses will be rendered obsolete, and how many new ones will be created? Within the answers to these questions lies your fortune.

As I've said since the first pages of this book, insight and perseverance are the only two things you need to achieve success. Spatial reality is your chance to create opportunity and maximize wealth in the quickest time imaginable. If you are serious about Future Proofing you, put everything you've learned thus far into action by following my M.O.V.E. method.

The M.O.V.E. Method

As you are brainstorming your plans for building a business to take advantage of the billions of dollars flowing into spatial reality, follow these four steps to guide you to success: Mindset, Obstacle, Void, and Execution.

1. **Mindset** *is everything.* Keeping a positive growth mindset, start dreaming about how your life can be even better living in an augmented world. Walk around with rose-colored glasses and visualize what data and imagines could appear in a heads-up display. The longer you let yourself "live" in this future world, the more real the opportunities will become.

2. **Obstacles** *are opportunities.* Revisit your *3 Problems a Day 30-Day Challenge* chart again. How will spatial reality solve your problems? What previously impossible task is now solved in the blink of an eye? Remember this is about applying a spatial reality overlay on top of everything we do. You don't have to be an engineer to visualize the solution.

3. **Voids** *will be created.* Just as the internet and smartphones created new solutions, they also created massive voids. What voids will smart glasses, 5G bandwidth, edge computing combine to create? If we are no longer limited by the size of our phone's screen, what could we see? Every empty room could become a new car showroom or a specialty shop. Every tourist destination or city could be customized to the needs of the viewer. The changes are so vast that focusing in on one void will get you thinking down a path with a logical conclusion. What major tech company would pay you millions to have your new app as a use case?

4. **Execution** *is the difference between a good idea and creating generations of wealth.* Find the right mentors, partners, and employees to bring your vision to life. The next two chapters will show you how to raise the capital and build a virtual workforce. No one has built

the first killer app for this new era; why can't it be you? Put your fears aside, apply your superpower, and be unstoppable. If you don't do it, I can guarantee that somebody else will.

The low-hanging fruit for augmented reality is entertainment. Today's video games and live experiences, early forays into spatial realty user interfaces, are introducing us to new ways of interacting within an augmented world. Niantic's Pokémon Go was the first AR commercial hit with more than 150 million players generating over $100 million in monthly revenue at its peak. "These next few years we will see a boom in smartphone AR thanks to developer platforms from the likes of Google, Facebook, and Apple," futurist Tom Emrich foresees. "These experiences will act as 'AR training wheels' for enterprises, developers, and consumers alike – preparing us for the need for a new head worn form factor while buying the time for the head worn technologies to become smarter, smaller, more cost effective and ready for widescale adoption."[1]

Just as the mouse changed computer user interface design, Siri and Alexa are training millions of humans how to talk to computers. Chatbots, meanwhile, are so advanced that soon an estimated 85 percent of all customer interactions will not involve a human. Education, corporate training, and healthcare will all be revolutionized by augmentation. Even industries like construction and manufacturing will undergo changes to their supply chains, automation, and safety departments that can only be provided by overlaying blue prints and underground pipe locations with augmented graphics. Firemen will be able to see through smoke, and even walls, to locate safe building exits. Construction crane operators will no longer have to work atop a 200-foot tall swaying mast, but rather can sit in a remote office and control cranes in cities around the world.

One of the most sweeping changes will be in the virtualization of consumer shopping. With over $1 trillion in annual consumer spending up for grabs, billion-dollar bets are being placed today on each parcel of this new augmented landscape. "This [Retail] is a sector where AR is revolutionizing the way we shop by bridging the gap between digital and physical worlds," Fashnerd.com Editor-in-Chief Muchaneta Kapfunde writes. "A radical store reinvention will offer retailers new ways to increase convenience and personalization, and consumers the opportunity to experience re-envisioned shops."[2]

It's a high-tech billion-dollar land grab with existential stakes for companies like Apple, Facebook, and Google. Over $3 billion in venture funding a year is going into building new enterprises to compete with today's tech giants, which are also spending billions to ensure their own future relevance. Converging technologies are spawning a clash of the titans, with mergers and acquisitions accelerating in both size and volume. As an industry, spatial computing is expected to expand from $11 billion in 2018 to over $60 billion by 2023 – a compound annual growth rate of over 40 percent! What piece of that is going to be yours?

The universe of spatial reality, including haptic gloves, intelligent wristbands, wearable cameras, earbuds, and smart clothing, extends far beyond visual augmentation. We're already living improved augmented lives with 3D bio-printed skin, bone, heart tissue, and corneas. Wearables give users greater control of their health, providing real-time analysis of biometrics. When combined with individualized genomic data, people will live longer, healthier lives. Robotic prosthetics and neural implants will improve and expand human capabilities. Exoskeletons and enhanced vision will change everything from the boardroom to the battlefield. The future, and your career's future, will be augmented!

"I do think that a significant portion of the population of developed countries, and eventually all countries, will have AR experiences every day, almost like eating three meals a day," Apple CEO Time Cook predicts. "It will become that much a part of you."[3]

The opportunities for new businesses, services, and products created by this revolution in computing will be an order of magnitude greater than the impact of the internet or mobile. How am I so sure of what is coming? Two reasons. First, the best way to predict the future is to hang out with those coding it. I have consulted on this field with dozens of industry leading companies including Microsoft, Google, and Facebook. I have also been retained by major corporations to help them prepare for and benefit from these changes. Nike's shoe fitting app and IKEA's furniture placement app are examples of AR going mainstream today, before glasses go mainstream. Spatial Reality is the one thing

I am certain of in this uncertain world. Second, I always follow the money.

In 2017, 40 percent of all venture capital investments were in spatial computing solutions. Why are Silicon Valley investors so confident in filling this void? Because they understand the stakes involved. Assume for the moment that I am correct about our smartphones staying in our pockets. In the near future, if you aren't buying your smart glasses from Apple, they potentially go out of business. If Google can't sell ads on your heads-up display or monetize search, it too goes out of business. If your AR glasses are your interface for social media, Facebook too is threatened if it misses out. With so many tech giants facing threats from spatial reality, it is investing tens of billions of dollars to fight for dominance in this emerging field. With the table stakes so high, who do you think will be willing to pay a massive premium to purchase your spatial computing startup company and prevent their competitors from buying it? Today's tech giants, if they want to stay giants, will be acquiring dozens of smaller players that fill new, emerging voids. That is why VCs are bullish and investing heavily. Best of all, most of these startups will be acquired before earning a penny in profits. Spatial reality is poised to be the greatest transfer of wealth in history and the opportunity of a lifetime.

I am so committed to this fourth revolution in computing that in addition to my column for *Fortune* magazine on this topic, I have authored the forward to two comprehensive books on the subject: Charlie Fink's *Convergence: How the World Will Be Painted with Data* and Gabriel René and Dan Mapes's *The Spatial Web: How Web 3.0 Will Connect Humans, Machines, and AI to Transform the World*.

Think back to the last revolution in computing – namely, the creation of the smart phone and the vast ecosystem of mobile applications it spawned. WhatsApp, Instagram, Snapchat, Twitter, and TikTok are all apps that created billion-dollar fortunes. With all that you know today, what app would you have created back in 2007 when Apple first launched the iPhone? How many millions or billions would you have earned with such foresight? You can't go back in a time machine, but you can make sure that you don't miss the boat this time around.

The opportunities for success in spatial computing are only limited by your imagination. The tech giants and telecommunication companies are building the operating systems, infrastructure, and devices. All you have to do is solve problems with the tools they've created. Rather than memorizing every species of fungus in a forest, smart glasses will tell us whether the mushroom you picked is edible or poisonous. Rather than waiting for the symptoms of a heart attack and then going to the hospital, a smart watch, which monitors your vital signs and compares them to all others in your cohort, can tell your autonomous car to take you to the hospital before you even realize you are having a heart attack. Your doctor will also be simultaneously notified and can provide customized instructions to the emergency room staff who will be sent your medical records in advance of your arrival. Smart cities can prioritize and move traffic out of your path to ensure the quickest travel time while digital micropayment systems will automatically pay other vehicles to get out of your way (or conversely, let you make extra income if you are not in a rush). Every medical procedure you undergo at the hospital will be immutably recorded onto your blockchain-based medical history. The spatial web will provide better patient care outcomes while cutting US healthcare costs in half (85 percent of present healthcare costs are caused by heart disease and diabetes which AI and wearables are better suited for managing patient preventative maintenance). The spatial web holds the key to fewer doctor visits, fewer medical tests and procedures, and a lower demand for prescription medications. Healthcare is just a small example of the power of spatial computing. It's time for you to MOVE into the future and start generating real wealth.

Digital supply chains will interface seamlessly with sensors in warehouses and on retail shelves. Just-in-time manufacturing will enable bespoke products delivered to your door. Today, you can customize your Tesla online. With IoT sensors, you'll be able to track your car's assembly and delivery as if it was an Amazon package. Maintenance crews can follow virtual arrows through buildings to find equipment in need of repair. Every mannequin in the department store will match your body dimensions and showcase the latest fashions accessorized by the clothing items you have previously purchased. Homebuyers can walk through potential homes virtually and see how their existing furniture fits the new home while getting the opportunity to purchase carpets and window treatments from vendors that already have the exact measurements of each room or window. Digital goods can be licensed to specific geographic locations and AI smart contracts will be able to make micropayments for a host of new goods and services. Trillions of dollars' worth of new companies and innovative products will enhance our daily lives. Now you know why I am bursting with excitement. I want to live in this world that you readers will create.

The spatial web holds so much promise for improving our lives that those companies failing to invest and embrace the future will go the way of Kodak, Radio Shack, and Blockbuster. The true potential of an augmented life is revealed when it provides us with the information we need, at exactly the right time and place. With so much information created daily, access to current relevant knowledge, not the arcane rote memorization of it, will be key to a functioning society. Hopefully, spatial computing resolves the growing imbalance between knowledge creation, accessibility, and dissemination. "Simply put, we believe augmented reality is going to change the way we use technology forever. We're already seeing things that will transform the way you work, play, connect and learn," Apple CEO Tim Cook envisions. "AR is going to take a while, because there are some really hard technology challenges there. But it will happen, it will happen in a big way, and we will wonder when it does, how we ever lived without it. Like we wonder how we lived without our phone today."[4]

"When you can't fail, you don't fail," Vin tells me as we celebrate his birthday. When we met to discuss his revenues for month eight, Vin was disappointed that he had just fallen short of hitting his $100,000 goal with *only* $98,644 in sales. I thought to myself, a few month ago he couldn't have imagined making $100,000 a year and now he was dissatisfied with his performance because he was 1.3 percent off his sales target! With two-thirds of the year in the rearview mirror, Vin felt like a first-time marathon runner at mile 17 on his way toward the *Future Proofing You* goal. He was tired, his body ached for a break, but his mind forced him onward toward the finish line. With $755,234 in cumulative

(continued)

(*continued*)

earnings, his mind wanted to congratulate himself on winning the race and dream about his vacation, which was just around the next bend, but could he maintain the pace?

While Vin had built up some steady referral income and revenues for *Ace the Game*, the Agency revenues were still mostly month-to-month. Four more months at $61,191 per month was less pressure than he had faced all year, but no cake walk, either. For Vin, it was still a marathon, but hopefully, one with no more mountains to climb.

Notes

1. Emory Craig, "10 Augmented Reality Quotes on the Coming AR Revolution," Digital Bodies (September 7, 2018), https://www.digitalbodies.net/augmented-reality/10-augmented-reality-quotes-on-the-coming-ar-revolution/.
2. Ibid.
3. Kif Leswing, "Apple CEO Tim Cook on Augmented Reality," *Business Insider* (October 3, 2016), https://www.businessinsider.com/apple-ceo-tim-cook-explains-augmented-reality-2016-10?op=1.
4. Oscar Raymundo, "Tim Cook: Augmented Reality Will be an Essential Part of Your Daily Life, Like, the iPhone," *Macworld* (October 3, 2016), https://www.macworld.com/article/3126607/tim-cook-augmented-reality-will-be-an-essential-part-of-your-daily-life-like-the-iphone.html.

11

Working Hard Doesn't Make You Rich

Capital is that part of wealth which is devoted to obtaining further wealth.
—Alfred Marshall, English Economist

PRIOR TO MOVING TO Texas from New York City, a boy arranged to buy a donkey from a farmer there for $100. The farmer agreed to deliver the donkey when the boy arrived in Laredo the following Monday. Come Monday morning, the farmer came to the boy's house and said, "Sorry, but I've got some bad news. The donkey died."

"Well then, just give me my money back," the city boy demanded.

"Can't do that as I already gone and spent it," the embarrassed farmer replied.

"Well, then just give me the dead donkey."

"Maybe you didn't hear me. The donkey's dead," repeated the farmer. "What in the world are you going to do with a dead donkey?"

"I'm going to raffle him off."

"You can't raffle off a dead donkey!" yelled the farmer.

"Sure, I can," the boy said. "I just won't tell anyone he's dead."

The farmer shrugged his shoulders, unloaded the dead animal, and drove off.

A month later the farmer bumped into the boy in town and inquired about the dead donkey.

"I raffled him off," the boy boasted. "I sold 500 tickets at $2 apiece and made a profit of $898."

"Didn't anyone complain?"

"Just the guy who won," the boy said with a smile. "So I gave him his $2 back."

The 27-year-old film school graduate's directorial debut had been a flop at the box office in 1971. In case his next film about a high school coming-of-age story flopped, he tried to sell his third movie before the second film hit the theaters. For his third movie, the director wanted to make a big-budget science fiction serialized cliffhanger. Sci-Fi movies, such as *Plan 9 from Outer Space*, were a money-losing genre, and every Hollywood studio but one passed on the young unproven filmmaker's project. So, when 20th Century Fox offered him only $50,000 to direct (with an additional $50,000 for writing and $50,000 for producing), he said yes on the condition that he owned the sequel rights. The studio never believed there would ever be a sequel and agreed to give George Lucas the sequel rights. When *Star Wars* became the highest-grossing film of all time in 1977 (and won six Oscars), Fox executives were desperate to make the sequel. Lucas agreed to give them the picture if he could also have merchandising rights to the entire franchise. Once again, the studio never believed that the movies would sell many toys and agreed to give Lucas the rights royalty-free. The *Star Wars* movies would go on to sell over $32 billion worth of action figures, games, clothing, bed sheets, costumes, lightsabers, Ewok Village playsets, and other licensed products making Lucas a multibillionaire. George Lucas made one of the most beloved movies of all time, but it was how he (and his lawyer Tom Pollack) structured the deal that made him wealthy, or as Obi-Wan Kenobi would say, "In my experience there is no such thing as luck."

Brandon Steiner was a 28-year-old New York sports fan who created a multimillion-dollar business from dirt. Literally buckets of it. In 1987, with just $8,000, a Mac computer, and an intern, Brandon started a business selling autographed baseballs. He was able to get the Yankees and the top athletes of every sport to work exclusively with him because of how he structured the deal. The athletes would get to keep 100 percent of all ball sales. How could any ballplayer argue for a better deal than that? Was Brandon an idiot? No, a business genius. Brandon makes his money selling a $40 plastic cube for collectors to display their signed ball that only costs him 19 cents to make. With sales of his autographed balls a homerun, Brandon then gathered buckets of dirt from baseball stadium infields and sold plastic ball-cubes with "real game dirt" beneath the autographed ball for an additional $100. In the years since, Steiner Sports has sold more than 1 million pieces of autographed sports memorabilia and today grosses more than $40 million per year.

Texas sisters Barbara Russell Pitts and Mary Russell Sarao were busy working moms trying to balance their jobs with raising children. One night, when Mary's ninth-grade daughter ran out of poster board after botching earlier attempts at making her school project, Mary made a 10 p.m. run to the store for more poster board. To make sure her daughter would get it right this time, Mary took a yardstick and drew light lines on it so that the words and pictures her child drew would be straight. Mary called her sister the next day with an idea for a new product, and Ghostline poster board was born. As an office administrator and a school teacher, the sisters didn't feel that they had the know-how or capital to set-up a poster-board company, so they contacted large school supply manufacturers with their idea. One executive told the women that if they filed a patent for Ghostline, his company would pay them a royalty. Months later, with no word from the company, Mary found out that the company had ripped off the sisters and was selling their invention. Their dreams were ruined, as they didn't have the resources to fight the thieving corporation. Undaunted, the sisters negotiated a win–win deal with the thief's competition. Carolina Pad offered to pay for the lawsuit if they could exclusively license the Ghostline patent. To date, the women have drawn over $15 million in royalties from those fine lines Mary drew on her daughter's poster board; not bad for an evening's kitchen-table inspiration.

Truth #11 – Working Hard Doesn't Make You Rich; Working Smart Does

What George Lucas, Brandon Steiner, and the Russell sisters' fortunes have in common is the creativity of their deal structure. Steven

Spielberg became a billionaire from getting a percentage of Universal theme park ticket sales, not from directing movies. McDonald's founder made his money from real estate, not selling hamburgers. Marc Benioff became a billionaire because he saw Salesforce's software as a service and not a product. As you build your business, you will quickly discover that how you structure a business opportunity is even more important than what you are paid. Mastering the creative ways to structure capital transactions has the potential to catapult you into becoming a millionaire or billionaire and *Future Proofing You.*

If you are currently being paid by the hour, you are never going to get rich. You would have to earn more than $500 an hour, full-time for a year to gross just a million dollars (and to put a billion dollars into a time perspective, one million seconds was just 12 days ago, while one billion seconds was 32 years ago). I can't tell you how many of my lawyer friends complain about this reality when it occurs to them too late in their careers to make a change. At the start of their careers, professionals make far more money than typical college graduates, but what most doctors, lawyers, and accountants can earn per hour hits a ceiling fairly quickly. For those stuck in this wage-slave world, their only way to amass wealth is to put their money to work for them (which we will cover later in this chapter).

It makes no difference if you are being hired to create online marketing, write a piece of software, or invent a new product. The truth is that working hard doesn't make you rich; working smart does. A well-structured deal can even make you the richest man in the world!

In 1980, when IBM was developing its first PC, the company needed an operating system to run its machines. As has often been told, Bill Gates acquired the Quick and Dirty Operating System (QDOS) from Seattle Computer Products and, in turn, licensed IBM a version of it known as PC-DOS. But the royalties from IBM are not what launched Microsoft revenues into the stratosphere and made Bill Gates a billionaire. Shrewdly, Gates (with the help of his attorney father) had a clause in their contract with IBM that allowed Microsoft to sell the same operating system to other hardware makers under the MS-DOS brand name. As more and more personal computer manufactures copied IBM's hardware, MS-DOS became the standard and the dominate computing platform worldwide. "Without this seemingly minor clause in this pivotal contract," writes tech historian Marcel Brown, "the history of the PC era could have been quite different than it was."

In order to know how to negotiate smart deal structures, you first must understand the important role capital plays in the success of your business and in the growth of your personal fortune. For anyone trying to become a millionaire, there are three stages of your financial development that will have the biggest impact on your becoming wealthy: deal structure, raising capital, and reinvesting profits. This chapter will try to demystify each of these components of wealth creation.

Deal Structure

Deal structure comes into play with each and every negotiation you enter in business. The terms under which you hire employees, contract with vendors, or sign new clients put you in control of your financial destiny. As I coached Vin from the very start of the World's Best Agency, each new work-for-hire client has the potential to become a long-term recurring revenue stream. Vin's marketing campaigns are key to his clients' financial success. In a typical client-agency relationship, Vin could be hired for a flat $20,000 a month to create and manage an online marketing campaign. If Vin was marketing a new Instagram celebrity's lipstick, for example, millions of units could be sold and his client could then make tens of millions of dollars profit from Vin's expertise. Sounds like a great deal for the client. But in this scenario, the client is also taking all of the risk and therefore is entitled to all of the reward. If Vin spends three months on a campaign that doesn't convert into sales, the client is out $60,000 with nothing to show for it. Vin would have made money, but the client could potentially go broke. This is a risk many smaller brands are unwilling to take. But if Vin believes in a product, and his ability to market it, Vin can offer to share the risk in return for a percentage of the sales he generates. Since Vin is building the online click-through funnel, he has the data to know exactly how many units are selling and what marketing channels are yielding the greatest ROI (return on investment). While Vin might be forgoing a guaranteed $60,000 payday, he could end up making 10 times that amount or more in commissions. With each new client opportunity, the amount of guaranteed revenue Vin is risking is always a finite amount while the potential upside is virtually unlimited. To become *Future Proof*, Vin needed to risk some of his time for more lucrative compensation.

As an entrepreneur starting out, your goal should be trying to generate recurring revenue streams instead of one-time gigs. Take every chance you can to bet on yourself and to have your compensation be tied to your performance. Even today, when companies ask for my assistance, I forgo the huge monthly fees most consultants with my experience command for a piece of equity in the company. I believe that if I can be instrumental in building a multimillion-dollar company, then I should be entitled to a piece of the value I am helping to create. Most clients agree with this approach because this structure also aligns both parties' goals: each only makes money if the venture is a success. In my career, I have earned sweat equity stakes in over 60 companies. Sure, there are times when I walked away from thousands of dollars in consulting fees for companies that didn't make it, but there are startups where I have made millions of dollars by taking a piece of equity that had little or no value before I became involved. My biggest payday using this technique came in 1999 when a startup offered us a 50 percent stake for our help, and 90 days later we launched an initial public offering on NASDAQ valuing their company at $440 million. Your risk is always finite, while your reward has infinite potential.

When Facebook was just starting out, company president Sean Parker tried to make the social network offices look cool. Parker wanted to hire graffiti artist David Choe to paint murals throughout their new headquarters. "My prices had been going higher and higher and I was like, 'Yeah, I mean, if you want me to paint the entire building, it's going to be 60, you know, 60 grand,'" Choe recalled. Wanting to preserve startup capital, Parker offered Choe the $60,000 in stock. When Facebook went public in 2012, Choe's stock options were worth $200 million. Today, the spray-painter's shares are worth nearly a billion dollars, making him perhaps the richest painter in the history of the world!

If you are not founding your own company, you still have the opportunity to have a huge Facebook-like payday downstream.

Whether you are doing a project or working full-time for any small startup, always ask for equity as part of your compensation package. You never know how big a startup can become. Remember, Google was once just two guys working in a Palo Alto school teacher's garage. When Google went public in 2004, more than 1,000 employees became multimillionaires because they had negotiated stock grants and options that became worth more than $5 million per person. Even Google's in-house masseuse, Bonnie Brown, became a millionaire!

Most of the millionaires in the tech industry aren't founders nor investors. They are employees who took lower salaries in exchange for equity. Microsoft is estimated to have created at least 12,000 millionaire employees (and at least three billionaires). If you don't understand stock options or how to structure an equity agreement, it is worth it to spend the money and hire an attorney to help you craft your agreement. Depending on where you live, there can be tax consequences with taking equity, so don't forget to speak with your accountant as well.

When neither a percentage of sales nor equity are available in a deal, you still have several other ways to earn upside on your performance. The first is a performance bonus. Reach an agreement in advance with your client that if your performance meets or exceeds certain metrics, you will earn a bonus. Whenever I negotiate this type of performance bonus, I also include a crazy stretch goal with an equally insane bonus amount. You never know which product is going to hit it out of the park. Would anyone have predicted that the Scrub Daddy from *Shark Tank* would sell more than $50 million worth of sponges?

The second bonus opportunity, which no client should ever turn down, is a continuity bonus. Imagine for a moment that the work you did made the company a huge success. Once they are a known entity, the business can hire someone to do the same job you did for less. You'd be shocked how many corporations aren't loyal to the vendors, suppliers, and employees that made them millions. Your only way to prevent this from happening is to structure a performance renewal clause in your initial contract. For as long as you continue to hit or exceed mutually agreed upon targets, your contract gets renewed for another year. This clause also prevents every would-be competitor from undercutting you and stealing your clients away.

So, before you take your next job, or agree to work on your next project, take a moment and focus on how best to structure the relationship to align goals in a way that gives you the most upside potential. Conversely, when hiring employees and vendors, structure the financial arrangement in a way that best motivates them to exceed goals and gives them a piece of the upside. Remember, it's better to own 50 percent of the Pacific Ocean than all of Lake Tahoe.

Raising Capital

If you are going to go the next step and start your own business, the biggest challenge entrepreneurs face is understanding how to get the money they need to launch and grow their companies.

Raising money is the second place where entrepreneurs must focus on how they structure their terms and work with capital. Too many first-time entrepreneurs blindly sign venture capitalist or angel investor term sheets without fully understanding the long-term implications in those agreements. Day one, you may have given away your company without even knowing it.

The first company you start may be the most profitable idea you will ever have in your life. It would be a tragedy if after you slave away for years to make it a success, everyone but you became rich. While I have had great success raising millions of dollars from venture capital firms and made millions more by partnering with them, many disgruntled founders refer to them as *vulture capitalists*.

When founder Lane Becker raised $10 million for his startup Get Satisfaction from a VC in 2011, he couldn't have been happier. Four years later when his company was acquired, he didn't get a penny, even though the VC and later-stage investors made millions. The complex terms of the VC investment forced Becker to lose control of his company. "I understand venture capital is a game and we lost," Becker told an interviewer after it happened. "Although I admit I thought it was more a game of chess and it's more a *Game of Thrones*."[1]

"Taking VC is like getting the world's worst boss: Shitload of opinions, undue level of influence, never actually shows up for work," tweeted Becker. While I haven't reviewed the specific paperwork that

Becker signed, let me share one example of a potentially predatory clause in venture capital deals. For years, in an effort to increase their profits, venture capital firms included a 3x liquidation preference in their contracts, which means that the VC gets paid three times what they initially invested before founders and employees see a penny. So, for example, if you founded a company with $10 million in venture funding and one month later sold it for $30 million, you would make nothing and the VC would make a quick $20 million profit. Another confusing area in these agreements is how your stock – in the very company you founded – vests. Some investors, in order to ensure that the founder stays around, will require that you relinquish your ownership of your company and have your equity vest over the next four years. So even if you only sold the VCs ten percent of your company, you would be giving back your 90 percent to the board. Again, if your company gets acquired for one hundred million dollars in the first year, you potentially could get nothing. Now single and double trigger vesting clauses can ameliorate this problem to some extent, but this gets into the minutiae of contract law. Suffice to say, sophisticated investors have had legal counsel write their agreements to favor their own interests. You need an equally experienced lawyer to look after your interests.

Having heard dozens of horror stories over the years from naïve founders who felt they got screwed, here are a couple of online resources that can better educate you on the process. For raising small rounds of angel capital, the incubator Y Combinator has posted on their website (ycombinator.com/documents) standard templates that they named SAFE (simple agreement for future equity) documents. The conditions outlined in these forms are intended to be fairly neutral and a good starting point for both parties to negotiate in good faith. SAFE agreements will save you time negotiating standard clauses and save you money having lawyers draft terms that have been used many times before. The second resource is a site dedicated specifically to the needs of founders. Created by the Founder Institute's Adeo Ressi, The Funded (thefunded.com) is a community of over 20,000 CEOs and founders who rate venture capitalists and discuss various financing issues. As a founder, you need to get educated on how the business of venture capital works. Too many founders get so busy working in their business that they forget to work on their business. You won't get wealthy building a successful company if you fail to hold on to it.

In balance, I should say that most venture capital firms provide founders with so much more than just money and are often the unsung heroes in a startup's overall success. Experienced VCs can guide a founder through the various stages of growth, introduce them to strategic partners, and help negotiate their exit with an acquirer. I owe much of what I've learned from VCs that sat on my companies' boards and took the time to explain aspects of the business world that I was unfamiliar with at the time. Scores of founders of some of the biggest tech companies in the world wouldn't be where they are today without the mentoring of VCs like Ron Conway, Bill Gurley, Vinod Khosla, Fred Wilson, Ben Horowitz, and Mark Suster. "One of the great things about young entrepreneurs is that they don't know that something can't be done," Fred Wilson noted. "So they try something that's so audacious and usually end up pulling it off."

You may know your subject area of expertise better than anyone else in the world, but that doesn't mean you have the know-how to handle every challenge that faces your fledgling company. As your company grows, you will have to negotiate facility leases, banking credit lines, international distribution contracts, SEC investigations, and lawsuit settlements. Many VCs are also former startup founders that understand the pressure and challenges you will face as a boss and employer. VCs, whose sole job is to fund risky ventures that average a 90 percent failure rate, may be the only way for you to raise large amounts of money quickly. If you understand the relationship you are entering into, a VC can be a trusted advisor and confidant.

I teach how to build a high-tech startup and work with several startup accelerators to assist new CEOs. I had a twenty-something student, who had never run a company, with a brilliant idea for a startup. I accompanied her up to Sand Hill Road in Silicon Valley where all the major venture capital firms have their offices and helped her pitch her idea. One week later she closed a $9 million Series A round. To date, VCs have funded her company with over $40 million and she still remains in control of her company. One cautionary thought from venture capitalist Marc Andreessen is to remember that, "Raising venture capital is the easiest thing a startup founder is ever going to do."

Obviously, the longer you can go building your company without needing investors, the more of the value you will get to keep when you eventually sell your business. Wayfair, an online home furnishings retailer, was profitable from the start. (The secret of the company's success was the founder bought hundreds of inexpensive domain names that aligned with popular search terms rather than burn vast sums of money on Google ad words.) But after a decade of profitability, the company hit a growth inflection point and raised $165 million from VCs just prior to going public at a $4 billion valuation.

Other founders delayed taking on investors by selling anything, anywhere they could. Never be too proud to raise money any way you can. Airbnb founder Brian Chesky and his cofounders tried funding their startup with just credit cards. When they quickly maxed out a binder full of credit cards, they needed to generate $20,000 fast in order to pay their monthly bills. With the 2008 US presidential election in full swing, the Airbnb team made two types of collectible cereal boxes: Obama O's and Captain McCain. After hot-gluing a thousand of the boxes together in their tiny apartment, the team sold $40,000 worth of cereal in one day.

Whenever candle and scent website Scentsy was short on cash, they sold their inventory at local swap meets. Packing up their inventory to sell directly to swap meet customers not only gave the company quick infusions of much-needed cash, but it also gave employees a chance to speak directly with customers to learn what they liked or disliked about the products. Being flexible and frugal in the beginning smells sweet today, as the self-financed e-commerce site now grosses more than $500 million a year.

Though I strongly recommend not using credit cards to fund your startup (I did it in my twenties and the debt I was drowning in from the high interest rates and penalties felt like torturous waterboarding), for many founders this may be the quickest way to cover some small early expenses. University students Mike Cannon-Brookes and Scott Farquhar were about as far away from Silicon Valley as one can get when they launched their company Atlassian in Sydney, Australia. Bootstrapping for as long as they could, the team amassed $10,000 in credit card debt before revenues came in for their Jira project management software. Even with robust sales of over $50 million, it took

Atlassian eight years to raise venture capital. Just four years after Accel Partners invested $60 million in growth capital, the Australian company went public on NASDAQ with a value of $4.37 billion.

One last cautionary tale. The only thing worse than credit card interest rates are payday loans. With interest rates and fees, some of these loans can have 1,000 percent per year interest rates. Veteran Elliot Clark used $2,500 payday loans after a medical emergency. His interest payment after five years had totaled a whopping $50,000. As a result, he and his wife lost their home. Do not, under any circumstances, bury yourself with this predatory evil lending practice.

The key lesson from raising capital is to make sure you understand what your business is and what it will take to scale it before you jump in and add the complexity of dealing with investors. Even if you are raising funds from friends and family, communicating with investors is just one more job for a busy founder. Graphic arts teacher Lynda Weinman, like so many YouTube stars today, used online video as a way to reach more students for free. As she built up her audience and content library, her site evolved into a subscription-based service. Needing capital to rapidly expand and capture the online market, Lynda raised $103 million from VCs. When she had the opportunity to further expand her course library by acquiring other content providers, Lynda raised an additional $186 million from private equity firm TPG Capital. The hypergrowth strategy paid off, and in 2015 Lynda.com was acquired by LinkedIn for $1.5 billion.

Another source of capital, which doesn't require founders to give up any equity, is preselling products on crowdfunding sites such as Kickstarter, GoFundMe, and Indiegogo. The game Cards Against Humanity, which was launched with a modest $15,700 crowdfunding campaign, went on to do $12 million in sales the very first year. Crowdfunding works best when you have a fan base from which to build awareness (and therefore funding). "Before you even start building your crowdfunding page," Command Partners' Roy Morejon suggests, "Start building a crowd first."[2]

Crowdfunding can even make you a billionaire. Perhaps the greatest crowdfunding success story of all time exceeded reality. When Palmer Luckey went on Kickstarter with the goal of raising $250,000 for his virtual reality Oculus Rift headset, he couldn't have dreamed of the response. Not only did he crowdfund over $2.4 million without giving away any company equity, two years later Facebook acquired his startup for $2.3 billion in cash and stock.

In the United States, the 2012 JOBS Act (Jumpstart Our Business Startups Act) greatly reduced the cost and regulations associated with raising startup funding. Title III of the act, more commonly referred to as the Crowdfund Act, became law in 2015 and raised the offering limits to $50 million while still using these simplified regulations. From 2015 through 2018, 107 companies used the new Reg A+ to raise a total of $1.5 billion. Companies such as Crowdengine, Startengine, and SeedInvest can help guide entrepreneurs through this new regulatory process.

All startups are risky. But by paying careful attention to how each deal is structured and the terms under which the capital is raised, founders can maximize their chances for success. Understanding what to do with your eventual profits is the final step in your financial development.

> If you don't find a way to make money while you sleep, you will work until you die.
>
> Warren Buffett

There is a popular internet meme with two pictures of Dr. Dre. One photo was taken at the start of his career and the second picture is after he became a billionaire. In the younger photo, the flashy hip-hop artist is in his twenties, wearing everything he owned in gold bling around his neck. In the second photo, taken after Dre sold his company Beats for $3 billion, the 49-year-old seasoned executive is dressed modestly with no hint of wealth. "It's not how much money you make. It's how much money you keep," Robert T. Kiyosaki teaches in his bestseller *Rich Dad Poor Dad*.[3]

Reinvesting Profits

The surest way to earn a million dollars is by starting to invest your money early in your career and putting your capital to work for you. That's why it's called capitalism. The very first thing I did when I made my first $1 million check was run out to Hollywood Magic and by a twenty-dollar card trick as a reward. The second thing I did was invest the rest. Don't go buying things you don't need with your early profits, because you never know when your income stream could dry up. Professional football players work hard from their teenage years on in order to achieve their dream of playing in the National Football League. Yet, according to *Sports Illustrated*, 78 percent of these NFL players are either bankrupt or are under financial stress within two years of retirement. Professional basketball players don't fare much better, with 60 percent of them going bankrupt within five years of leaving professional sports. Despite having career earnings in excess of $400 million, heavyweight boxer Mike Tyson declared bankruptcy in 2003 when he was just 37 years old. These athletes' big mistake was not making their money work as hard as they did. "It's not your salary that makes you rich," according to financial expert Charles A. Jaffe, "it's your spending habits."[4]

"You have to have a small amount of money and invest it regularly for a long time, and live to get to be old. That's how you get rich," says Ron Baron, the billionaire founder of Baron Capital, which has nearly $26 billion in assets under management. "If you invest $5,000 a year for 30 years, it's worth $890,000 (based on historical stock market returns)."[5]

The earlier you start out investing, the more you will earn over time. Investing in the beginning isn't about trying to beat the market or make brilliant stock picks, it is about leveraging the power of compound interest. The principal capital that you put in the first year makes money. That new earned capital is then reinvested, and it makes more money. This compounds over time, earning you interest on interest. Mathematically, an investment earning just 1 percent per month would earn 12 percent per year with simple interest, but actually earns 12.68 percent per annum when calculating compound interest. It is never too late to start. Genius investor Warren Buffett made 99 percent of his $90 billion after he was 50 years old.

By not buying what you don't need today, just as Elon Musk did by living off of $30 a month, you can earn enough passive income to never have to work again and be *Future Proofing You*. Think of your nest egg as an employee you hired. At first, it takes more energy on your part to manage the new employee and make her productive. But over time, the employee gets momentum and will eventually eclipse your earning power. When you can't, or don't want to, work, your employee continues to earn for your lifetime and beyond. By reinvesting profits, the Vanderbilt, Mellon, Hearst, and Rockefeller families have been *Future Proof* for generations. With proper stewardship, these wealthy families will be *Future Proof* for generations to come.

No matter what investment strategy you decide to pursue, remember, never put all your eggs in one basket. As your wealth grows, diversify your holdings both in terms of asset class (stocks, bonds, real estate) and geography (US, major foreign markets, and emerging markets). The more you spread your investments around, the less likely a major catastrophe like the 2008 sub prime housing fiasco or the 2020 pandemic will impact your overall wealth.

Vin came to me with his plan for investing his profits. Given how successful he was working in the cryptocurrency field, he was going to become a crypto day trader. This, I warned him, is the most common mistake people make with investing. If you are spending 100 hours a week working in a particular field, you are already heavily invested in both time and earning potential in that sector. Your livelihood is already too concentrated into one sector of the economy. You should therefore diversify and make sure your hard-earned capital is deployed in a completely different field. Vin believed his personal knowledge of the major players in the crypto field would minimize his investment risk. I don't know if I could have convinced Vin on my own not to speculate on crypto trading, but on December 17, 2017, when Bitcoin went from $19,666 a coin to $8,094.80 in one day, losing 59 percent of its value, he got the message loud and clear.

Whole books have been written about investing, but for Vin, the investment advice I wanted to impart was that diversification is part of his overall strategy of becoming *Future Proof*. Vin needed to work smart on structuring his agreements and let passive income be a co-worker. The more revenue streams you have, the greater the likelihood of achieving your long-term goals.

Nine months into our experiment, Vin had developed four steady revenue streams. The bulk of his revenue was coming from clients of the World's Best Agency. Within the agency itself, Vin was being careful not to rely too much on any one client or any one business sector. Client diversification helped him weather the storm of Facebook and Google banning ICOs and forced him to canvas new, emerging areas for new clients. In addition to the $63,240 he made from his agency, Vin's *Ace the Game* e-Book earned him $24,970. As part of the sales funnel for his growth-hacking book, Vin created an upsell for personally mentoring subscribers. This yielded an additional $7,000 in the month. Where Vin dropped the ball was affiliate referral fees. In the prior month, he made $24,800 just by referring work he couldn't handle to other vendors, but counteracting the effects of the Facebook ban on his clients' products took so much time and effort, Vin made zero affiliate revenue. Vin still was turning down small jobs, but he wasn't following through with handing the projects off to others in his network.

Lesson learned, month nine still had a great outcome, with total revenues from all sources of $95,211. Vin had made it through three-quarters of the year and 85 percent of the way toward his million-dollar goal. With $847,445 already earned, Vin just needs to average around $50,000 per month for the next three months to become a millionaire. Keeping him focused through the beautiful southern California summer was our next challenge. But with the wind now to his back, Vin was sailing toward his goal by not having to start each month's revenue from zero.

Notes

1. Alyson Shontell, "The Founder of a $50 Million Startup Sold His Company and Got Nothing," *Inc.* (April 14, 2015), https://www.inc.com/business-insider/the-founder-of-a-$-50-million-startup-sold-his-company-and-got-nothing.html.
2. Jonathan Chan, "16 Crowdfunding Experts Share Their Top Tips and Advice on How to Crush Your Next Crowdfunding Campaign," *Foundr* (November 21, 2016), https://foundr.com/crowdfunding-experts.

3. Robert T. Kiyosaki and Sharon L. Lechter, *Rich Dad, Poor Dad What the Rich Teach Their Kids about Money - That the Poor and Middle Class Do Not!* (United States: Plata Publishing, 2002), 124.

4. Dan Fourmier, *The Young Investor* (Bloomington, IN: Trafford Publishing, 2008), 21.

5. Matthew J. Belvedere, "Any Patient Investor Can Turn $5,000 a Year into Nearly $1 Million, Says Billionaire Investor Ron Baron," CNBC (November 10, 2017).

12

Remote Workers Are Your New Competitive Advantage

To win in the marketplace you must first win in the workplace.
                    —Doug Conant, co-author Touch Points

IF YOU EVER HAPPEN to visit Woodside, California, along a narrow
tributary of Bear Creek, nestled in an old grove of oaks, sits a world
renown restaurant. Buck's Restaurant of Woodside is not famous
because of its BBQ Bacon Burger or Bodacious Hot Fudge Pie; though
both are local favorites. It's not famous for its wild décor complete
with an eclectic array of flying machines dangling from its ceiling,
a human-size Statue of Liberty holding an ice cream cone, or the
giant wooden sculpture of a spawning salmon out front. What makes
Jamis MacNiven's zany eatery famous is the legendary role it has
played in Silicon Valley startup history. Located just four miles
from Sand Hill Road (where iconic venture capital firms such as
Sequoia Capital, Accel, Greylock Partners, Menlo Ventures, Kleiner
Perkins, Andressen Horowitz, Draper Fisher Jurvetson, and others are
headquartered), many startups without offices of their own had some
of their earliest meetings at Buck's. Hotmail, Netscape, PayPal, Tesla,
and many others met with VCs here. So large is the fabled status
of this restaurant that venture capitalist Bill Draper begins his book

The Startup Game: Inside the Partnership between Venture Capitalists and Entrepreneurs with a chapter titled "Breakfast at Buck's."

Restaurants aren't the only places to hatch startups. HP, Disney, Amazon, and Google all started in small garages. Dell, WordPress, Snapchat, Dropbox, and Facebook all began in dorm rooms. Yankee Candle, Martha Stewart Living, Fortnite/Epic Games, and Under Armor all worked their way out of someone's basement. Even global company Microsoft was once run out of a motel room in Albuquerque, New Mexico. From the humblest of places, global multibillion-dollar companies started. To save on rent and overhead, many startups try to work from restaurants, home, and shared working environments for as long as possible so as not to squander what little capital they have. The one truth that Covid-19 exposed to the business world was that in the twenty-first century, there is no longer a need for big, expensive corporate offices.

Truth #12 – Remote Workers Are Your New Competitive Advantage

When the impact of the pandemic hit the United States, businesses had to scramble to find a way to continue functioning and keep their employees safe. Insurance company Nationwide quickly shifted nearly all of its 32,000 employees to working from home. "We've been investing in our technological capabilities for years, and those investments really paid off when we needed to transition quickly to a 98 percent work-from-home model," Nationwide CEO Kirt Walker said. "Our associates and our technology team have proven to us that we can serve our members and partners with extraordinary care with a large portion of our team working from home."[1]

Amazon, Facebook, Google, and Microsoft gave all employees the option to work from home. Twitter CEO Jack Dorsey went so far as to tell his employees that they could work remotely forever and never be required to work from the office again. According to the Centers for Disease Control and Prevention, 46 percent of companies implemented some form of remote working policies during the 2020 pandemic. With many businesses being able to easily adapt to remote workers, Barclays CEO Jes Staley predicts that centralized offices with thousands of employees "may be a thing of the past." Echoing that belief, Morgan Stanley CEO James Gorman predicts that his bank will need "much less" real estate in the future. While most companies survived the 2020 pandemic, the era of the mighty corporate headquarters has died.

With the remote-work genie out of the bottle, most employees are looking for a way to maintain the flexibility of working when and where they choose. This is the competitive advantage of any startup; you can let people work from their homes. You now have access to a global talent pool eager to maintain their freedom. Employees can travel the world while still maintaining a full-time job and not have to wait until they retire to enjoy life. Understanding the evolving needs of today's wage earner gives you the best chance at competing for the top talent. "Remote work isn't a privilege or a special accommodation," cautions Atlassian's Head of Talent Programs Nickie Bellington. "It's a way of working, and that's a strong statement for some people. It shouldn't be a question of rewarding top performers with the ability to work remotely."

Of those employees required to work from home during the pandemic, three in five US workers would like to continue working remotely even after the health concerns have passed. A study by Owl Labs concluded that 80 percent of employees would like to work from home at least part of the time.

With so many corporate employees working from home, you can also leverage big company employees looking to earn some extra cash from a side hustle. Just as 99designs gave startups access to thousands of graphic artists (many of whom have full-time jobs working for ad agencies), you now can access very skilled, specialized expensive talent and just pay for them when you need them. Obviously you don't want employees to violate any employment agreement they may have signed, but plenty of graphic artists, engineers, researchers, and salespeople are permitted to moonlight. Your virtual company, propelled by a phalanx of virtual talent, can't be beat by large companies dragged down by massive overhead and costly payrolls. With the right management tools, a virtual workforce is so efficient that it can save you from needing to raise millions of dollars and dilute your company ownership.

The concept of telecommuting, as it used to be called, started in the 1970s. The problem with working from home back in the pre-internet days, was that the telephone was the only means of communication and all documents had to be either mailed or couriered back and forth. With today's communication and management tools, people began to recognize that work is something you do, not something you travel to. The desire for a better quality of life is so strong, that according to Gallup's State of the American Workforce poll, 35 percent of employees would change jobs if they could work remotely full-time. Among millennials the desire to work from home is even stronger with Gallup finding 47 percent would switch jobs for the opportunity. A flexible work environment is so important to millennials, the same survey concluded that it was a bigger employment incentive than student loan or tuition reimbursement. If you need to compete with the corporate giants for talent, be more flexible and responsive to people's needs.

With 78 percent of American workers willing to take a pay cut to work from home, the truth is that having distributed workers is the new competitive advantage. Leveraging this advantage, and powered by a whole new generation of online tools and apps, virtual companies are flourishing around the world. Software developer Scopic Software grew to over 200 employees without having an office. Basecamp, Buffer, Clevertech, and Articulate are all finding that they can provide better service to their customers, and a better quality of life for their employees, by being 100 percent remote working companies.

Benefits of Employees Working from Home

Improved employee moral isn't the only benefit of having a distributed workforce. Intuit estimates that employers save more than $11,000 per remote worker by needing less office space, electricity, equipment, and furniture. Being freed from constant co-worker interruptions, numerous studies have shown that remote employees get more work done each day. According to a 2020 Harris Poll, 65 percent of remote workers report being more productive at home than in the office.

An even more important benefit of remote working is the size of the talent pool you get to draw from. Instead of being limited to those employees who live within a commuting distance from your office, you can now hire the best employees from around the world. "Do you want to access talent everywhere, or just in specific markets?" HubSpot's

Chief People Officer Katie Burke posits. "If the answer is everywhere, you need to be at least open to the possibility of remote work — it opens doors to attracting and retaining talent around the world, literally and figuratively."[2] With foreign worker visas to the United States being harder to attain, foreign workers can join the team without moving to America.

Allowing for such flexibility will help you recruit better talent, too. Employees put such importance on having the freedom to work remotely that they are more loyal, have less turnover, and are more productive. Employer benefits of remote working are only half of the value equation.

According to recent studies, employees save between $2,500 and $4,000 per year by working at home just half the time. Workers also save the equivalent of 11 workdays per year that they otherwise would have wasted commuting. For big cities like New York, daily commutes average 81.6 minutes roundtrip per day, which at New York's minimum wage would translate to $5,324 in lost wages/productivity per worker per year. By forgoing traffic, congested trains, and urban noise, remote workers report being less stressed and able to spend more quality time with family and friends.

Commuting is also bad for the environment by releasing harmful chemicals and greenhouse gases into the air. Commuters are exposed to as much as twice the particulate matter in the air that causes oxidative stress in humans than during other parts of the day. Prolonged exposure can lead to respiratory and heart disease, as well as cancer. "We found that people are likely getting a double whammy of exposure in terms of health during rush-hour commutes," according to Michael Bergin, professor of civil and environmental engineering at Duke University. "If these chemicals are as bad for people as many researchers believe, then commuters should seriously be rethinking their driving habits."[3]

Remote working is also one of the easiest ways for companies to reduce their carbon footprint. According to a study by the Telework Research Network, if just 40 percent of Americans who could work remotely did, the nation would save 280 million barrels of oil per year – the equivalent of taking 9 million vehicles permanently off the road. Leverage workers' desire to protect our environment as a competitive advantage when recruiting new talent.

Additionally, both employers and employees may have possible tax savings by working from home. Many communities have incentives to reduce commuter congestion, and some employees may be able to deduct their home office expenses on their state or federal taxes. Flexible working arrangements also provide more diversity in the workplace by being more accommodating for single parents, those taking care of elderly relatives, or individuals with disabilities that are unable to easily travel to a workplace.

The advantages of leveraging a remote workforce will make your startup able to respond to changing market conditions faster, launch new products and services with less capital, and expand into new territories seamlessly. But none of these advantages will come to fruition if your virtual company isn't managed properly.

Five Techniques for Managing Remote Workers

Building a remote-worker company takes planning and preparation. Many of the management techniques that are utilized in an office environment (stopping by someone's office, grabbing a coffee together, or celebrating a co-worker's birthday), can't be used with distant workers. Additionally, a global remote workforce must be managed across a wide range of time zones and cultures. To best succeed and get the most out of a dispersed team, here are five techniques I recommend for managing remote workers:

1. *Trust and transparency.* If you hire people that you trust, then trust the people you hire. If you find yourself micromanaging employees, then you hired the wrong people. The most successful remote workers are self-starters; so look for people who have either worked remotely in the past or have run their own businesses. The more goal-oriented the person, the better they will be able to govern their progress and know how to ask for help when they get off track. If you are holding your employees to certain performance metrics, you must be transparent with your expectations. Employees are no more psychic than you are, so spell out exactly what the job is and isn't. Without being able to walk around the office and casually check in on progress or problems, you need to set up consistent

one-on-one sessions with each member of your team. These meetings aren't just for you to get your questions answered, but should be opportunities to solicit honest feedback about how you and the company can better support each employee's needs.

"One way in which dispersed teams can ensure they get off to a good start is to engage in a formal launch process," recommends Harvard Business School Professor Anthony Mayo in his online course *Leadership Principles*. "Even if a face-to-face meeting isn't possible, it's critically important to be deliberate and intentional in launching the team and collectively agreed upon norms to govern the work you do together across locations. Through this process, team members get to know each other in a meaningful way, and that helps lay the foundation for working together more effectively in the future."[4]

2. *Create shared values.* Whenever possible, instill a sense of shared purpose in your team. The more mission driven the company, the more sharing and collaboration will grow among team members. Without the team building that organically happens from people having lunch together or chatting in the hallway each day, it is important to create a community among all the employees. Set up virtual treasure hunts or trivia contests with prizes. For all company interactions, encourage video communication over faceless conference calls. If your company is a hybrid of office and remote workers, keep a live video chat line open around the office coffee machine so remote workers can pop in and say hi to those taking a break at headquarters. I have found this technique especially helpful with remote teams halfway around the globe. A person in Los Angeles and Warsaw can grab a coffee together even though one is just starting their day and the other is ending theirs.

"You can never overcommunicate enough as a leader at a company, but at a remote company, nothing could be truer," suggests Know Your Team CEO Claire Lew. "Because you don't physically see people in person, information doesn't spread in the same way, so leaders need to do the heavy lifting for evangelizing the message."[5]

Celebrate victories and promotions companywide. With a shared purpose, when one team member succeeds, everyone succeeds. Having a purpose unites employees toward a goal and against the external competition. And at least once a year, schedule a global face-to-face conference somewhere fun and exotic. When I was working at the global music company EMI, Special Markets President Eli Okun set a sales goal and a stretch goal for his division each year. In addition to the traditional raises and bonuses that came from hitting the sales goal, if the stretch goal was met, everyone in the entire division and their significant others were sent to Hawaii to celebrate. Eli's plan was such a great motivator that most years the team went to Hawaii.

3. *Work on your emotional intelligence.* So much of our normal workplace communication is nonverbal. When you go to an office every day, you can tell by just looking at someone how their day is going. *Are they stressed? Do they look unwell? Are they dressed differently that they usually appear?* Managing remotely will require some new communication and emotional intelligence skills. Don't be afraid to take a personal development course online or to get coaching from someone who has managed remotely before. As your team grows internationally, be sensitive to local customs and be accommodating to other people's time zones. Lastly, don't assume that every country celebrates the same holidays as you do. The more you embrace cultural diversity, the more loyalty you will engender. "One of the secret benefits of using remote workers," Basecamp CEO Jason Fried discovered, "is that the work itself becomes the yardstick to judge someone's performance."[6]

4. *Promote a healthy work–life balance.* Without the traditional rhythms of arriving at the office and leaving to go home at night, your employees will need you to respect their boundaries. Encourage people to share with the team what hours they are working and when they can't be reached. Conversely, employees need to normalize their remote work day as if they were in the office. Children and other family members have to respect your work hours, and boundaries need to be set with them as well. When I ran my first company out of my home, my sons were in preschool, so I created the "Who can stay quiet longer? game" whenever the phone rang. Even at that young age, they learned to understand when Daddy could or could not play. And every workday should have a hard stop to it to avoid burnout. Everyone has a to-do list of

projects around the house, but personal household errands should be accomplished during the time that otherwise would have been wasted commuting. With proper scheduling and boundaries, remote workers will get to enjoy more quality time with loved ones and reduce their level of stress.

5. *Invest in remote management tools.* With the thousands of dollars a month remote workers are saving you in office overhead, it is critical to invest some of that savings into remote management software. Distributed workforces have become so mainstream that hundreds of tools have been developed for every aspect of the job. There are project-oriented tools for collaboration, workflow automation, and content management. There are managerial tools for time tracking, productivity analysis, and time zone converting schedulers. Cloud storage and shared drives can be leveraged to utilize their robust security systems, and password managers can track access to shared software licenses and apps. Virtual private networks, virtual call centers, and conference calling software can help track and memorialize meetings. There is even software for onboarding of new hires and processing freelancers' invoices. There are two tools that I find invaluable with remote teams. *Krisp* is a noise-cancellation app that works with Zoom, Slack, and most of the other communication platforms. Meetings are more enjoyable and productive when background noise is eliminated from every caller. Getting honest feedback is often a challenge when managing remotely. *Chimp or Champ* is an anonymous weekly employee happiness meter. You can't improve morale if you don't know you have a problem.

For all of the many advantages of building a virtual company, there are some risks. Not everyone is suited for remote working. Many remote employees complain of feeling disconnected from their in-office coworkers and dissatisfied with their job as a result. A study by software maker Buffer reports that loneliness was a challenge for 19 percent of remote employees.

For first-time remote workers, there is a period of adjustment. Many come into the job with a preconception of being able to travel the world and work from the rainforests of Costa Rica or the beaches of Phuket, Thailand. You should suggest that working from a local café with less distractions might be a better place for new hires to start. Remote employees also feel more pressure to prove themselves. Rather than slacking off, many remote workers put in longer hours and burn out quickly. That is why communication and time tracking is so important. By having one's company promote a healthy work–life balance, most remote workers find that they would prefer to never go back to a nine-to-five office again.

From the start of our *Future Proofing You* experiment, Vin made use of all the advantages of using remote workers. First, he never rented an office for his agency and saved all the associated costs. Since he was working out of his apartment, Vin could only hire remote workers. This gave him access to less-expensive skilled talent in Eastern Europe and Asia. Given Vin's lack of management experience, he had to learn quickly how to track employees' progress and replace those unable to work efficiently. Whenever possible, Vin also tried to hire people for a specific project rather than full-time employment. If they were great, he had more work to throw at them. If they were subpar, he didn't have the cost and hassles of firing them.

Unfortunately, 10 months of nonstop grinding threw work–life balance out the window for the year. Vin was burnt out and emotionally spent. He had not seen friends, gone on a date, or even been to a movie for the better part of the year. He missed his family in England terribly. Knowing that working 24/7 had a hard stop date was the only thing, in my opinion, that kept him from losing it completely. Best of all, with $90,227 in revenue for month 10, his year-to-date total revenue was now $942,016. He only needed to make $28,992 of each of the next two months to hit his goal. Having built up recurring revenue from his agency clients, Vin knew that if no one cancelled on him, he already had $60,000 in commitments for month 11 on the books.

(continued)

(*continued*)

Vin realized he had achieved his goal with two months to spare. Vin could quit now and achieve $1,000,000 with just the projects already in hand or continue working to exceed his goal.

"WOW. What a shocker ending; hitting the goal in 10 months," I wrote him in an email. "You crushed it!!"

For the first time all year, he felt free. Vin had the freedom to continue pushing as hard as he could or just coast to the finish line. After spending months fantasizing about all the places he was going to travel to when this experiment was over, Vin decided to stick it out and work for the next two months. He was a champion, and champions don't ease up.

Notes

1. Adedayo Akala, "More Big Employers Are Talking about Permanent Work-from-Home Positions," CNBC (May 3, 2020), https://www.CNBC.com/2020/05/01/major-companies-talking-about-permanent-work-from-home-positions.html.
2. Sophia Bernazzani, "How HubSpot Is Building Remote Work into Its Company Culture," OWL Labs (February 4, 2019), https://www.owllabs.com/remote-work-interviews/katie-burke.
3. Robert Preidt, "Rush Hour Pollution May Be Worse Than Thought," *Health Day News* (July 28, 2017), https://live.healthday.com/u/robertpreidt.
4. Antony Jay, "How to Run a Meeting," *Harvard Business Review* (March 1976).
5. Tim English, "Working from Home? These 10 Inspiring Quotes Are for YOU!" Inkonit.com (March 19, 2020), www.inkonit.com/blog/working-from-home-these-10-inspiring-quotes-are-for-you/.
6. Jason Fried, "Working from Home Boosts the Quality of the Work," *Inc.* (October 28, 2013), https://www.inc.com/jason-fried/excerpt-remote-workers-boost-quality.html.

PART

II

Future Proofing Your Business

While the prior chapters focused on *Future Proofing You* and launching a business, the final section of the book focuses on Future Proofing your new business and understanding how you and your new company fit into the broader context of society.

13

Using Mergers and Acquisitions for Future Proofing You

You've got to know when to hold 'em
Know when to fold 'em
Know when to walk away, and know when to run.
—The Gambler, *lyrics by Don Schlitz*

FROM THE START, Eric Baker's story reads like every entrepreneur's fantasy. While a student at Stanford University, Baker co-founds StubHub. The American online ticket exchange quickly grows into the largest secondary-market for event tickets, selling tens of millions of tickets per year. As with many fast-growing businesses, the two founders had different visions for the company and Baker was fired from his own company. Angry, and still believing in his vision for online ticketing, Baker flies to London and launches a similar service, Viagogo, in Europe. Viagogo is an instant success and grows quickly. Meanwhile, the same board that had fired him sells StubHub to eBay for $310 million, making Eric Baker rich but unhappy to see his creation owned by strangers. Baker continues to grow his European event ticketing business, and on November 27, 2019, exacts the revenge every fired founder dreams about: Viagogo acquires StubHub from eBay for $4.05 billion. "It's personally satisfying to have my two babies together and be able to reunite them," Baker said in announcing the deal. His happiness wouldn't last long.

By the time the deal closed in February 2020, the world – and definitely the world of live events – had drastically changed. With the Covid-19 pandemic shuttering theaters and stadiums across the globe, the two companies lost over 90 percent of their revenues and had to furlough the majority of their employees. Talks of bankruptcy were bantered about in the press and financial analyst Moody's downgraded the company's status to negative. "It's rare that you can judge a deal within months of completion," Noah Kirsch wrote in *Forbes*, "but the verdict on this one is absolute: Baker's purchase of StubHub will go down as one of the worst deals in history."[1]

Events outside of one's control can take any entrepreneur from hero to zero in the blink of an eye. For every story of a founder like Mark Zuckerberg turning down a $1 billion buyout from Yahoo! and going on to make tens of billions more, there are thousands of examples of life-lasting regret. There are two sides to every deal. With the shoe on the other foot, how brilliant was eBay's board to unload StubHub before it became a costly drain on its bottom line and net billions of dollars off an asset that might soon be worthless?

Yahoo! foolishly turned down a $44.6 billion offer from Microsoft. One-time internet darling Groupon turned down a $6 billion offer from Google in 2010 and today is worth just a half a billion dollars. And in 20/20 hindsight, does anyone believe that in 2003, Friendster should have rejected Google's takeover stock offer that is today worth more than $1 billion?

Most founders spend all their energies raising capital and building their companies, with little regard for how to maximize the return on their investment of time and money. Many consider their creations as their children and can't imagine parting with them. Understanding how exits happen and then taking the steps to make them happen is the only way a founder stands a chance of becoming Future Proof.

The Art of the Exit

In the four decades since I founded my first startup, I have been on both sides of exits. I have sold companies to larger corporations and I have acquired smaller startups. I have taken companies public and I have worked on mergers between equals. I have been on the winning side and I have been on the losing side. I have completed complicated deals in record time and been left at the alter after months of due diligence. In this chapter, I want to demystify the process and arm you with the knowledge I have accumulated so that you will have the best chance of a positive outcome.

I wish I hadn't learned my lessons the hard way. When I was in my early thirties, just a few months after my startup released its first video games, a more established company offered a third of its stock for acquiring my startup. Not wanting to lose control of my baby, I turned down the offer. Today, Activision Blizzard, the company that offered us a 33 percent stake, is worth $61 billion. I have had much success in my career, but I have to confess that 25 years later, making a billion-dollar mistake still stings.

My lasting lesson from that first experience is to not be afraid to sell early. Very few startups go public. Of those that don't go out of business, 97 percent are acquired. Often times, the very first offer for your company may in fact be the best offer that you will ever receive. A TechCrunch analysis of VC-funded companies shows that 40 percent of startups are acquired after their series A funding and most other companies will go out of business. The reason for this is simple – VCs invest in sectors that are perceived as hot. The attention the startup gets after announcing its first funding from a major VC will alert everyone looking at the space. If the young company deploys its new funds wisely, the value of the company can grow exponentially in a matter of months. So, if a major company needs to enter that same market, the sooner it purchases the startup, the more time and money the acquirer will save.

Why Large Companies Acquire Small Companies

To fully understand the acquisition process, it is important to comprehend the motivation of a public company CEO. Though it may appear that CEOs make obscene amounts of money, in reality, most have a modest base salary and a huge upside for making their company more profitable and their company stock more valuable. With so much of their executive compensation tied to very strict metrics, most CEOs are rewarded for short-term thinking. The result of this thinking is that many CEOs would rather cut the expense of long-term research and development to make quick profits now. With the majority of public company CEOs keeping their jobs for less than five years, the job becomes a series of 13-week quarterly sprints and not a well-paced marathon. Without the costly investment in new products, large companies have in essence outsourced research and development in the form of acquisitions. Google didn't invent its advertising business; it acquired DoubleClick for $3.1 billion. Google didn't invent video sharing; it acquired YouTube for $1.65 billion. When the world migrated from desktops to mobile, Google didn't invent Android; it acquired it. One of the reasons Google continues to thrive is that it has attained products and services from the more than 200 acquisitions it has completed.

CEOs have many other reasons for buying startups. Defensively, they may buy a startup to prevent a competitor from getting into their space. A company may buy your startup just to acquire your talent (this is commonly referred to as an acq-*hire*). I also have seen CEOs, whose stock is languishing, acquire companies for the press value of making their company look like it is making big moves.

So, it goes to reason that if VCs invested in a sector set to explode, other established corporations are also looking at the space for the reasons just mentioned. I was on the board of a pre-revenue startup that a company offered $100 million to purchase just days after our $9 million funding round was announced. The founders, both in their twenties, would have been financially set for life. I tried everything in my power to explain why this was a fantastic deal and why they should take it. But with billion-dollar dreams in their heads, they turned down the offer and I resigned from the board. The following year, competitors sprung up like daisies in summer, and the founders were forced to raise additional capital to stay afloat. With each subsequent cash infusion in the unprofitable company, their equity stake is reduced. The company's sector is no longer the focus of the industry and growth has stagnated. Eight years later, the business has no exit in sight, but if the owners had taken the money they were offered in their first month, that $100 million invested in an S&P index fund would now be worth at least $159 million.

Since that unfortunate experience, I ask every startup founder, before they launch their company, "What amount of money would it cost to buy your 'idea' today?" The purpose of the question is to get people thinking about how much money they really want (or need) before crazy dollar amounts get blogged about online. Would $10 million change your life? Would $20 million be enough for future proofing you? What could you buy with $1 billion that you couldn't buy with $100 million? With 75 percent of venture-backed startups failing; how big does the bird in hand need to be to satisfy your desires?

"Selling starts on day one and is a leadership-only function; work out who will be your buyer," suggests former Ubiquisys CEO Chris Gilbert who sold his company to Cisco for more than $300 million. "Only the CEO can do this. Constantly articulate why a company should buy you."[2]

Before considering any offer, you need to understand your personal goals and motivation for both starting and selling your company. Would you like to become wealthy when you are old, or would you like to start enjoying life now? Did you start the company to solve a problem or to become wealthy? Does the acquirer have the resources to take your mission further or are they buying the company to just acquire talent? The clearer you are in your mind as to your goals and purpose, the easier it will be to evaluate any deal that emerges.

Selling a company is a huge distraction and will take up a great deal of your entire management's time, so be certain that you are mentally committed to selling before entering negotiations. "All of your ability to run day-to-day operations of your company will grind to a halt," warns Justin Kan who sold his company Twitch Interactive to Amazon for $970 million. "You should only enter an acquisition process if you are certain you want to sell the company and you are likely to get a price you can accept."[3]

Valuing a startup is more of an art than a science. Since companies are bought and not sold, the company is either valued on its future cash flow/profit or its strategic value to the acquirer. CFOs, investment bankers, VCs, and a host of corporate experts will create an array of metrics – such as cost per user or net enterprise value – to justify whatever number is being offered.

Getting an Offer

Especially in Silicon Valley, where every major tech company has scores of corporate development people, anyone can say they are interested in buying your company. Unless the offer is accompanied by a detailed term sheet (usually with an expiration date), it is just talk. Rarely do offers come out of the blue. Most begin as conversations. The more you are able to expose yourself and your company to decision makers at the top of potential acquirers, the better your odds. What seems like an open conversation with your mentor or a key investor, may lead to them sharing your story with key contacts of theirs. Once someone is seriously interested, act swiftly. Time kills all deals.

I was CEO of a public company when a much larger competitor came in with an acquisition offer 40 percent above our current market cap. With such a fantastic outcome for our shareholders, I was eager to accept and close the deal as soon as possible. When the due diligence process dragged into months because the executive leading the acquisition had fallen out of favor with their CEO, the deal died. If your goal is to someday sell the company or take it public, then you need to run it professionally from the start and have all your diligence materials ready at a moment's notice. No acquisition goes through without due diligence. The more your books are in order, the smoother the process will be. Is your cap table up to date? Have you filed all of your taxes? Have all your employees signed nondisclosure and noncompete agreements? Keep accurate records and use bookkeeping software from the moment you open your first company bank account. That extra process in the beginning, when you have extra time, will save you from scrambling when your business is on fire and you don't have time to worry about paperwork.

Before you share any diligence material, you need to protect yourself and your company. Unscrupulous pretend acquirers may be looking to steal your customers or key employees, reengineer your source code or understand your cost structure. Always require any suitor to sign a nondisclosure agreement. If violated later, that agreement will enable you to sue in court for damages. In 2017, a jury determined that Oculus had to pay game maker ZeniMax $500 million for violating their nondisclosure agreement.

Outside of the record keeping, there are three pieces of information that every acquirer is looking to gather. First, do you own the intellectual property (IP) the company is using? Not to get too technical, but many acquisitions have fallen apart when it is discovered that the startup is using "borrowed" code. Next, an acquirer wants to gauge the capabilities of your team. "Instead of taking the opportunity to hire individual talent, some companies are buying for the talent and discarding the product," says Shekhar Purohit, a managing director at executive-compensation consulting firm Pearl Meyer & Partners in San Francisco.[4] If the company is buying you for your products and services, then they really need to make sure that your customers are going to stick around after the acquisition.

You may know more about your company than anyone alive, but your business is not mergers and acquisitions. You will need legal and tax advice. The earlier you bring in the experts, the more control you will have over the process. The acquirer's term sheet may seem straightforward, but unless you have been through this process multiple times before, you may not know what isn't in the term sheet that could protect you. If your acquisition price is more than $100 million you may also want to consider hiring an investment banker. Though expensive, often they take 1–2 percent of the overall deal, investment bankers know how to structure deals better than most attorney's because that is all that they do. When the US Department of Justice Antitrust Division blocked AT&T's purchase of T-Mobile, T-Mobile received a $6 billion breakup fee that its bankers had included in the deal. Not a bad profit for a failed acquisition.

Be as transparent as possible. "Right from your first conversation through to every piece of documentation, be absolutely clear and transparent with the business you are selling," Nicole Munoz, founder of Nicole Munoz Consulting, Inc., says. "It can be as difficult to purchase as it is to sell, but having a clear and transparent process is key."[5] Many potential suitors may not want word to get out about the possible deal, but that doesn't mean you should keep it a secret from company management and major investors. Secrecy builds distrust, starts internal rumors, and causes unhealthy office politics. In order to shepherd an acquisition through, a founder needs to build consensus for the deal. The last thing you need is a potential deal getting scuttled because of a shareholder lawsuit.

Lastly, when the deal looks like it is nearing completion, work with the acquirer to jointly inform key business partners and clients. You don't want to have unhappy customers and lose business because people felt blindsided. By seeking their input ahead of time, the process of integrating the two companies will go much smoother.

One last cautionary tale about the acquisition process. The acquirer holds all the cards. At the beginning of the process, when you sign the term sheet, it is only natural to have visions of how you are going to spend the millions of dollars you are getting. Many founders will have shared the news with spouses or family. In your mind, it is a done deal, and you are psychologically committed to the exit. Knowing this, the night before the deal is scheduled to close, the acquirer tells you that changing market conditions have spooked their board, and they lower the agreed upon price by $38 million.

That's exactly what happened to the Travelscape founders the night before they were to announce the deal had closed. Some corporate bullies believe that no one is going to walk away from the table at that stage after having spent a month dreaming about being rich. Most entrepreneurs cave to such pressure tactics. Travelscape's Tom Breitling and Tim Poster walked away from the table and, luckily, later sold their company for more money.

Depending on the pace of the acquirer, even simple deals can take a long time to get done. Turner Media's purchase of Bleacher Report for $200 million was an eight-month journey. "It went from something that seemed out of reach, to something that was remotely possible, to something we thought might happen, to something we thought would probably happen, to something that seemed almost certain," Bleacher Report co-founder Bryan Goldberg says. "You go to bed every night thinking there's a really good chance this deal is going to go through, and knowing at any minute it could come apart for the smallest, most abrupt of reasons."[6]

The easiest acquisition to complete is when the telephone rings. By staying in dialogue with key industry leaders, promoting your company's accomplishments in the press, and making yourself accessible, inbound offers will come. If you have already thought through what you really want, and have your house in order, the process should be quick and painless.

Vin chose not to focus on selling his business and rather, wanted to mothball it for a year. Seeing how time-consuming coaching was, Vin shuttered this revenue stream to focus on building a conference speaker business and started to book an international tour of speaking gigs. Vin downsized staff and cut costs for his core marketing operations as he recognized that he was going to be taking some time off at the end of our experiment.

With a month to spare, Vin had achieved his goal by earning $1,033,802. Far from coasting across the finish line, month 11's $91,786 in revenue was actually an improvement over month 10. Much to his surprise and mine, $69,000 of the revenue had come from affiliate sales. This revenue stream, coupled with his online book sales, would mean that Vin would continue to earn substantial revenues as he traveled the world and recuperated from his year of sacrifice. Just as Warren Buffett had famously recommended, Vin was now making money while he slept and was Future Proof.

Notes

1. Noah Kirsch, "The Worst Deal Ever," *Forbes* (May 27, 2020), www.forbes.com/sites/noahkirsch/2020/05/27/worst-deal-ever/#2e23644888d1.
2. Benjamin Joffe and Cyril Ebersweiler, "What Every Startup Founder Should Know about Exits," Tech Crunch (July 31, 2018).
3. Justin Kan, "The Founder's Guide to Selling Your Company," Justinkan.com (November 10, 2014), https://justinkan.com/the-founders-guide-to-selling-your-company-a1b2025c9481.
4. Susan Johnston, "How to Ease Acquisitions from the Acqui-Hired Founders," *Entrepreneur* (August 28, 2012).
5. Scott Gerber, "18 Key Considerations to Make When Selling a Business," business.com (May 28, 2020), https://www.business.com/articles/considerations-when-selling-a-business/.

6. Alyson Shontell, "What It's Like the Moment You Sell Your Startup for Tons of Money," Yahoo! Finance (September 25, 2013), https://finance .yahoo.com/news/moment-sell-startup-tons-money-152121781.html?guc counter=1&guce_referrer=aHR0cHM6Ly9kdWNrZHVja2dvLmNvbS8&guce_referrer_sig=AQAAAHlBH32r9xpeo1I_lJIlZI6Rywv8ZIlrSdRxA2pvz3Po3e3kg6gVMjeWC8IoBe0LuDUeepk_w4plOAygCH2Oiqn6VwEwzAPDrDyvYg6D1OJoVd_09z5pzz4gBPZJCdaLpUnpYLJFOvrdEZJ5VOvfcTub199WQXCuWIJC8q-Si-Gs.

14

Fulfilling the Need for Profitable Sustainability

Only when the last tree has died and the last river has been poisoned and the last fish has been caught will we realize that we cannot eat money.
—Chief Seattle, leader of the Suquamish and Duwamish people

BLACK FRIDAY, THE FRIDAY after Thanksgiving in the United States, is the traditional kickoff of the Christmas shopping season, which accounts for 20 percent of most retailers' annual sales. With the average American spending approximately $1,050 on gifts, the competition to lure customers into one's shop with heavily discounted Black Friday doorbuster specials is intense.[1] By running costly ad campaigns for their reduced price one-day bargains, stores create a frenzy of rabid consumers lining up and even camping out overnight. Against the backdrop of all this clamoring for a piece of the $7 billion being spent on this one day, imagine the shock readers of *the New York Times* experienced in 2011 when they saw a full-page advertisement with the massive headline "Don't Buy This Jacket."[2]

Beneath the photo of a Patagonia jacket, the ad read "It's Black Friday, the day in the year retail turns from red to black and starts to make real money. But Black Friday, and the culture of consumption it reflects, puts the economy of natural systems that support all life firmly in the red. We're now using the resources of one-and-a-half planets on our one and only planet." The ad went on to explain that while Patagonia would like to be in business for a long time, it was more important to leave the world inhabitable for our kids. "We want to do the opposite of every other business today. We ask you to buy less and to reflect before you spend a dime on this jacket or anything else."

What Patagonia and its founder, billionaire Yvon Chouinard, recognized was that even if its garments were organic or made from recycled materials, each article of clothing they produce emits several times its weight in greenhouse gases, generates at least another half garment's worth of scrap, and draws down copious amounts of fresh water. Chouinard, a committed environmentalist, said that it would be hypocritical to work for environmental change without encouraging consumers to think before they buy.

The R2 jacket in the ad, one of Patagonia's best sellers, uses 135 liters of water to be produced (the equivalent of three glasses a day for 45 people). Its production generated 20 pounds of carbon dioxide and created two-thirds its weight in waste. By educating their customers, and hopefully all the readers of *the New York Times* that day, on the true cost of consumerism, Patagonia launched the Common Threads Initiative. The initiative encourages all consumers to reduce, repair, reuse, recycle, and reimagine. Reduce waste by purchasing quality products that last a long time. Patagonia promised to repair any of its gear that may have been broken or damaged from use. The company pledged to find a home for customers' old clothing items and to recycle gear that was worn out, and asked consumers to pledge to keep old stuff out of landfills and incinerators. And the company added one new "R" to the ecology movement – it wanted everyone to *reimagine* a world where we take only what nature can replace.

More than an attention-getting stunt, the *Don't Buy This Jacket* campaign reflected that sustainability was a core value of the company. In 2002, Chouinard founded the *1% for the Planet* initiative and became the first business to commit 1 percent of its annual sales to the environment. What Yvon Chouinard recognized is that capitalism as we have known it is broken, and even with his billion-dollar fortune, he alone can't save the planet. You can't become Future Proof without Future Proofing our world.

Human activity is killing the life on this planet. Dozens of plant and animal species go extinct every day. By 2050, between one third and half of all species on Earth will have vanished.[3] Climate change is overheating our world and may cause the sixth mass extinction on the planet. According to the World Meteorological Organization (WMO), 20 of the warmest years in recorded history have happened in the past 22 years.[4] Carbon emissions continue to rise unabated each year and yet the UN Climate report warns that global carbon pollution must be reduced by 50 percent to avoid a catastrophic end to civilization this century.[5]

As more and more consumers awaken to the need for more sustainable business practices, corporations have begun to embrace social responsibility. Unfortunately for many businesses, the more companies make consumers aware of their impact on our environment, the more corporations get blamed for society's failures. The Occupy Wall Street movement grew out of the growing chasm between the needs of the public and the needs of the boardroom. The root of the problem isn't that corporations and their executives are evil villains determined to destroy our planet, but rather, that our current measurement of success, both corporate and personal, is outdated and out of touch with ecological realities. The solution is sustainable capitalism, and businesses from startups to multinationals are rapidly responding to this societal need.

Sustainable Capitalism

Sustainable capitalism is a new paradigm where societies weigh the true cost of a product (resource depletion, environmental impact, etc.) in calculating profitability. In our current form of capitalism, when a company like Hooker Chemical (now known as Occidental Chemical Corporation) dumps 21,800 tons of carcinogenic toxins and chemical byproducts into Love Canal, New York, harming the health of local residents, the US taxpayer pays $400 million to clean up the disaster.[6] With sustainable capitalism, the lifecycle of everything manufactured – including dealing with the waste it creates – is factored into a product's true cost. This is demonstrated in both large companies and local businesses just getting off the ground, such as when your local sandwich shop stops using plastic containers and straws.

Currently, with shareholders able to move their money instantly to whichever company they perceive to be the most profitable at the moment, CEOs have been forced to maximize for short-term quarterly profits over any longer-term societal goals. This profit bubble ignores the well-being of customers, the depletion of natural resources, and the long-term economic impact instant gratification is having on all living things. Extending beyond just ecological issues, focusing on short-term profits also drives down wages and shifts jobs to locations where people are willing to work for an unsustainable wage and further undercuts the buying power of the very customers to whom the company is trying to sell its products. This vicious cycle of cutting costs at any price is unsustainable for people, communities, and the environment. Profit at any cost isn't profiting society.

If modern capitalism isn't broken, then how else can one explain that Walmart's low-wage employees, who don't earn enough salary to survive, cost taxpayers more than $6.2 billion a year in public assistance such as food stamps and Medicaid. Walmart is just one of many examples of the growing trend of having taxpayers subsidize corporate workforces. "America's fast-food companies have quietly outsourced a significant chunk of their labor costs to the taxpayer, with more than half of the industry's 3.65 million low-wage workers on public assistance at a cost of $7 billion each year," according to Forbes.[7] A National Employment Law Project report estimates that the 10 largest fast-food corporations in America are responsible for nearly 60 percent, or $3.8 billion, outlaid by taxpayers for low-wage workers. "Anyone concerned about the federal deficit only needs to look at this report to understand a major source of the problem: multibillion-dollar companies that pay poverty wages and then rely on taxpayers to pick up the slack, to the tune of a quarter of a trillion dollars every year in the form of public assistance to working families," Former Senator Tom Harkin of Iowa explained. "Seven billion of this is just for fast-food workers, more than half of whom, even working full time, still must rely on programs like food stamps and Medicaid just to make ends meet."[8]

The solution to this systemic societal problem is perhaps the biggest void or problem that smart entrepreneurs and corporations need to address. Companies must move beyond the attention-getting public relations focused, but low-impact, corporate social responsibility programs of today. The next generation of sustainable companies need to evolve their business practices to ones of shared values. Shared value companies understand the need to generate the right kind of profits. Profits that enhance society, not diminish it. As more consumers make conscious choices in their spending, more investors will move their capital to companies whose prosperity is not at the expense of society at large. As capitalism evolves, the definition of value creation must expand beyond short-term profits.

Purpose-Driven Profits

Burger King, the fast-food giant, is a great example of implementing sustainable business practices. As humorous as it may sound, the United Nations' Food and Agriculture Organization estimates that 14.5 percent of all global greenhouse emissions comes from cattle flatulence (aka cow farts). Recognizing their role in serving 2.4 billion hamburgers each year, Burger King began adding 100 grams of lemongrass to cows' diets, which reduced methane emissions from cattle by 33 percent – a small action with a huge global impact.

In addition to consumers and investors, employees are growing more socially aware about the impact their jobs have on their environment and community. A 2019 poll from Gallup and Bates College highlighted the fact that 95 percent of four-year college graduates "considered a sense of purpose" important in their work.[9] "This 'purpose gap' is a glaring problem for the younger work force, as millennials place a higher priority on purpose in their lives than previous generations, and they look to work more than other sources to find it," according to Bates College president A. Clayton Spencer. "The purpose gap is also a challenge for employers because of a strong correlation between employees' purpose and engagement and an organization's bottom line."[10]

Sustainable capitalism isn't driven by marketing needs or charity, but rises from a deeper understanding of what true value creation can be. Sustainable capitalism, powered by a range of new technologies, is fueling innovation across virtually all sectors of business. Consumers are expecting societal and economic costs be thought of if corporations are to maximize *true* profits.

Kansas-based startup Greenfield Robotics, of which I am the chairperson, is a personal example of how shared values and technology can address unmet market needs while helping improve our environment. Agriculture, according to the Environmental Protection Agency (EPA), accounts for nearly 10 percent of all greenhouse gas emissions.[11] To reduce the impact of farming on the environment, many farmers are now switching to no-till regenerative farming, which lowers greenhouse emissions, conserves water, and increases crop yields per acre. Unfortunately, not tilling the soil leaves farmers no choice but to rely on poisonous herbicides for weed control.

Greenfield Robotics' aim is to use herds of small, autonomous robots to destroy weeds without damaging broad-acre crops such as wheat, soy, sorghum, and cotton. Much like releasing a herd of goats onto a grassy field, Greenfield's robots use machine vision to direct themselves up and down rows of crops and cut down the weeds so that crops can grow. Using robots-as-a-service is less expensive for farmers than spraying crops and does away with using toxic herbicides such as glyphosate (Roundup) and dicamba, which are hazardous to people, pollinators, wildlife, and aquatic organisms. With over 2 million farmers planting 915 million acres a year, the value created by the company goes far beyond financial profits. Our company motto at Greenfield is "Healthy people, healthy planet."

In addition to creating awareness around the plants in our lives, rethinking the pet food business also creates new opportunities for sustainable growth. Mars Petcare, the global leader in the pet-food industry, reimagined its purpose as "a better world for pets." Looking beyond the pet food aisle, the company began to look at the totality of having a healthy pet. Valuing pet health drove the companies' board to acquire Banfield Pet Hospital as well as BluePearl, VCA, AniCura, and Linnaeus veterinary services. The *better world for pets* approach transformed Mars Petcare into the largest and fastest-growing division of Mars Inc.[12]

Similar reimaginings are transforming drug stores into medical clinics to provide end-to-end solutions for customers' health. CVS, with nearly 10,000 retail locations, introduced MinuteClinics, where nurse practitioners and physician assistants can perform health screenings, provide wellness services, as well as diagnose and treat minor health conditions. With the US facing a shortage of nearly 122,000 doctors in coming years, diagnostic wearables – think a super Fitbit that monitors a myriad of bodily functions such as glucose levels, heart rate, and blood oxygenation – will launch a new wave of health-related devices and services that not only improve users lives, but reduce healthcare costs and hospital overcrowding.[13]

The Sharing Economy

The sharing economy is another great example of how corporate values, sustainability, and technology are fueling innovation. Uber and Airbnb are the flagships of the sharing economy. Fewer people will need to own cars as ride sharing becomes ubiquitous. Airbnb makes more efficient use of underutilized existing structures, thereby reducing the need to build more hotels. According to the Brookings Institute, the sharing economy will expand massively from $14 billion in 2014 to a third of a trillion dollars ($335 billion) by 2025.[14] Mobile phones, machine learning, and data analytics enable sharing across a wide range of business sectors from peer-to-peer lending, crowdfunding, couch surfing, car-sharing, co-working, bartering, talent-sharing, and even dog walking. What all these new companies have in common is using technology to reduce or reuse our impact on the environment.

Rover connects pet owners with dog sitters, walkers, and doggy daycare providers. Similarly, SitterCity offers caregiver services for kids instead of critters. Reviews and background checks assure the more than 7 million parents using SitterCity that their little ones are in good hands.

JustPark is an innovative parking space sharing company that connects people not using their home or apartment parking space with commuters in congested cities frustrated by limited or costly parking. Apartment tenants make extra income while they are away, or at work, from the over 2 million drivers who use the app.

Instead of begging friends to help you move heavy furniture, paint the living room, or decipher the 40 plus steps to assemble IKEA's Hemnes dresser, TaskRabbit will help you find local experienced labor. The gig economy, as it is commonly referred to, lets people leverage technology to create part-time or full-time income.

No part of the sharing economy became more vital during the Covid-19 pandemic than food delivery services such as DoorDash, GrubHub, UberEats/Postmates, and Caviar, which were used by more than 40 million Americans in 2020. Internationally, Deliveroo, Delivery Hero, Takeaway, DiDi, and Rappi allowed millions more to shelter-in-place without starving. The delivery of meals has grown into such a major business that it created an entirely new sustainable sharing business: the ghost kitchen.

Rather than have food couriers waste gasoline driving around to dozens of franchise locations, ghost kitchens are shared spaces in lower rent areas built just for delivery-only food preparation and can house many restaurant brands under one roof. The concept is so popular that it in turn spawned the creation of virtual restaurant brands such as Califlower Pizza, Ginger Bowls, Krispy Rice, Plant Nation, and F#CK Gluten that actually have no retail locations at all. By leveraging shared commercial kitchens, and not having to invest hundreds of thousands of dollars to open a brick-and-mortar location, virtual brands are a low-cost way to keep up with the ever-evolving consumer palette and test new cuisine concepts before opening a real restaurant. More than 4,500 virtual brands now exist and are reshaping America's $863 billion restaurant industry. Recognizing the symbiotic relationship between delivery services and ghost kitchens, Uber cofounder Travis Kalanick launched startup CloudKitchens to incubate more ghost kitchens.

The sharing economy is more than just sharing resources; it is about sharing values and community. With this philosophy in mind, Camille Rumani and Jean-Michael Petit created Eatwith. Connecting travelers with every day people that host meals, cooking classes, and food tours, Eatwith builds communities around a culinary experience. The company, which has quickly expanded to over 130 countries, grew out of the founders' frustration of traveling abroad without actually meeting local residents or experiencing local cultures. "We felt very disconnected from the places and the cultures we were visiting so we wanted to create a platform to facilitate the connection between travelers and locals by serving up great food and great company in an intimate atmosphere," Rumani explains, adding, "I think Eatwith truly empowers women because it helps them tell their stories about who they are, what they want to achieve, their culture and tradition, and their abilities and creativity."

As the world's population nears 8 billion people, now more than ever, every business needs to focus sharing resources, benefiting the entire community, and building profitable sustainability. If you want to live a purpose-filled life, what better goal to guide your career is there than saving the planet? To help align your personal goals with those of your business and society at large, one should ask these four questions when creating or managing a sustainable business.

Four Questions for Creating Sustainability

What Beliefs Are Core to Your Company?

From its founding, Google's unofficial motto was "Don't be evil." As simple as that phrase is, it recognizes the power that computers and software have over our lives. With that as a foundation, Google employees focus on providing unbiased information. When companies stray from their core beliefs, employees and customers take notice. In 2020, when Facebook's inconsistent policies regarding hate speech were brought to light by unhappy employees and users, advertisers responded with the Stop Hate for Profit campaign. Over a thousand advertisers (including Coca-Cola, Diageo, Honda, Levi Strauss, Starbucks, Unilever, Verizon, Patagonia) on the platform paused their social media advertising in a boycott that caused Facebook's stock to plummet 8.3 percent in one day and removed $56 billion from the company's market cap. Facebook discovered the hard way that values are now core to a company's reputation and profitability.

Clearly articulating what guides your company, as Patagonia's Common Threads campaign illustrated, not only builds customer loyalty and helps recruit like-minded talent, it leads the company into making longer-term decisions that balance near-term profits with long-term sustainability.

What Is Your Value Proposition?

For too many startups, this question was narrowly framed as, "What financial value do you provide customers?" Being the cheapest product or service may not reflect the true cost of your business to the broader community. What is the impact on the community if the jobs you create do not provide your employees a living wage? What impact does unlivable wages have on poverty, crime, and homelessness? My friend Dan Price, founder of Gravity Payments, made international headlines when he announced that he was mandating a $70,000 a year minimum wage at his company. Knowing the high cost of living in Seattle and how many employees had to juggle student loans and other debts, Price concluded that employees distracted by personal financial problems would be less productive and not provide the level of service that built Gravity's business. "For me, having empathy is one of the most powerful things I can do to improve as a leader," Price said.

To fund the raises, Price cut his $1.1 million salary to $70,000. Most of the business world thought Price was crazy. "I hope this company is a case study in MBA programs on how socialism does not work," Rush Limbaugh asserted on Fox News, "because it's gonna fail."[15]

But having a strong value proposition caused an amazing result. Even with higher payroll costs, corporate profits increased because of a 30–40 percent boost in employee productivity. Gravity's employee retention rate also rose to 91 percent and the company has no trouble attracting new talent because people want to work at a business that values its employees.

How Do You Measure Success?

Solely focusing on financial profit is what created much of the mess the world is in today. In a world struggling with diminishing resources, endless growth is not an economic feasibility. Bottom-line management is bottoming out. As management consultant Peter Drucker aptly noted, "If you can't measure it, you can't improve it."[16] When you take a holistic view of your business, take a critical view toward all the ways it impacts the planet and its people – from waste and raw materials, through to energy usage and greenhouse gas emissions. If reducing the company's carbon footprint is a component in factoring an employee's bonus, they will focus on it.

Every time you search for something on Google, a server some-where is using electrical power. When Google made it a priority to measure its data center's energy consumption, it was able to reduce its rates to half of the industry average. The result of constant mea-suring and improved efficiency has made the company carbon neutral for over a decade. Google has also embedded circular economy prin-ciples into server management to reduce waste. By working with the vendors in its supply chain, Google reuses, refurbishes, and reman-ufactures the old hardware in its centers. With a long-term goal of zero waste, Google's management is measured by its commitment to sustainability.

How Do Your Sustainability Goals Compare to the Rest of Your Industry?

It is great to have internal goals, but your company is not operating in a vacuum. As more and more corporations are publishing annual sustainability reports, your customers, suppliers, investors, and employ-ees will want to know how you compare. Since goals of having a zero waste, zero carbon footprint are more aspirational than achievable in the beginning, understanding who the sector leaders are in your indus-try and what methods they are employing to achieve their performance will help you succeed faster.

Walmart management realized that after labor, electricity was the company's largest cost. In an effort to increase profits, Walmart set a goal of reducing greenhouse gas emissions by 20 percent as measured by the total energy intensity per square foot (kWh/sq. ft.) by the year 2023.[17] Seeing this as a benefit to the planet, and not a competitive advantage, Walmart partnered with General Electric, the US Department of Energy, and a host of other suppliers to develop solutions for the entire industry. Having a public commitment of this size from a retailer with over 11,000 stores sparks startups to invest in pioneering new energy-efficient solutions because they know there is a massive customer waiting. As of the writing of this book, Walmart has already installed over 1.5 million LED fixtures in more than

6,000 stores for an energy saving of $100 million per year. "The ripple effect from these LED conversions throughout the business is truly staggering," Walmart's Vice President of Energy Mark Vanderhelm explained. "We believe that by continuing to reduce one of our biggest operating expenses, we're supporting future innovation and delivering on our promise of Every Day Low Prices."[18]

When one industry leader prioritizes sustainability, the entire market is forced to respond. Walmart's success at energy efficiency put a bull's-eye on the energy consumption of its rival, Target. Trying to "out green" the competition, Target installed rooftop solar panels on a quarter of its stores. According to the Solar Energy Industries Association, Target is now ranked number one among corporations in on-site solar for three years in a row, with 25 percent of its locations using 100 percent renewable energy.[19]

Procter & Gamble aims to lead the packaged goods industry on sustainability with their Ambition 2030 program by committing to reduce its carbon footprint by 50 percent, purchase 100 percent renewable electricity, and strive for circular solutions to reduce plastic usage so that none of its packaging ends up in our oceans.

Just as competition drives innovation in business, it has the same impact driving sustainability across virtually every industry. Nike and Adidas are competing on reducing waste, minimizing carbon footprint, and creating a greener supply chain.[20] Unilever and Nestlé are improving in product life cycle, water efficiency, and the use of organic palm oil in products. Faced with international concern over water usage, both Pepsi and Coca-Cola are focusing on water stewardship and have targets on groundwater replenishment.[21]

By having sustainable capitalism as a framework, even the smallest of startup companies can reduce energy usage and waste, which boosts profitability. Purpose-driven companies have increased employee morale, productivity, and retention rates. Lastly, companies that focus on sustainability today stay ahead of inevitable new environmental regulations that may catch their competition off guard. Being ahead of future government restrictions also ensures that their responsible supply chains will be available to meet the future needs of the company.

Working every single day and night is unsustainable. After 12 arduous months, Vin really needed a break. Having surpassed his million-dollar goal in month 11, Vin stopped hustling for new business and spent his free time planning out his well-deserved year of traveling the globe. He booked future speaking gigs in Slovenia, Denver, and Italy. He finished up ongoing work for existing clients and even went clothes shopping for the first time in 12 months. Final-month revenues tallied $35,729, bringing his yearly total to $1,069,531 and our *Future Proofing You* experiment to an end.

Notes

1. "Winter Holiday FAQs," *National Retail Federation.* https://nrf.com/insights/holiday-and-seasonal-trends/winter-holidays/winter-holiday-faqs. Accessed August 31, 2020.
2. Marc Gunther, "Patagonia's Conscientious Response to Black Friday Consumer Madness," *Green Biz* (November 28, 2011), www.greenbiz.com/article/patagonias-conscientious-response-black-friday-consumer-madness.
3. University of Arizona, "One-Third of Plant and Animal Species Could Be Gone in 50 Years." *ScienceDaily* (February 12, 2020), www.sciencedaily.com/releases/2020/02/200212150146.htm.
4. "WMO Climate Statement: Past 4 Years Warmest on Record," World Meteorological Organization (November 29, 2018), public.wmo.int/en/media/press-release/wmo-climate-statement-past-4-years-warmest-record.
5. Elizabeth Weise, "End of Civilization: Climate Change Apocalypse Could Start by 2050 If We Don't Act, Report Warns," *USA Today* (June 5, 2019).
6. Michael Parrish, "Occidental Agrees to Pay $98 Million in Love Canal Case: Environment: In a Key Civil Lawsuit over Buried Toxic Waste, the Company Will Also Take Over the Cleanup Effort," *Los Angeles Times* (June 22, 1994).
7. Clare O'Connor, "Reports: Fast Food Companies Outsource $7 Billion in Annual Labor Costs to Taxpayers," *Forbes* (October 16, 2013).

8. Ibid.

9. Jeremy Bauer-Wolf, "Purpose as Well as Paycheck," *Inside Higher Ed* (April 11, 2019), www.insidehighered.com/news/2019/04/11/gallup-bates-report-shows-graduates-want-sense-purpose-careers#.

10. Ibid.

11. Thin Lei Win, "Fighting Global Warming, One Cow Belch at a Time," Reuters (July 19, 2018), www.reuters.com/article/us-global-livestock-emissions/fighting-global-warming-one-cow-belch-at-a-time-idUSKBN1K91CU.

12. "Mars Petcare Marks Strategic Entry into European Veterinary Care Sector as Anicura to Join the Business," *Business Wire* (June 11, 2018), www.businesswire.com/news/home/20180611005394/en/Mars-Petcare-Marks-Strategic-Entry-into-European-Veterinary-Care-Sector-as-Anicura-to-Join-the-Business.

13. Association of American Medical Colleges (AAMC), "New Findings Confirm Predictions on Physician Shortage," (April 23, 2019), www.aamc.org/news-insights/press-releases/new-findings-confirm-predictions-physician-shortage.

14. Niam Yaraghi and Shamika Ravi, "The Current and Future State of the Sharing Economy," Brookings India (March 2017), www.brookings.edu/wp-content/uploads/2016/12/sharingeconomy_032017final.pdf.

15. Annie Reneau, "The CEO Who Gave Everyone a $70K Minimum Salary in 2015 Has a Message for the Doubters," *Upworthy* (August 24, 2020).

16. Steve Katzman, *Operational Assessment of IT* (Boca Raton, FL: CRC Press, 2016), 135.

17. GE Current, "Walmart Continues Retail Energy Efficiency Leadership with 1.5 Million LED Fixtures Now Installed," https://www.gecurrent.com/ideas/walmart-continues-retail-energy-efficiency-leadership. Accessed August 31, 2020.

18. Ibid.

19. Bruce Horovitz, "From the Rooftops, Big Box Stores Are Embracing Solar," *The New York Times* (October 7, 2019).

20. Knut Haanaes, "Why All Businesses Should Embrace Sustainability," IMD.org (November 2016), https://www.imd.org/research-knowledge/articles/why-all-businesses-should-embrace-sustainability/.

21. Ibid.

15

Pay It Forward

In the order of nature, we cannot render benefits to those from whom we receive them, or only seldom. But the benefit we receive must be rendered again, line for line, deed for deed, cent for cent, to somebody.
                                    —*Ralph Waldo Emerson*, Compensation

CHARLES MULLI IS THE most remarkable man I have ever met. Mulli was born into a typical family in a small rural village in Kenya. One morning when he was just six years old, he awoke to find that his entire family had moved during the night, leaving him behind in their abandoned hut. Alone and without food, Mulli walked 43 miles to the big city of Nairobi in search of work. Although Nairobi streets had many orphaned youths, Mulli was lucky to find a private home that fed him and offered him a job doing domestic chores. Working many odd jobs, by the time Mulli was 22, he had saved enough money to buy an old van. With one vehicle, he started a business of transporting workers between the towns of Eldoret and Nyaru. As his transportation business grew, he continually reinvested his profits into more vehicles and became very wealthy.

Happily married with eight children, one evening when driving through the city, he saw a small boy who was a street orphan, just as he had been years before. Moved to tears by the experience, he took the child and his two friends home. Mulli greeted his shocked wife by telling her that they now had three more kids. As kind and generous as this selfless act was, what makes Mulli so remarkable is that he repeated this act over and over. Selling all his businesses and using up all his life savings, Mulli and his wife, Esther, adopted and raised over 23,000 abandoned children. They had to move to the countryside, build dormitories, and grow their own food. They had to dig wells to find water when there were no rains to sustain their small farm. Now known as the largest family in the world, Mulli's children have grown up to become doctors, teachers, engineers, and business leaders. In meeting with Mulli, I was moved by what a kind and modest man he is. He takes no credit for his heroic acts of generosity and just thanks God for the children. I can think of no greater example of paying forward one's success in life.

Just as practicing gratitude helps you to develop a growth mindset, committing yourself to paying it forward enriches your soul. Paying it forward is not about grandiose gestures, but in refocusing your perspective on making every day count. At 95 years old, former president Jimmy Carter still teaches Sunday school and swings a hammer building Habit for Humanity shelters. Since retiring from the White House, Jimmy Carter and his volunteers have built more than 150 homes for poor families. Superstar rocker Jon Bon Jovi's JBJ Soul Kitchen restaurants were opened to make sure that everyone had access to a hot, nutritious meal, regardless of financial circumstances. There are no prices on the menus at his New Jersey eateries. Instead, patrons are offered the choice to make a financial donation or volunteer at the restaurant. Each hour worked cooking, waiting tables, or washing dishes earns volunteers a three-course meal. "One in six people in America are suffering at night and going to bed hungry, and one in five families live at or below the poverty line," Bon Jovi said. "What this restaurant is truly meant to do is empower. You don't come in here with a sense of entitlement. You come in here and volunteer because we need your help."[1]

Even if you don't own a restaurant, you can still pay it forward every time you dine out. My wife and I live in a part of Los Angeles that is frequently devastated by wildfires. Though having fortunately never lost our home, local firefighters risk their lives combating these fierce infernos. Our local neighborhood restaurant is also just a block away from the fire station. Whenever we dine there, if we see firefighters eating, their meal is on us. (Many times, I am unable to pay for the firemen's meal because another patron has beat me to the cashier.) Detroit's Sister Pie owner Lisa Ludwinski encourages customers to "pie-it-forward."[2] A coupon is placed on the wall for each prepaid pie, and any consumer can walk in and redeem the coupon for a free pie – no questions asked. To the best of my knowledge, the record for restaurant customers paying it forward by paying for the next person in line's coffee goes to a Starbucks in St. Petersburg, Florida. In 2014, one woman's act of generosity motivated the next 377 customers to buy a stranger a cup of coffee.[3] Lasting unbroken for 11 hours, this random act of kindness has spawned thousands of more chain events around the world.

When I was struggling in my twenties with my first software company, we didn't have the money to make donations to charity, but we had the time. With more hours in the day than paying work to fill them, each year we selected a philanthropic project to do for free. Using the skillsets of our entire team, we created everything from some of the very first software for learning-disabled children to designing interactive exhibits for museums. Decades later, when I bump into former colleagues from my old startup, we don't reminisce about our bestselling games, but, rather, the impact we were able to make with our collective efforts.

This experiment with mentoring Vin was one of the most rewarding experiences of my life and a validation that every individual – regardless of where they start – has the power to achieve. Beyond the intrinsic rewards of helping others, our society needs more mentors and entrepreneurs. Globally, the middle class is shrinking, not growing. Many of the gains of equality and freedom achieved in the twentieth century are eroding as our society becomes more disjointed and the chasm between the haves and the have-nots deepens. In sharing this experiment with the world, I put my reputation on the line – not for self-gain or aggrandizement but with the fervent desire for this book to ignite that spark in a million readers. We all need to get involved, help others achieve their dreams, and solve the myriad of problems facing humanity. By sharing my 12 truths and showing the impact that a year with a growth mindset can have on one person, I hope to empower each reader to not only Future Proof their career but to share what they have learned with others.

Writing books, speaking at conferences, and consulting with major corporations has given me a platform to shine a spotlight on the amazing works that people like you are doing across the globe. Please email me (jayalansamit@gmail.com) so that I can share your story with others. Only by helping each other can we be future proofing our world.

Notes

1. Laura Colarusso, "Soul Food: Jon Bon Jovi Is Opening an Innovative New Community Kitchen to Fight Hunger," *Daily Beast* (July 13, 2017), www.thedailybeast.com/soul-food.
2. Melissa Kossler Dutton, "Giving Chains: Holiday Customers Enjoy Paying It Forward," Daily Herald (November 15, 2016), www.dailyherald.com/article/20161115/news/311159926/.
3. Times Staff Writer, "Nearly 400 People 'Pay It Forward' at St. Petersburg Starbucks," *Tampa Bay Times* (November 21, 2014), www.tampabay.com/news/humaninterest/more-than-250-have-paid-it-forward-at-local-starbucks-and-the-chain-is/2193784/.

Epilogue – Vin's Reflections

A FEW MONTHS after our *Future Proofing You* experiment ended, I asked Vin to write a few words about the experience of earning his first million dollars. The following are his thoughts:

I went into this thinking it would be totally impossible, but even if I failed, I'd get a chance to learn from Jay so it would be a win–win. But at the same time, I didn't want to be one of those people who goes to America and it doesn't work out as I didn't try hard enough, or apply myself correctly. I do like the idea that someone might read this and see it's possible for them, too. Many of the top business talking heads were helped massively by their parents when starting out, went to a top university, or had a great network. My parents had little money, we grew up on housing estates, and I myself was on social welfare just before I started my entrepreneurial journey. And then I came to America and had no real contacts, and it was like starting from zero, but I felt I had something to prove.

The key is to say yes and do what they say when you're working with an (experienced) mentor/coach (even if you don't agree with them). They have been there and done it, and this served me well. A couple of times I did not follow Jay's advice and learned some painful lessons I will never forget, and I do not wish that to happen again.

One of my main takeaways has been the freedom that what I achieved gave me. When you're under pressure to make enough money to pay bills and survive, you have little freedom with your time, let alone to look better at opportunities. Having completed this challenge, I was able to be more selective on the projects I took on, allowing me to take on projects that are truly fulfilling, not because I needed the money (I used to say yes to everything, leading to some very stressful moments taking on bad clients!).

Being future proof means being confident that you have the skills for whatever life will throw at you. Having a growth mindset gave me the confidence to compete in a world I had no business being in. Growing up without much money, not going to a prestigious university, not really working any jobs of any note, not having connections didn't happen as soon as I started using the internet as an engine and believed in myself. In the old days, you would need money to start a company or connections to get you started. Now, you just need an internet connection and to be using the strategies I used.

There's always going to be obstacles and problems as you progress. The key is to see them as opportunities. When I was on welfare, I started an online magazine. I had no money to promote the site so I had to learn how to create viral content, teach others how to make it (so I wouldn't have to write the articles myself), and then how to make them go viral (for free) using other websites. This led to 25,000 visitors in the second week, 300,000 visitors a month within six months, and one million visitors a month and an investment of $250,000 within one year. That would have cost an astronomical amount of money using traditional methods (PR etc.).

During my year with Jay, there were moments where things were difficult and it looked unlikely anything would happen at all, but I kept believing in the process and found ways through to the other side. I no longer look at these setbacks as failures – more part of a learning process. When I look back at each consecutive year, I don't remember the failures, just the successes. The learning process compounds over time and the wins get bigger.

Are you no longer afraid of not having a job or by future proofing yourself do you realize that you'll never need to work for someone else again? A lot has changed for me. I remember the days of applying to jobs online and getting no replies for weeks on end. Since I started this entrepreneurial journey and by future proofing myself, I have no fear of not working again. I won't need to work for someone else, as I can create my own opportunities using the skills I've acquired. This experience allowed me to see the world as a place where opportunity is available anywhere you put deep focus. After I completed the challenge, I was able to take off for the first time in years, confident that offers would come in as of the work I'd done (and they did, better offers than ever). It's a liberating feeling.

At the moment, I'm looking to pay it forward and help other companies and entrepreneurs just as Jay helped me. Speaking on stage has always been a great way for me to inspire and educate around the world, as well as advising companies on how to become future proof themselves. Since completing the project in this book, I have worked on marketing campaigns that have generated seven-figures+ for one of the biggest companies in the world, and have worked on content and marketing campaigns with some of the biggest music artists in the world, among other projects I've been working on.

My mission is to future proof as many people as possible from everything that has happened recently. I love the idea that there are people out there who want to do what I did with Jay, and I can now be the person to help them or their company get there.

Vin Clancy
vin@vinclancy.com

About the Author

INTERNATIONAL bestselling author Jay Samit is a dynamic entrepreneur and intrepreneur who is widely recognized as one of the world's leading experts on disruption and innovation. Described by *Wired* magazine as "having the coolest job in the industry," he raises hundreds of millions of dollars for startups, advises Fortune 500 firms, transforms entire industries, revamps government institutions, and for three decades continues to be at the forefront of global trends.

The former Independent Vice Chairman of Deloitte Consulting, Samit helped grow pre-IPO companies such as LinkedIn, has been a Nasdaq company CEO, held senior management roles at EMI, Sony, and Universal Studios, and pioneered breakthrough advancements in mobile, e-commerce, digital distribution, and spatial reality that are used by billions of consumers every day. Called the "guru for the entire industry" by *Variety*, his list of partners and associates reads like a who's who list of innovators, including Bill Gates, President Bill Clinton, Pope John Paul II, Steven Spielberg, Steve Jobs, Reid Hoffman, David Geffen, Sir Richard Branson, and Paul Allen.

Samit's previous book, *Disrupt You! Master Personal Transformation, Seize Opportunity, and Thrive in the Era of Endless Innovation* (MacMillan, 2015), is currently published in 12 languages. He has also written for such publications as *Fortune, Harvard Business Review,* and *the Wall Street Journal.*

A sought-after conference speaker and consultant, Samit provides disruptive solutions for such corporate clients as Adobe, American Express, AT&T, Best Buy, Coca-Cola, Disney, Ford, GE, Google, IBM, Intel, McDonald's, Microsoft, Procter & Gamble, Visa, and dozens more.

Samit is a Magna Cum Laude graduate of UCLA, a Presidential Fellow, and an adjunct professor at the University of Southern California's Viterbi School of Engineering.

Acknowledgments

FIRST, I REALLY must thank all of the thousands of readers of *Disrupt You!* who have taken the time to write me, write reviews, and share the book with their co-workers. I am touched by the community of friends I have made around the world through my writings. These friendships are an unexpected joy and one of the highlights of my life. A heartfelt thanks to superfans David Dattoli, Daniel Ibri, Paulo Ibri, Romualdas Isoda, Rubina Mumtaz, and Francisco Vergara for working tirelessly to get my book published in their native languages.

While I truly love hearing from grateful readers sharing their success stories, the inspiration for this book came from an email I received from a frustrated reader of *Disrupt You!* While he found the book motivational, he didn't believe it was possible for **him** to achieve success. Not being able to convince that one person set my mind on a path of wanting to prove my thesis that we live in a world where everyone is capable of Future Proofing their lives and achieving lasting success.

This book wouldn't have been possible without Vin Clancy. His journey became our journey to share. While his persistence and ingenuity are outlined in the book, it is hard to capture the character of the man. Vin is a man on a mission to make the world a better place, and I am confident that he will accomplish his goals. I also want to thank him for being fully open and transparent in sharing his feelings during our year journey together and keeping meticulous records.

I so appreciate Tom Bilyeu, not only for being generous with his time and talent in writing the introduction for this book but also for the daily motivation and inspiration he provides to entrepreneurs everywhere. I also want to give a belated thanks to Reid Hoffman for the amazing introduction he wrote for *Disrupt You!* (Due to the order things were turned in to my publisher last time, I never got the opportunity to thank him in print. Reid, I am forever in your debt.)

I want to thank Clint Brauer and the entire of team at Greenfield Robotics for allowing me to practice what I preach by working together to build a company based on sustainable capitalism principles. For me, *Healthy Food, Healthy Planet* is more than a company slogan. It is a promise I am making to my granddaughters, Naomi and Valerie, to make our world a better place.

Having worked with other publishers, I am indebted to Mike Campbell and his team at Wiley for making the process of publishing a book seem effortless.

Lastly, I want to thank the three most important influences in my life: my muse, my best friend, and my wife. I am so blessed to have them all in one person.

Index